GENESIS – (VOL 1) FALL FROM REST, CALL TO REST

GENESIS – (VOL 1) FALL FROM REST, CALL TO REST

David Benjamin

Dedication

To the "Beaten Sheep"

Contents

Introduction:

From Genesis to Revelation, there's a singular set of themes spanning all the scriptures, with consistent language, metaphors, comparisons, allegories, and word usage. Genesis, with all its different types, essentially defines the Bible's vocabulary for its major themes. God's design in spreading major doctrines and themes throughout various parts of Scripture encourages a comprehensive understanding of His Word. As diligent students, we need to explore the entirety of God's counsel and "connect the dots" between different passages and themes. This kind of study assumes a unity in the scriptures held together by supernatural design.

As Peter says, "No prophecy is a private interpretation. Holy men of old wrote as they were moved upon by God." They used consistent language through the scripture to speak of the same things. This is how we know these things. We search the scriptures (2 Peter 1:20-21).

In this pass through Genesis, we have taken these principles for granted and have determined to see Christ represented on every page. This time we discovered a singular and thoroughly neglected point to the narrative in Genesis - Christ as our Rest! My intention is to help believers see the "smiling face" of God in these chapters.

Chapter 1: Introducing the Bible's Design (Prologue)

It fascinates me that from Genesis to Revelation, there's a singular set of themes spanning all the scriptures, with consistent language, metaphors, comparisons, allegories, and word usage. Chuck Missler often stated that we have 66 books written over thousands of years by more than 40 authors in three different languages. Yet, we find it is an "integrated message system written from beyond our time domain." He emphasized that every detail exhibits supernatural design. He did have a unique ability to show us how powerfully the Scripture is constructed, proving it is supernaturally designed. Sadly, I cannot recommend his teachings as he veered off into Galatian error, especially later in his ministry.

The Law of First Mention

Genesis, with all its different types, essentially defines the Bible's vocabulary for its major themes. There is a principle called the "law of first mention," which states that the first use of a word related to one of the major themes in the Bible governs its context throughout the Scripture and defines it. For example, the first use of the word 'sin' is with Cain and Abel, as we'll see when we get to Genesis 4. Sin is pictured as a lion, crouching, ready to devour him. It is depicted as a principle more powerful than Cain, acting even without his decision to do something. Sin is first presented as a principle before it's itemized into transgressions in the Bible. This is confirmed and elaborated as doctrine in Romans 7:17, where we encounter the 'law of sin' in our members.

Another striking example, and one of my favorites, is the word Love. The first time we see this in the Bible is when God told Abraham to take his "only son, whom you love," and sacrifice him.

"And he said, Take now thy son, thine only son Isaac, whom thou lovest, and get thee into the land of Moriah; and offer him there for a burnt offering upon one of the mountains which I will tell thee of. And Abraham rose up early in the morning, and saddled his ass, and took two of his young men with him, and Isaac his son, and clave the wood for the burnt offering, and rose up, and went unto the place of which God had told him."

Abraham's willingness to sacrifice his only son, Isaac, clearly foreshadows the Father's future offering of Jesus Christ. This event serves as a type of God the Father offering His only begotten Son as a sacrifice for the sins of the world.

We're told in Hebrews 11 that Abraham believed that even if Isaac were sacrificed, God would raise him from the dead. This points to the resurrection of Christ, who was sacrificed but rose from the dead, fulfilling God's promise and redeeming mankind. The location of this event, Mount Moriah, is seen by most as a significant foreshadowing of the crucifixion of Jesus Christ. It is believed to be the same mount where Jesus was later crucified. When Isaac, the seed of Abraham (and definitely a figure of Christ), ascended the hill with His father, Abraham (whose name means Father of nations), he carried the wood himself. He was approximately 30 years of age.

Isaac asked, "We have wood and fire, but where is the sacrifice?" Abraham's response was, "God will provide Himself a sacrifice." This is a play on words (and there are many of these in the scripture). God not only provided a sacrifice in the place of Isaac, but He provided *Himself* as the ultimate sacrifice.

When Abraham was interrupted by the Angel, he looked up, and a ram was caught in a thicket by the horns. Jesus Christ also was crowned with thorns, a thicket. The thorns are a symbol of the curse from Genesis 1.

While Abraham acts out the role of the Father and Isaac the Son, another character remains back with the donkeys. He is referred to as Abraham's servant. From other places, we know that this is Eliezar. Eliezar means "comforter." Eliezar was the steward in Abraham's house, sometimes acting out the role of the Spirit, our paraclete, our comforter. Whenever he acts out this role, he is nameless. Genesis calls him the servant rather than by his name. This is because the Spirit does not speak of Himself but only what He receives of Christ, He tells us. (Genesis 24:2-4)

John 16:13-15 Howbeit when he, the Spirit of truth, is come, he will guide you into all truth: for he shall not speak of himself; but whatsoever he shall hear, *that* shall he speak: and he will shew you things to come. (14) He shall glorify me: for he shall receive of mine and shall shew *it* unto you. (15) All things that the Father hath are

mine: therefore said I, that he shall take of mine, and shall shew *it* unto you.

The next time we see Eliezar in Genesis incidentally, is again as the "nameless servant", typifying the Holy Spirit, where he is sent by Abraham on behalf of Isaac to gather a bride from Laban's house. On the way back, he showers her with gifts, exhibiting the riches of the glory of Abraham's house while telling her of the goodness of Isaac, whom she has yet to meet and will soon see. This is very much a picture of the Spirit sent by the Father in the name of Christ to receive the Bride and bring her home on a journey into the knowledge of Christ while showing forth His riches He has received from the Father as gifts to her. (Genesis 24:10-53)

Even though Ishmael was also Abraham's son, God's choice of language in the text makes Isaac appear as if he were the only son of Abraham. "Take now thy son, thine only son.." What about Ishmael? We learn from the story that it is a 3-day journey from the time that God commanded him to sacrifice Isaac and when he is said to have received him "back as a figure" as one raised from the dead per Hebrews 11.

So the first presentation of the word, "love" in the Bible sets its tone, and the story its presented in contains all the themes and elements of the redemption in Christ. It is a picture that describes, not of our love for God, but God's love toward us.

The biblical definition of love is not about our love. As John says, "Herein is love, not that we loved God, but that he loved us, and sent his Son to be the propitiation for our sins" (1 Jon 4:10). According to the law of first mention, the first time a primary theme or even a word that has much significance is presented, all the surrounding elements will also be consistently seen throughout the scripture. Almost every item in the story relates to the propitiation, which Romans 5 says is the demonstration of God's love for us. "God commends His own love toward us, in that while we were sinners, Christ died for us." Commends mean to "recommend" and to display and point to, and emphasize!

Expositional Constancy

In addition to the law of first mention, there is also the principle of **expositional constancy.** This means that a word or theme's initial definition and context will be consistent throughout the Bible.

For example, when Paul speaks about building with wood, hay, and stubble compared to gold, silver, and precious stones, we can interpret the spiritual significance behind the materials by looking at their use in scripture. The Bible uses consistent imagery. Gold represents faith in the divine nature, silver signifies redemption, and precious stones symbolize transformation and the building up of God's dwelling place (1 Corinthians 3:11-15).

Take silver. It is consistently associated with innocent blood as seen in the betrayals of Joseph by his brothers and Jesus by Judas for thirty pieces of silver (Genesis 37:26-28; Matthew 26:14-16). In the Tabernacle, silver's use underscores redemption, as each person is required to contribute a shekel of silver at birth symbolizing their redemption (Exodus 30:12-16). When Peter asserts that we are not redeemed by perishable things like silver or gold, but by the precious blood of Christ, the message underscores the eternal nature of our salvation (1 Peter 1:18-19).

The consistent usage of these symbols across the scriptures is indicative of divine meanings and God's definitions that far surpass our natural understanding. We uncover these definitions by examining the connections these symbols make to various themes throughout the Bible. The language and themes in the Bible demonstrate a remarkable consistency, indicating a supernatural design.

We must consider the broader context of the scriptures when examining the meanings of symbols. It is crucial to remember that God often imparts meanings to words that may diverge from human concepts. Therefore, relying solely on theological dictionaries can lead to cultural bias and misinterpretation. Secular dictionaries, likewise, are unsuitable for answering theological questions. Our aim should be to comprehend how God uses words in scripture. The law of first mention and the principle of expositional constancy guide us in this journey, enabling us to identify connections and comprehend the overarching themes that God seeks to convey.

Studying the Whole Counsel of God

To effectively employ expositional constancy, we have to immerse ourselves in diligent study of the entire Bible. God's design in spreading major doctrines and themes throughout various parts of Scripture encourages a comprehensive understanding of His Word. As diligent students, we need to explore the entirety of God's counsel and "connect the dots" between different passages and themes. This kind of study assumes a unity in the scriptures held together by supernatural design.

As Peter says, "No prophecy is a private interpretation. Holy men of old wrote as they were moved upon by God." They used consistent language through the scripture to speak of the same things. This is how we know these things. We search the scriptures (2 Peter 1:20-21).

God designed the word to distribute His teaching throughout the whole system. For example, there's not a single chapter that comprehensively covers any doctrine of the Bible. The major doctrines are not established in one chapter but sprinkled throughout the whole message system. This means you have to be a diligent student, looking at the entirety of scripture, the whole council of God's word, to understand the themes.

For instance, if you want to understand baptism, you can look at the flood and the decree that God made there concerning man, his judgment of man, and the end of the human race. You can learn what a good conscience is and how Noah represents that, as discussed in 1 Peter (1 Peter 3:21). You also can see the clear teaching in Paul's writing who says we are baptized into the death of Christ (Romans 6:3-5).

Moreover, what about the nature of that death? Is it suffering for us? Its significant that the cross was in the garden, where there was also a tomb where Jesus was buried. You have to see that it's a kind of planting; He was a seed planted in the earth in his death in that garden tomb

(John 12:24-25). We were planted there with Him and can emerge from His resurrection as His multiplication (Colossians 2:12-13). We were buried with Him in baptism (Rom 6:4). Our entrance into His death is a position of rest and repose, in a garden, where life is anticipated! All of those truths are contained in baptism and more.

What's the key to understanding these things? We consider the entirety of scripture rather than focusing on isolated verses. This isn't to say that we disregard what Peter or Paul have written; instead, after we glean the understanding of the immediate context of the verses, we may broaden our search to understand the vocabulary. Then our understanding develops by absorbing a bit of wisdom "here and there" (Isaiah 28:10, 13

Today, I had a conversation with an individual who was finding it challenging to comprehend the concept of our death with Christ. They were seeking instant clarity, yet I suggested that the understanding unfolds with continuous interaction with the Word over time. As Jesus once said, "If you continue in my word, you are truly my disciples, and you will know the truth, and the truth will set you free" (John 8:31-32).

The goal isn't merely to amass knowledge but to experience a spiritual transformation as you explore the Word and meet God within it. The idea is for the Word to nurture you. This isn't a process you can rush through as if you're reading a textbook. It's about patiently and sincerely studying the scriptures, praying, and maintaining a humble spirit and a strong desire to receive understanding. For example, it took me several years of studying Romans 6 through 8 to start truly comprehending it. It wasn't until I started understanding that I had died with Christ that things started to make sense. Realizing that there is no death to sin without death to the law was a pivotal moment. But to experience the freedom described in Romans 8, we need to come to terms with God's judgment about the flesh.

Similarly, understanding Romans 8's "righteousness of the law" as God's righteousness blessing us with the spirit of sonship, bearing witness with our spirit that we are children of God, and providing the life and peace that floods our minds when we align ourselves with Him, not as a matter of being 'better.' God's Word is meant to be savored, bit by bit. It's through repeated engagement with the Word that spiritual understanding evolves. The gospel is everywhere in the Bible, and God has ensured its message is clear and accessible. Even if parts of the Bible were removed (which wouldn't happen, thanks to God's sovereign protection), the gospel message would still be evident. It's like a jigsaw puzzle – even if a few pieces go missing, you can still see the whole picture. This is because Jesus is everywhere; you can't silence His voice.

As we explore books like Genesis, our quest is not merely for knowledge. Our deeper longing is to commune with God, to let the Word feed our spirits and draw us nearer to Him. The goal here is not to turn the Word into a chore, but to allow it to be a source of delight. This journey isn't about ticking off boxes; it's about discovering and savoring the sweetness of God's message in the Word.

In sharing these principles, my intention isn't to heap an added burden onto your studies, or to imply that you must follow these methods rigidly to gain any truthful insights. Nor am I advocating for a "patchwork" approach to studying the Word, where you're leaping from scripture to scripture, wrenching them out of their context in an attempt to unearth some "hidden meaning."

Understanding the Word requires seeing how different scriptures fit together like pieces of a puzzle, showing us the consistent use of language and themes by God. However, it's equally important to consider the immediate context of a verse to grasp its true meaning. Instead of quickly jumping between passages using Bible verse links and word studies, take time to understand a verse within its own context. To fully comprehend a verse, look at the entire chapter it belongs to, and to understand the chapter, consider the book it's a part of. Understanding words and language involves searching for consistent explanations and broader themes. It's about grasping the Word in both its immediate context and in the broader scope of God's message.

God has organized the word in a way that there is no way to truly understand it without actual encounters with Him. God orders your steps so that you won't learn about Him without Him interacting with you and dealing with you. That's why God designed it this way and why He protects the message system. The great news is that the gospel is literally on every page. So, if something were to happen to the Bible, (and God has sovereignly protected it so it wouldn't) but if you take pages out, or take chapters out, or take whole books out, it doesn't dissolve the message. You've still got it in every part. Jesus is everywhere; you cannot shut Him up. You lose a little resolution if you take some of the chapters out, but you can still understand it and will have everything you need. Genesis is a great book to show us many of these major themes. I don't know how many of the things we're going to get into, but my hope is that the word really does become food for us. That we enjoy God through it, it brings us into fellowship with Him, and we see Jesus Christ. What else is there? There is nothing else to pursue. There's a taste of the sweetness of God in the word.

Chapter 2: Life, Resurrection, Image, and Dominion in (Genesis 1-2)

The Focus of Genesis 1 and 2 Life and Resurrection, Image and Dominion

Now we come to Genesis 1, which records the world's creation or restoration, depending on your perspective. As I mentioned, my focus on this pass through Genesis is on something other than cosmology, physics, or whether the earth is flat or curved. Instead, my focus is on *life,* which ultimately means Christ Himself.

In my view, the significant event related to life occurs on day three when God brings the land out from the sea and begins causing life to come forth. This day represents resurrection, so it's noteworthy that God brought dry ground out of the waters of death on the day of resurrection.

"Let the waters under heaven be gathered into one place and let the dry land appear, and it was so. God called the dry land earth, and the gathering of the waters was called seas. He said it was good. Let the world bring forth grass and herbs yielding seed, and the tree yielding fruit after his kind, whose seed is upon it in itself. So, the principle of life and multiplication upon the earth, and it was so. The earth brought forth grass and herbs yielding seed after its kind, and the tree yielding fruit whose seed is in itself after its kind. God saw it was good, and the evening and the morning were the third day."

On the third day, with the ground appearing, we have the beginning of life and see a presentation of life in increasing complexity and richness of consciousness. It starts with the herbs, trees, and grass, which possess the least complex form of consciousness.

Then on the fourth day, celestial bodies and the beginning of times and seasons bring more light. The fifth day sees the rise of birds, animals, and sea creatures, all forms of life with higher consciousness than that of herbs, grass, and trees.

Interestingly, there must first be more light for these kinds of life to emerge. The more complex life of the fifth day does not come forth until the fourth day lights are established. Light is related to knowledge in the Bible, and I believe God told the story to show the order of complexity of consciousness leading up to the creation of man on the sixth day.

On the sixth day, we ssee man. Man is the highest of the created consciousness and can know and walk with God. He is unique, made in the image of God, unlike all other animals, which were created after their kind. Adam was referred to as a son of God, and man is the only life created after another kind. However, man is not the highest life form in the order. He is the highest created life of the first six days, but on the seventh day, "after God finished all His work," another life is present, represented by the Tree of Life.

The highest life, with the highest consciousness, is the Divine Life. This is represented by the Tree of Life, which also points to God's purpose. On the 7th day, God puts man in front of the Tree of Life, representing God's own life. This is a picture of God's intention. He wants to work Himself into man and become a part of man. God's will in the universe allows man to become His expression and reign as His representative. For this reason, God created man in His image and gave him authority with His likeness. He gave man dominion over everything. But we know the story: man didn't eat from the Tree of Life. Instead, he ate from the other tree and corrupted himself. As a result, his image was no longer in the likeness of God. Despite this, God didn't take away man's authority.

Ever since this event, the earth has been corrupted. Death and sin have reigned, and man is corrupted in his image and needs to be redeemed and recreated. To achieve this, God sent Jesus Christ to partake of flesh and blood like us, made a little lower than angels for the suffering of death (Hebrews 2:9). In the resurrection, Jesus makes Himself available again as food, saying, "Unless you eat my flesh and drink my blood, you have no life" (John 6:53).

God's intention has not changed since the fall. His desire is to put His life in man and form man in His image, maintaining that image so that man expresses not his own life but God's life. That's what God wants. That's what the sons of God are, and that's what Christ is - the God-man. We are born of God because we receive Jesus Christ, the Tree of Life. God's life comes into us, and He brings us into the new creation, which is created in the knowledge of Christ, in true righteousness and holiness, after His image (Ephesians 4:24, Colossians 3:10). In regeneration, the image of God is restored in our spirit. Eventually, our body will also be transfigured (1 Corinthians 15:49). Everything is earthly first, then heavenly.

First the Earthly, then the Heavenly

1Co 15:46-49 Howbeit that was not first which is spiritual, but that which is natural; and afterward that which is spiritual. (47) The first man is of the earth, earthy: the second man is the Lord from heaven. (48) As is the earthy, such are they also that are earthy: and as is the heavenly, such are they also that are heavenly. (49) And as we have borne the image of the earthy, we shall also bear the image of the heavenly.

Man was created from clay out of the dust of the ground, but was meant to express God on earth This first man, Adam, was given dominion over the whole earth (Genesis 1:26-28). This is an earthly picture, but there is a Second Man, represented by Christ Himself. The second man from heaven, Christ in resurrection, doesn't just have authority over the earth but also over the heavens! He's been raised, exalted, and seated in the heavens, far above everything in heaven and on earth. He's been given a name above every name, far above the principalities, far above the angels, at the right hand of God (Eph 1:23; Heb 1:1-4) There's a man there as the representative head of a *new humanity* that will be recreated in His likeness (Rom 8:28-29). This man becomes the life of those who are members of His Body. This is who we are as we are also raised up together with him and seated with him in the heavens. We are destined to be glorified with him, like unto his heavenly glory, to reign with him as heirs not only of the earth but also of the heavens.

First, it's the natural, which we see in Genesis, and then it's the heavenly, which we see in Revelation (1 Corinthians 15:46-49). In Genesis, there's an earthly garden; in Revelation, there's a heavenly city. So again, there is this developing of a theme through scripture, first in types set in natural settings on the earth and then fulfilled in the reality that comes from heaven and remakes us in a heavenly way.

In Genesis we see God, creating man in His image and likeness, and setting the Tree of Life before him. This picture has both a literal and symbolic meaning. It represents an earthly reality and serves as a shadow of a more heavenly reality revealed later (Genesis 2:7).

For us, the fulfillment of this picture is heavenly because we are made for heaven. It's not just about God breathing life into clay and setting mankind before the Tree of Life to rule on Earth. The reality is that God, in Christ, went through incarnation, human living, death, resurrection, ascension, and glorification. He is now deified and clothed in His divinity. He is spiritual and heavenly.

When Jesus appears to the disciples in John 20, He shows up in the upper room without using a door or anything physical to transport Himself into that room. And yet, He's still flesh and bone. He breathes into them and says, "Receive the Holy Ghost." That was when the Church was really born. Although we say that the Church was born in Acts 2 when the Holy Spirit came down as a clothing of power, I believe that the disciples were regenerated when Christ breathed Himself into them. Those disciples received Christ, the life-giving spirit, as He breathed Himself into them (John 20:19-23).

This event is analogous to when God breathed into Adam to make him alive. But instead of just becoming alive as mere men, they became active as the sons of God. They became alive with the divine life, able to enter into the Kingdom of God and partake of His affairs.

I'm getting ahead of myself, but the focus in Genesis 1 is a focus on life, from first bringing out the earth and setting up the dry ground so that life can be multiplied. That being on the third day is a type of resurrection out of the tomb. He separated from the waters, which I believe are a picture of judgment and death.

To see the land on day 3 as a type of resurrection does require that we see the waters as a type of death, and even judgment, which may sound strange to us if our frame of understanding for Genesis is a creation account. However, in the next chapter, I will share a little more from my own perspective (with scriptural evidence) that this may be both a creation and arestoration account after a previous judgment.

Chapter 3: Man's Creation - A Divine Response? (Genesis 1)

The Creation of Man - a Response?

I believe in the literalness of the scriptures, but I believe in their unity as a whole, and often something that is presented in one part of the scripture takes the whole of scripture to understand. I hold the view that Genesis is more than a creation account. It speaks a restoration and hints at something that preceded it. This view is mine, and you're not required to embrace it. However, for context, it does help to revisit some of the details in the beginning of Chapter 1.

> **"In the beginning, God created the heavens and the earth and the earth was without form and void.." (Gen 1:1).**

What we see in Genesis 1 is that God created the heavens and the earth. It does not say that He created darkness. Darkness, throughout scripture, signifies judgment It just says, "darkness was upon the face of the deep." Then, the next thing God did was to say, "Let there be light." This could be viewed as a "response" on God's part.

The Hebrew word used in Genesis 1:2 ("and darkness was upon the face of the deep") is "hayah," which can be translated as "was," "became," or "came to be." Therefore, the phrase "The earth was without form and void" can also be understood as "The earth became without form and void" (Genesis 1:2).

Both Paul and John cast the darkness in creation in a negative light and correlate it with ignorance and evil. John refers to it in his more mystical beginning of the Gospel of John. "In the beginning was the Word, and the Word was with God, and the Word was God. The same was in the beginning with God. All things were created through Him, not apart from Him. Not one thing that was made was made without Him." Then he adds, "In Him was life, and the life was the light of man. And the light shines in the darkness, and the darkness didn't overcome it." (John 1:1-5)

In one sense, John is reminding us of the creation account to show that Christ is the reality. This is a picture, but Christ is the reality. God did create the heavens and the earth. There was darkness, and He commanded light. But that speaking was His Word, and that Word is a person, which is Christ. He is the light, and in Him is life.

John also refers to the word of life which was in the beginning in 1 John (1 John 1:1), speaking of Christ as the manifestation of God as light and life, before he talks about darkness which he associates with the antichrists, those who have taken the way of Cain, who deny they have sin and who have no truth in them (1 John 1:6, 2:9-11, 3:10-15). They abide in death. John associates darkness with death, and light with life in both his Gospel and his epistle (John 3:19-21, 8:12, 12:35-36, 1 John 1:5-7, 2:8-11). Life that cannot be held by death and cannot be overcome by darkness is *resurrection*.

Paul speaks of God "calling light out of darkness" in 2 Corinthians 4 (2 Corinthians 4:6), saying that just as God called the light out of darkness, He has shone in our hearts to illuminate the glory of God in the face of Jesus Christ. Paul contrasts believers with those who are veiled and blinded by the God of "this world" so they cannot behold the glory of God (2 Corinthians 4:3-4). John and Paul both teach that the present world abides in darkness (Ephesians 5:8, Colossians 1:13, 1 Thessalonians 5:4-5, 1 Peter 2:9, 1 John 2:8).

The reason the light comes out is so that life can come. The focus in Genesis 1 is life. Light comes for life. But when the earth became formless and void, it denotes chaos and destruction, a result of God's judgment. The Hebrew words for formless and void are *"tohu"* and *"bohu"*. We find they only appear a few times and are always linked to chaos and destruction resulting from God's judgment.

God said in Isaiah 45:18 that He did not create the earth formless and void, but to be inhabited. This suggests to me that if I'm going to be consistent with the entirety of scripture, and He says He didn't create it that way, then it's more likely that something happened between when God created the heavens and the earth and when it became formless and void.

He didn't create it formless and void, He created it to be inhabited. So, what happened? Why was there darkness on the face of the deep? The Hebrew word for "deep" is *"tehom"*. It can also be translated as "abyss", "ocean", or "flood". Where did the deep come from? The deep, in scripture, is the abyss, the dwelling place of demons and fallen angels.

Darkness and Judgement

Darkness, consistently throughout scripture, signifies judgment. Water can symbolize either judgment or life, depending on the context. The flood of Noah is a reference to the waters of judgment. So, there was darkness, meaning there was no light, and there were waters - an abyss.

This is the basic premise of the "gap theory" - that there was a gap of time implied between Genesis 1:1-2, which represents a fall of a previous order (the fall of Angels) and a subsequent judgment. While we are concerned with the Biblical account of God's testimony concerning His Son, it is worth noting that there is a parallel "occult" history that inverts these events, and treats the darkness in Genesis 1:2 as positive and the responses of God to the darkness to shape and create order as negative and even evil.

Now, whether you want to believe in what is called the "gap theory" is up to you. This is how I view it.

It is said that G.H. Pember popularized the gap theory in his book "Earth's Earliest Ages". Although I have attempted to read it in the past, I cannot recall much of it. While I was introduced to this idea at some point, my understanding of it is mainly based on biblical accounts related Lucifer's fall. In Ezekiel 28:13-14, it is mentioned that Lucifer once walked upon the "stones of fire" in an Eden-like setting. But due to his numerous transgressions and greed, he was discovered to be iniquitous and was cast out from the holy mountain (Isaiah 14:12-15).

The question that arises is, when did Satan rebel? Was it after or before the fall of man? We know that when Adam and Eve were in the Garden, there was already a negative element represented by the tree of the knowledge of good and evil. Death was present, sin was there, and Lucifer, who had already fallen, was a serpent. He was the *"nakash,"* the shining one, the enchanter. He had already lied and sinned. He was sinning while he was lying to them, introducing them to death and sin. God warned them about death and sin.

Many people may think that the beginning of everything was perfect and without death, but scriptural evidence suggests otherwise. The darkness that covered the earth and the presence of an abyss indicates that some sort of judgment or catastrophic event had already taken place. These negative aspects are related to Satan's kingdom and God's judgment.

The Angelic Perspective

From Satan's perspective, although God desired to have man before the foundation of the world, man would have been perceived as a response to Satan's rebellion and displacement. Satan viewed himself as having authority over this world, being called the God of this world (2 Corinthians 4:4). Do you remember when he promised the kingdoms of the world to Jesus Christ? (Matthew 4:8-9) Was this an idle boast? But was it really his? Not originally! God gave it to man, who He created from the dust of the earth. God made man in His likeness and gave him dominion. This was an insult to the angels (Genesis 1:26-27).

The angels questioned God's decision. They wondered why God was mindful of man, who was made lower than the angels, yet was given dominion over all God's works.

Psa 8:3-6 When I consider thy heavens, the work of thy fingers, the moon and the stars, which thou hast ordained; (4) What is man, that thou art mindful of him? and the son of man, that thou visitest him? (5) For thou hast made him a little lower than the angels, and hast crowned him with glory and honour. (6) Thou madest him to have dominion over the works of thy hands; thou hast put all things under his feet:

According to Hebrews 2, this was an angel that spoke this. To them, it was a wonderful mystery. To some, it was an insult!

God has always worked on the principle, as stated in Corinthians, of choosing the foolish things of this world, the things which are despised, to confound the mighty and the strong. The angels were the first group to be offended by God's choice of "foolish" things. So-called foolish man will be instrumental in displacing Satan not only from the earth but the heavens as well. (1 Corinthians 1:27-28)

Currently, Satan can go back and forth, accusing us before God. But this will come to an end when he is displaced even in the heavens by the manchild, who has been given dominion. The redeemed, regenerated, transformed, glorified, heavenly, new creation man will occupy the highest place of honor.. When you really start digging into it, in his eyes, we have become his replacement. (Revelation 12:10-11)

We are given more than any angel because we are brought into God's heart and made one with Him. This is represented in Genesis 1, even though it is the earthly foreshadow by the Tree of life, which is God's life presented to man as food! I understand that not everyone agrees with this view.

For the record, I still believe in a seven-day creation model. However, there are even some mysteries to the 7 days if we are literal enough with the scriptures.

For example, the sun and the stars were set in place on the fourth day to set times and seasons (Genesis 1:14). We know a 24-hour period is dictated by the Earth's rotation with respect to the sun, but the sun and the stars were not put into their place to govern times and seasons until the fourth day. So, what governed the times and seasons for the first three days? Well, darkness and light, I suppose. I don't have all the answers. I just wanted to let you know where I stand on this.

As we will see, the 7th day is mysterious. Interestingly, it never ended. We are taught in Hebrews that this 7th day, which represents God's rest, is always held forth as "Today" (Hebrews 4:9-10), whether in Joshua's time, David's time, or now.

After the judgment of the angels or whatever this former cataclysm was, the earth was plunged into darkness. Peter mentions that the earth, which was then destroyed, was standing in and out of the water (2 Peter 3:5-6). He then talks about the earth that presently is. It's kind of strange.

These are some mysterious things that come from trying to be as literal as possible when reading the Word.

Principle of Separation

Regardless of whether or not you agree with my interpretation of Genesis as a "restoration" account following a previous judgment, the main idea is that we can see a pattern where darkness is present, then the Spirit moves, and God does something. As we will see, much of what God does from Genesis 1 through 12 is related to separation. He separates light from darkness, and dry ground from the sea, setting boundaries for the sea. He separates the people in what we will call the "line of life" from the people of the world in Cain's line, and separates Noah from the old world through the ark, and later separates the people of Shem's line by language from the people of that world. And as believers today, our hearts, which were once filled with darkness and alienation, become enlightened with the knowledge of Jesus Christ when God speaks the Gospel and shines His light into our lives. This shining continues to distinguish and separate, truth from error, darkness from light, the soul and the spirit, the earthly and the heavenly, the wisdom of God from the demonic wisdom from below.

In Genesis 1, in the midst of the darkness, the Spirit "broods". The Hebrew word depicts brooding like a mother hen over eggs to incubate them for life. (Genesis 1:2). Remember Jesus weeping over Jerusalem and saying how long He had longed to gather them as a chick gathers her hens (Matthew 23:37). Here, the Spirit is portrayed in the same way, hovering over the waters of the deep.

God calls light out of the darkness, and Paul says that this is how God works with us. Our hearts were in darkness. We didn't understand Jesus Christ at all. We didn't understand God's glory. We couldn't even see Him. He was just a historical figure that we discarded and mocked. That was my life. My heart was in darkness, but the Spirit was hovering over me. There were so many people in my life, Christians, that I persecuted and caused to suffer (Acts 9:1-2).

God responded through those praying for me. What was that? That was the Spirit hovering over me through the church. Eventually, He incubated a softness in me that allowed for life and light to come forth. God shined; He called light out of darkness and shined in my heart to illuminate the knowledge of the glory of God in the face of Jesus Christ.

Suddenly, Jesus Christ was "three-dimensional," in my view. He was risen; He was real in my mind. I couldn't stop dealing with Him. I had to contend with Him, and that changed my life and caused me to be born of God. When the light comes, life comes, and that was my eating of the Tree of Life. He made Himself available to me as a kind of food, and ever since then, He has been supplying me with Himself as life and light. And that's true of all of us as believers. This light is how he separates us out from the darkness around us. With it, comes life, and we grow in the knowledge of Him.

We must remember that just because Paul and John use an allegorical spiritual approach, it does not void the literal. This is a literal creation account. God literally created the Heavens and the Earth in seven days. I don't believe that the universe is super old or anything like that. I'm as literal as possible with the Bible. But I do believe that those first three days, there may have been more that happened than what the story portrays. Remember we are looking at this history through the lense of what God wants to tell us about His testimony concerning His Son.

Remember, time is a physical property that bends and changes. It moves at different rates depending on your place in it. It's even impacted by things like mass and gravity, and acceleration. But that's not the point. The point is not the cosmology. The point is the principle. For anything to happen when there's judgment, darkness, water, and death, God responds next with light and life. On the third day, he brings forth *dry ground where life can grow.* God calls forth light by speaking, and by His speaking, He separates the darkness from the light.

Separation

The principle of separation is evident in the first three days of creation. Through His spoken word, God separated darkness from light, heaven from earth, and dry land from water. This same kind of separation is necessary in our lives. God separates soul from spirit, the spirit of fear from the spirit of sonship, the clean from the unclean, and the old from the new. When we are saved and the knowledge of God's glory is revealed to us through Jesus Christ, a process of separation begins. God separates us from our former life by baptizing us into the death of Christ. He separates us from false teachings by washing us with His word. This process of separation is ongoing in our lives.

The Word is a two-edged sword. It is meant to divide. Hebrews says that the Word is living, sharp, and active, sharper than any two-edged sword, able to divide asunder soul and spirit and pierce even to the thoughts and intention of the heart (Heb 4:12). He searches us. The Word is a Person who searches us. Nothing is hidden from the eyes of Him with whom we have to do. This is another reason why the doctrine is strewn through the Bible. On the one hand, you're searching the Word. On the other hand, the Word is searching you!

This searching is for you to discern what's of the old and what's of the new, and is a critical aspect of our spiritual journey. There needs to be a separation. One of the reasons why Christians don't learn and grow is because they don't have that foundational understanding that separation is a good thing. Division is a good thing. Division is of God.

Often, it is said that there's unity in the body and so, therefore, we all need to be one. However, the unity of the body is enjoyed in fellowship, which is a group of people who have been separated out by the word and divided from all the darkness. Remember what Paul said to Timothy:

> **But in a great house there are not only vessels of gold and of silver, but also of wood and of earth; and some to honour, and some to dishonour. If a man therefore purge himself from these, he shall be a vessel unto honour, sanctified, and meet for the master's use, and prepared**

unto every good work. Flee also youthful lusts: but follow righteousness, faith, charity, peace, with them that call on the Lord out of a pure heart. (2 Timothy 2:20-22)

Separated individuals become vessels of honor who can discern the difference between the earth and the heavens, natural things and spiritual things. They have a fellowship that can build up the body of Christ. The oneness is a "separated out" oneness, not a general one. It's not unity for the sake of unity (Ephesians 4:15-16, 2 Corinthians 6:14-15).

Keeping the peace and letting darkness and light, heaven and earth, water and dry, all peacefully coexist is not the way. The word comes, and when the light comes, and when life comes, there's a separation. The dry land eventually is separated. If you want life to grow and the herbs and the grass and everything to start coming forth and generating fruit, you've got to be separate. For us this doesn't mean not watching TV or not dancing, or not wearing pants! It is a separation of being renewed in the spirit of your mind by the entrance of his word, which gives light. (2 Corinthians 7:1, Romans 12:2)

The entrance of the Word is light and gives understanding, and that understanding changes the course of our lives. We are going towards the new city of Jerusalem, moving steadfastly towards Christ. It may not seem like it sometimes, and if it's up to us, we might veer in another direction. But we've been given a faithful Shepherd who will not lose any of us and will bring us home to Glory. Meanwhile, He is providing everything necessary for us to grow in all things into Him, and that's His life growing in us. This is what it means to partake in His life. We are increasingly being molded into Him, and He is fitting Himself into us as He nourishes us with Himself as the Tree of Life (John 17:16-19, Colossians 3:10, 1 Peter 1:23-25, John 6:35-58, Galatians 2:20).

Chapter 4: The Triune God and Corporate Man (Genesis 1)

The Triune God and a Corporate Man For Fellowship

At the end of the sixth day, he had created man. After he made the beasts, he said "Let us make man in our image" (Gen 1:26).

> **Gen 1:26 And God said, Let us make man in our image, after our likeness: and let them have dominion over the fish of the sea, and over the fowl of the air, and over the cattle, and over all the earth, and over every creeping thing that creepeth upon the earth.**

Now, it's important to note that God here is referred to as Elohim, a *plural* noun. "In the beginning, God (Elohim) created the heavens and the earth." This plural noun infers the Godhead, the triune God.

It's also interesting to note that in the Hebrew, there is an untranslated Aleph and Tav untranslated after "In the beginning, God" (Genesis 1:1) and before "created the heavens and the earth".

This Aleph and Tav is not presented in the translations because it's not a word, it's just two characters. The Aleph is the first letter of the Hebrew alphabet, and Tav is the last. This corresponds to the Alpha and the Omega in Greek (Revelation 1:8). These symbols represent the first and the last, which is Christ Himself. I maintain that Jesus Christ is the God of the Old Testament.

This is something that you can see in an interlinear Bible:

"Genesis 1 (KJV) - In the beginning God created." Blue Letter Bible. Accessed 23 Jul, 2023. https://www.blueletterbible.org/kjv/gen/1/1/t_conc_1001

Christ is the creator of all things. Yes, Elohim is the Triune God, but in Christ dwells all the fullness of the Godhead (Colossians 2:9). That's how God has always "done" everything. All of the fullness dwells in Christ, and all of God's works have been done through Christ.

All things were made by him; and without him was not any thing made that was made. (John 1:3)

Consider Christ's words, "Do you not believe that I am in the Father, and the Father is in me?" (John 14:10) He is the only begotten Son "in the bosom of the Father (John 1:18)", and everything God ever did was through Him.

Colossians declares that He is the image of the invisible God (Colossians 1:15). By Him, all things were created, whether in heaven or on earth. In Him, all things consist (Colossians 1:16-17). He holds them all together and is the heir of all things. Everything was created for Him, by Him, through Him, and in Him. They're held together in Him.

Jesus Christ is the subject of the Bible, the Alpha and the Omega, the beginning and the end of God's alphabet. He is the beginning and the end of everything God has to say. He is everything God has to say. He is the Word. He is God's voice. He is the light and the life.

So God, Elohim, the Triune God, said, "Let us make man in our image," using the plural form, "after our likeness," again in plural. But it's one God, not three. They co-inhere and coexist. The Father, Son, and the Holy Spirit exist together as a unity. They cannot be separated and never have been. Everything God does is in the Son, through the Spirit.

God moved on the waters of the deep by the Spirit and then said, "Let there be light." That's how God moves. He moves by His Spirit to release things into existence by speaking. So, everything is the Father, by the Spirit, in the Son. We see this in Genesis.

Singular and Plural

God said, "Let us make man," but then He used "them," a plural term:

(27) So God created man in his own image, in the image of God created he him; male and female created he them.

So we see some kind of wordplay related to the Triune God and his plurality, and the creation of man as a "them" also indicates plurality. God created man in His own image, and in the image of God, He created him. This image is mentioned three or four times. Male and female, He created them. So, it's a singular man, but it's also a plural man, male and female, just like God is. "Let us make man in our own image," God is a plural noun, but it's used in a singular tense. God said it, and He creates man, both plural and singular.

Why? Because he is interested in fellowship. What he wants is to multiply the fellowship. That's why John wrote, "These things we write to you, that you may have fellowship with us, and our fellowship is with the Father and with His Son, Jesus Christ." (1 John 1:3). The mystery of the triune God is profound, but the root of the mystery, and its reason, is simple: Fellowship.

In principle, God deals with everyone by dealing with one man, whether Adam or Christ. Who we are "in" determines our position before God, our inheritance, and our destiny. When God created Adam, everybody was created in him. The principle is that although you were individually thought of by God, you existed in Adam. That's why when he fell, you fell; when he died, you died; when he sinned, you sinned. We are all in Adam, and now we need to be in Christ. He created the first human race in Adam and created the second, the heavenly human race, in Christ. That's why being 'in Christ' is so important versus being 'in Adam'.

This concept is supported by scripture references such as Romans 5:12 and Romans 5:19, which state that "by one man sin entered the world, and death by sin; and so death passed upon all men, for that all have sinned" and "by one man's disobedience many were made sinners, so by the obedience of one shall many be made righteous".

We need to see the doctrine of the two men in these verses. Because of one man's transgression, all of us died. Because of one man's obedience, all are made alive. You're either in Adam or in Christ. That's the difference between the old creation and the new creation, the flesh and the spirit, the old man and the new man.

The only way to get into Christ is to be baptized into His death, to die with Him, and be crucified with Him (Romans 6:3-5). God terminated and put an end to Adam in Christ, the "Last Adam" (1 Cor 15:45). As we will see, this decision was made back in Genesis 6 (Genesis 6:6-7). As we'll see, He already said He repented that He made man, and He judged him. But then, He started calling people out of the Adamic world, starting with Noah, with a view, ultimately to bringing forth a new race in the resurrection of Christ.

Through His human living, death, and resurrection, the Seed of the Woman, the Seed of Abraham, the Seed of David and the Last Adam, Jesus Christ, was clothed in incorruptibility. Afterward, He came and breathed Himself into the church to make them born of this new, incorruptible life that will eventually clothe them and fit them for a new, incorruptible heaven and earth (John 20:22; 1 Cor 15:53). The purpose of this new city, the New

Jerusalem, is fellowship (Rev 21:3). God and man will dwell together forever - God as the Father, with His many sons; the Bridegroom with the Bride, whom He loved and gave Himself for; the Son with His brothers, conformed to His image and glorified.

This is the ultimate destiny of every redeemed person and these people, brought together in Christ are made into "One New Man" (Col 3:10; Eph 2:14-17). God began with a "him" that was a "them" with Adam, and in the new creation, the Body of Christ, the New Man is one, a He (Christ) and they (the many sons of God) who are members of Him and have His life. We will see more of this when we come to Genesis 3.

But as mystical and profound as this is, the underlying root is very simple. Even in the types, we see multiple designations, the core motivation is relationship and fellowship. The driver for the desire to fellowship is to know and be known, understood, shared, appreciated, and loved. And this is eternal life. Remember, Jesus said, "This is eternal life, that they may know You, the only true God, and Jesus Christ whom You have sent." Even the presentation of life in the Bible, whether created or Divine, is related to consciousness and knowledge because, at the root of all of this, there is a communication of God to His beloved creation. Even "dead matter" is for communication - theheavens declare the glory of God!

Chapter 5: Dominion at the End of the Sixth Day (Genesis 1)

The End of the Six Day is Dominion

Gen 1:26 And God said, Let us make man in our image, after our likeness: and let them have dominion over the fish of the sea, and over the fowl of the air, and over the cattle, and over all the earth, and over every creeping thing that creepeth upon the earth.

While the root of everything in this account is a desire for fellowship, there is still the matter of restoration and subjecting negative elements brought in through the collapse (discussed previously) and the fall. This is what the Kingdom of the Heavens is all about. Man is given dominion over everything on the earth. It's an earthly dominion. As we've said, "First the natural, then the spiritual. First the earthly, then the heavenly." Imagine yourself as an angel watching this, as Lucifer watching this. He was inflamed, he was angry, he was jealous, he was filled with rage at man's creation, and would have seen it as an insult and as a response. Man is not a response to Satan in the long term, man was God's focus the whole time. But Satan would likely have seen it as a strategic response. Man now had the authority and was told to "subdue" the earth and "replenish it." Again, I believe these hint that there was already "Trouble in Paradise."

Six in the Bible is associated with man and is often said to be his number. This 6th day ends with man, created in God's image and given authority. The end of the 6th day establishes a dominion where things are subdued, and in my view there is a hint of something negative here. But the beginning of the 7th day, as we will see, is the blessing of rest with the Tree of Life as its center. We will focus quite a bit on the 7th day and its meaning and spiritual significance as we move through these chapters in Genesis.

The Kingdom of Heaven and the Kingdom of God

These two "days" (the 6th and the 7th) can be related to two aspects of God's kingdom, known later in the Bible as the Kingdom of Heaven and the Kingdom of God. Let's take a closer look at the difference between the kingdom of the heavens and the kingdom of God. The kingdom of the heavens, even though it contains the word "heavens," is actually related to the earth and the affairs of the realm in which man lives. I believe it began with giving authority to man. The term really shows up in Matthew (Matthew 3:2, Matthew 4:17, Matthew 5:3, Matthew 5:10, Matthew 5:19-20, Matthew 6:10, Matthew 7:21, Matthew 8:11) and refers to Christ, the seed who was promised to Adam and Eve, coming to inherit the Throne of Glory promised Him as the seed of David (2 Samuel 7:12-13; Psalm 89:3-4; Isaiah 9:6-7). Christ is the Seed of the Woman (Genesis 3:15), the Seed of Abraham (Genesis 12:7; Galatians 3:16), and the Seed of David (Jeremiah 23:5-6; Acts 13:22-23).

These titles all refer to things that were spoken about the One who was to Come, who is the "seed to whom all the promises were made" (Galatians 3:16). He is the heir of the kingdom of the heavens and the one who will ultimately accomplish its purpose. Where Adam Failed, the Last Adam, the Second Man, succeeds (1 Corinthians 15:45). These titles include all of the promises related to our great salvation, from crushing the head of the serpent (Genesis 3:15) and dealing with sin (Hebrews 9:26), the curse (Galatians 3:13), the fall of man (Romans 5:12-19) to the ruling of the nations with the rod of iron (Psalm 2:8-9; Revelation 2:27; Revelation 12:5) and subjecting them to God (1 Corinthians 15:24-25). In this kingdom, Christ will rule the nations making His authority known to all (Revelation 11:15). It is a kingdom characterized by judgment (Matthew 13:41-42; Matthew 25:31-46) and the subjugation of negative influences (1 John 5:18-20). From the perspective of where we stand in time, this kingdom is still yet to come in its fullness.

The **Kingdom of God,** on the other hand, manifests in the 7th day and is a realm where God's life operates unfettered. It's an intrinsic sphere of influence that is timeless and limitless (the 7th day never ends and is always "today", as we will see.) Its primary focus is God's life and divine authority, as opposed to material aspects or visible demonstrations of power. A believer becomes part of this Kingdom when they partake in God's grace and life and truly come to know God. Righteousness, peace, and joy in the Holy Spirit are the distinguishing features of this Kingdom (Romans 14:17), emphasizing the spiritual and relational aspects of the divine life.

In this Kingdom, believers are ushered into God's household and family, attesting to the intimate, familial relationship between God and His people. Jesus expressed this when He said, "But the kingdom of God is within you" (Luke 17:21, KJV). He reminds us that this kingdom isn't about external, material things; rather, it's about an inner reality of peace, joy, and righteousness in the Holy Spirit. Another scripture that supports this understanding is Colossians 1:13 (KJV), which says, "For he hath delivered us from the power of darkness, and hath translated us into the kingdom of his dear Son." Here we see that believers have been transported into a different realm altogether, where they partake in the divine life of the Son.

In contrast, the Kingdom of the Heavens represents the outward manifestation of God's kingdom on earth, specifically connected to the throne of David. This kingdom primarily focuses on God reigning through His people and the establishment of His will on earth. The divine life operates through human life in this Kingdom, creating a unique union of the divine and the human, but is a condescension on God's part to involve Himself with the affairs of men in human terms.

The Kingdom of the Heavens is envisioned as the Kingdom of God applied to the earthly sphere, bringing the divine life into humanity's daily experiences. This is beautifully captured in the Lord's Prayer: "Thy kingdom come, Thy will be done in earth, as it is in heaven" (Matthew 6:10, KJV). Jesus promised His followers a place in this Kingdom, saying, "And I appoint unto you a kingdom, as my Father hath appointed unto me" (Luke

22:29, KJV). The ultimate manifestation of the Kingdom of the Heavens is prophesied in Revelation 11:15 (KJV): **"The kingdoms of this world are become the kingdoms of our Lord, and of his Christ; and he shall reign for ever and ever."**

While these two Kingdoms overlap and are interrelated, they serve distinct purposes and possess unique features. The Kingdom of God emphasizes the operation of God's life and divine authority, and it can be accessed by believers here and now, while the Kingdom of the Heavens points to the future realization of God's reign on earth through His people. However, both represent different facets of God's comprehensive rule and provide a complete picture of His dominion, where love, grace, and intimate fellowship between the Father and the Son are the ultimate realities.

When I talk about the difference between the kingdom of God and the kingdom of Heaven in my teachings, I often emphasize that the kingdom of God has to do with a kind of life and its affairs. To help illustrate this point, I like to use the analogy of a cat watching me as I pay bills at my desk. The cat belongs to the feline kingdom and has its own set of affairs and concerns. As I write checks, the cat may see my pen moving around and interpret it as an attempt to play with him. However, the cat cannot understand that I am actually engaged in managing the household economy of the human kingdom, paying bills that contribute to the well-being of our family and the establishment of our kingdom.

Similarly, the kingdom of God is not just about an outward rule or an earthly throne, such as the establishment of the Davidic throne on earth. Rather, it is about entering into God's life and experiencing his divine affairs. Jesus taught that in order even to perceive or enter the kingdom of God, one must be born again, born of water and of the Spirit (John 3:5). This new birth is not just a change in status or adherence to rules, but a transformation that enables us to partake in God's life and understand his purposes.

In the kingdom of God, we become partakers of God's divine nature (2 Peter 1:4) and are brought into his household and family. We experience righteousness, peace, and joy in the Holy Spirit (Romans 14:17). It is a realm where we fellowship with the Father and the Son, sharing in their love and intimacy. This fellowship is not limited to an earthly kingdom with outward rules, but a deep, intimate love affair between Christ and his church, flowing from the eternal love of the Father and the Son in the Spirit.

While the kingdom of the Heavens begins with the man appointed to subdue and replenish the earth and ends with a rod of iron and dealing with nations of people who cannot perceive the kingdom of God, the kingdom of God is eternal in nature. and belongs to God's life. It is not limited to a specific time or place. In fact, even after the kingdom has been delivered to the Father, life will go on forever in the realm of the kingdom of God. It is an everlasting reality where righteousness dwells, and there will be no more death or pain. It is a kingdom based on God's love and grace, where we experience the intimate fellowship between the Father and the Son.

When Christ delivers the Kingdom (which I believe refers to the Kingdom of the Heavens) to the Father, and God is "all in all," I think this will mark the beginning of something new - the ages to come. In these ages, God will no longer condescend to deal with human affairs; instead, humanity will have been fullyuplifted to participate in divine matters.

Chapter 6: From Elohim to Jehovah Elohim (Genesis 2)

Elohim Revealed – Jehovah Elohim

Now we move on to Genesis 2, which begins with the setting apart of the 7th day. The way this chapter presents makes some people think that there is a second creation account Adam and Eve, but that's not really it. I believe that it's just "zooming in." In Chapter 1 we saw God speaking everything into existence, defining it, declaring, and separating and setting boundaries. You could think of Genesis 1 as a series of definitions. But in Genesis 2, those definitions manifest as reality for man in the Garden on the 7th day. Another way to view it is to see that the view is "zooming in" and bringing everything described in the first 6 days into "focus" on the 7th day.

There is something else introduced here. God begins His interactions with man not as God Elohim, but as Jehovah Elohim. As we saw in our messages on chapter 1, everything accomplished in Chapter 1 was the work of God (Elohim). But we saw that by the inclusion of the Aleph and Tav after the name Elohim, Christ was implied. Perhaps we could say "Christ was concealed" in Genesis 1. Then, starting in Day 7, you'll notice that it is the "Lord God" in the KJV. This is the english for Jehovah Elohim. This is the one who interacts with man and reveals Himself to Him. (Genesis 2:1-3; Genesis 2:4-7). Genesis One has

Christ concealed (Elohim and a hidden Aleph Tav) and Genesis Two revealed Jehovah Elohim.

The second chapter begins with a sanctified seventh day. We will explore the concept of the "Sabbath Rest." This corresponds with God's revelation in the holiest to a man no longer separated from God by the veil. In the Old Testament, God was hidden within the veil in the Tabernacle and in the temple, and people could not access Him. But in the New Testament, the holiest has been opened. God has been revealed in the person of Christ and is now accessible to us. Likewise, in Genesis 1, Christ is unknowable. The works of creation are coming forth from the mysterious God, Elohim. But in Genesis 2, God sanctifies the seventh day and interacts directly with man, as Jehovah Elohim. This is Christ revealed. The basis of the reality of the "Sabbath Rest" is the revelation of Jesus Christ and faith in Him.

Jehovah is a transliteration of the unpronounceable YHVH. Jehovah Elohim is the pre-incarnate Jesus Christ who walked with Adam in the cool of the day and had a human form. He is known as YHVH, which is unpronounceable because He has not fully revealed Himself. Although in Hebrew, a pictographic alphabet, each character in the alphabet has a symbolic representation of something related to Christ. If you are unfamiliar with this, you can google paleo Hebrew and the name of YHVH to find many resources. This is the person who appeared to Moses and spoke to him as a man, even as a friend. Jehovah, the God of the Old Testament, is Jesus Christ. He said to the Pharisees, " Abraham rejoiced to see my day. He saw and was glad." They then questioned, "You're not even 50 years old. How can Abraham have seen your day?" He replied, "Before Abraham was, I am." He declared to them that He was the God of the Old Testament. He was the voice in the burning bush that proclaimed, "I am," to Moses. (John 8:56-58; Exodus 3:14)

Furthermore, He is the man who appeared to Abraham in Genesis 18 and shared a meal with him. This is Jehovah. This is Jesus Christ, Jehovah Elohim. He is the one who will interact with the Adam that He created in the Garden on the seventh day. The Hebrew word for Eden is עֵ֫דֶן (pronounced ay'-den). The word can be translated as "delight" or "pleasure," but it is also related to the word "rest" or "abode." So while "rest" may not be the most common translation, it is valid. God starts dealing with man in rest, and man begins in rest. We have talked a lot about rest in our studies of Hebrews. we'll see it in Genesis as well. The blessing of rest will be a major theme as we will see in these first few chapters off Genesis. (Genesis 18:1-8)

The Seventh Day of Creation and God's Rest:

> **Thus the heavens and the earth were finished, and all the host of them. And on the seventh day God ended his work which he had made; and he rested on the seventh day from all his work which he had made. And God blessed the seventh day, and sanctified it: because that in it he had rested from all his work which God created and made. (Genesis 2:1-3)**

Notably, 'created' and 'made' are two different Hebrew words. 'Created' refers to His speaking things forth out of nothing, while 'made' usually refers to Him fashioning something out of something that already exists.

God created the heavens and earth, but then He made all these things. The idea is that He created everything out of nothing, but then He made things on what He created out of existing materials, including man. 'Let us make a man in our own image,' He said, but He when He made man, he used His own hands and existing materials (clay). The rest of the things God made by speaking them forth. With man things are kinetic, tangible and personal. How much more personal can God be than breathing life's breath into man's nostrils?

The Significance of Entering God's Rest:

Now the view has shifted and we are in the 7th day. Each of the previous days was marked by an evening and a morning. There's been debate over how long these days were. Some assume they were 24-hour periods. I don't have a problem with that. God could have accomplished everything in one day, but He chose to break it down into seven periods, each marked by a cycle of darkness and light. It's fascinating to observe that darkness follows as a response after God does something. Night, often associated with negative things in the Scripture - drunkenness, sleep, judgment, spiritual blindness - follows each divine act in Genesis 1. It definitely seems like a struggle of light and darkness. There is no fellowship between the two.

According to the scriptures, the seventh day of creation was not a 24-hour period, and it has not ended. In Genesis 2:2-3, it says that God ended his work on the seventh day and rested, blessing and sanctifying it. However, unlike the previous six days, there is no mention of an evening and morning for the seventh day. This suggests that the seventh day is ongoing and everlasting.

In Psalm 95:7-11, the author urges the reader not to harden their heart as the Israelites did in the wilderness. The author reminds the reader of God's promise of rest and warns them that they will not enter that rest if they grieve God and do not heed his voice but harden their heart (in unbelief). The author is referring to the seventh day of rest mentioned in Genesis and suggests that it is still available to God's people.

Similarly, in Hebrews 4:1-11, the author warns the reader against the disobedience of unbelief, which can cause them to miss out on the present enjoyment of God's rest. The author explains that the seventh day of rest mentioned in Genesis foreshadows a present rest that is available to believers. The author encourages the reader to strive to enter that rest and not to fall short by disobedience.

Thus, according to Psalm 95 and Hebrews 4, the seventh day of rest mentioned in Genesis is still available to believers and can be entered through faith. The writer of Hebrews represents that today is the day:

Seeing therefore it remaineth that some must enter therein, and they to whom it was first preached entered not in because of unbelief: Again, he limiteth a certain day, saying in David, To day, after so long a time; as it is said, To day if ye will hear his voice, harden not your hearts. For if Jesus (Joshua) had given them rest, then would he not afterward have spoken of another day. There remaineth therefore a rest to the people of God. For he

that is entered into his rest, he also hath ceased from his own works, as God did from his. Let us labour therefore to enter into that rest, lest any man fall after the same example of unbelief. (Hebrews 4:6-11)

the writer of Hebrews is arguing very plainly from the scripture that if Joshua had really brought the people into rest when he brought the into the land, how could David in teh psalms, hundreds of years later, present the rest of God as "today?" Because God's rest is always today. It is a present reality.

Based on this seven-day model setup in Genesis 1, God instituted the Sabbath with all of its seven-day cycles for Israel's prophetic timelines, a commemoration of all of God's accomplishments, but especially a commemoration of the significance of the "Rest" of God. It is amazing to me how many people spend their time arguing that the earth was created in 7 literal 24 hour periods and yet never encourage anyone to enter rest, and often rail against it.

The old creation culminated on the seventh day when God rested from everything He created and made. This rest is what God wants His people to enter into. The Good land, in the old testament was often referred to as the 'rest' for God's people. The Holy of Holies in the temple and the tabernacle is also known as God's resting place, serving as a symbolic representation of rest. God's ultimate goal as a shepherd is to guide His people into rest.

Psa 23:1-2 The LORD is my shepherd; I shall not want. (2) He maketh me to lie down in green pastures: he leadeth me beside the still waters.

The seventh day sanctifies the completed work of God. God completed His work, blessed it, and sanctified it. In the Old Testament, it is true the severest punishments were for not keeping the Sabbath, which symbolizes rest. Butt he Pharisees had turned the Sabbath into a burden, imposing restrictions on even the most minute infractions. However, Jesus taught the true significance of the Sabbath. Jesus corrected this, "stating that the Sabbath is for man, not man for the Sabbath." God provided man with a rest to liberate him from burdens, not to impose them! (Exodus 20:8-11; Matthew 12:1-14; Mark 2:23-3:6; Luke 6:1-11)

In their feast system, the Israelites observed the Sabbath as a reminder of the significance of rest. They were to rest in the finished work of God. The most faith was required to keep the seventh Sabbath year, also known as a week of years. They were to plant the field for six years, and on the seventh, they were to let the field fallow, living off the provision from the six years. This required faith and was a signifier that they understood God as the provider, not their labor.

The judgment on the nation and their captivity in Babylon was related to this (2 Chronicles 36:21). For 490 years, the people of Israel did not keep the Sabbath, and God punished them by bringing them into Babylon for 70 years. This allowed the land in Israel to rest for 70 years, which were the 70 years of rest that they owed God (Leviticus 26:34-35). In other words, working on the Sabbath was a significant transgression because it violated God's principle of rest. It required faith to let the land lay fallow, particularly for farmers, because it meant foregoing profit from their work. They failed to do so, and God eventually punished the nation not only for this, but for other transgressions as well (Jeremiah 25:11-12).

The point is, God set these severe penalties in place for Israel to teach them about His desire for humanity to enter into a state of rest. To enter rest, in this context, means to enter into one's inheritance and a recognition that everything comes from God, and that He supernaturally supplies.

An inheritance is something that's provided for you without your labor. For New Testament believers, death of the testator has occurred, and now we have a testament, an inheritance. Our salvation is an inheritance, and it was symbolized by the good land. This land was an inheritance for the children of Israel and was called their rest. (Hebrews 9:16-17, Hebrews 9:15, Hebrews 4:1-11, Hebrews 11:8-16, Deuteronomy 12:9-10)

According to the passage, the rest of God is symbolized by the Holy of Holies, where God Himself dwelled (Hebrews 9:3-8), and it is called His rest. Believers are encouraged to enter this rest and enjoy God as their portion (Hebrews 4:1-11). This rest is not a burden, but an enjoyment. Unfortunately, Christianity and religion often turn what God has provided as a rest and enjoyment into a burden (Matthew 23:4).

This is how you can discern whether you should listen to a Bible teacher. Do they make the Christian life a burden, or do they bring you into rest? Christ is here to be our rest. He said, **"Come to me, you who are weary and heavy-laden, and I will give you rest. I am meek and lowly,**

and I will rest your souls." He's our shepherd. What does a shepherd do? He leads us beside still waters and makes us lie down in green pastures. He puts us to rest, anoints our head with oil, and gives us a feast in the presence of our enemies. He promises that we'll dwell in the house of God forever. That's our inheritance. He makes us heirs and brings us into rest. That's His intention, that's what the gospel is for, and that's the reality of the Christian life: entering into rest.

If you want to be disobedient and grieve God, then don't enter rest. Stay in unbelief, don't obey the gospel, and remain in your own labors, toiling and putting burdens on others. That's how you grieve God. People talk about pleasing Jesus with works, but the way to truly please Him is by enjoying Him as your rest and providing Him to others as rest. This is your stewardship, your ministry, and this is actually our "work".

Chapter 7 God's Rest and Man's Purpose
(Genesis 2:1-3)

The creation account is not merely about the formation of the world; it's God dealing with man and the principle of rest. He brings man into a garden where everything has been provided for him - a place of rest. God gives man something to do, tending the garden, but nothing is strenuous about it. Man isn't out digging in the dirt, bringing forth thorns and thistles by the sweat of his brow to get bread. Instead, he's simply pulling fruit and herbs from trees, consuming what's provided.

God's intention for man's existence was not burdensome toil. Unfortunately, after the fall, Cain thought it was. He worked in the cursed earth, not resting at all, having no vision of rest. He believed God actually desired the cursed fruit of the ground and the result of his toil. Cain didn't understand that such toiling was a result of the fall. God's intention wasn't for man to sweat, toil, and be burdened. His intention in salvation is not for us to be burdened and heavy-laden, but to bring us into rest, as he did when he first created man.

God created and prepared everything, then placed man in the garden on the seventh day. On the sixth day, he did make man, but on the seventh day, he revealed himself to man and put him in the garden. This is where we see God interacting with man, and it's an important principle. For example, where did one have to be in the Old Testament to interact with God? In the Holy of Holies, which was their rest, God's rest. To enter rest is to be in the presence of God.

God's Interactions with Man in the Seventh Day

In the Holy of Holies, interaction with God wasn't available to them because of the thick veil. They had to work in the holy place, tending the tabernacle, and only the high priest could enter the Holy of Holies. Only the high priest could commune with God. This was a picture, according to Hebrews 9:8-9, because as long as that holy place stood with all of the works and labor of the priests, it showed that the way into the holiest was not yet manifest.

Christ has entered the holiest, ripped the veil, and taken it out of the way. He has made his own flesh a new living way to bring us into the presence "within the veil", where we can be at rest again. You can only have fellowship with God at rest, in the Holy of Holies. If you are laboring, burdened, and heavy-laden in the holy place, keeping the sacrifices, maintaining the incense altar, the showbread, and the lampstand, it just shows that you have not been brought into the holiest. In the holiest, there's nothing for man to do. God is his rest.

Yet, the holiest becomes a very active place because Christ is living. Hebrews says that the blood of Jesus is to purge our conscience from dead works to serve the living God (Heb 9:14). How? By bringing us out of the holy place with all the works and burdens and into the holiest, with the presence of the living God. The dead works are cast out, and through the death of Christ, which terminated all of them, we enter the place where the finished works of God are manifested in resurrection.

During the days of the Tabernacle, the priests were laboring in the Holy Place, but the Living God resided in the holiest, and that's where we yearn to be. Now we have access. Coming back to Genesis, it's crucial to understand that God reveals Himself and communicates to Adam in the rest on the seventh day, not on the sixth. If you're still in the sixth day, which symbolizes man, work, and creation, God is still working, and you're also expected to work. There's no communication with God on the sixth day in principle. You must be in the seventh day.

Furthermore, the revelation of God occurred on the seventh day. It was not just God (Elohim) speaking to Himself ("let us make"), but Jehovah God, Jehovah Elohim, speaking to humanity. He introduced Himself and walked with Adam in the cool of the day, indicating that fellowship is found in rest, salvation is in rest, and God's intention is rest. His desire is for us to be at peace. He arranged circumstances so that humans would interact with Him beginning on the seventh day.

Those who constantly focus on works, living in the "sixth day," also speak about God but rarely mention Christ. They do not extol the person and work of Christ because, in the sixth day, He is only implied. On the other hand, those who live in the "seventh day" by enjoying their privilege as sons and heirs based on faith in the finished work of Christ, possess a detailed knowledge of Christ. Their discussion of spiritual matters is marked by a focus on Christ.

This seventh day never ended; it's always available today to enter into rest by faith. God is still in the seventh day. The generations of the heavens and the earth were created in the day that Jehovah Elohim made the heavens and the earth.

Creation and Manifestation in the Seventh Day

Gen 2:4-6 These are the generations of the heavens and of the earth when they were created, in the day that the LORD God made the earth and the heavens, (5) And every plant of the field before it was in the earth, and every herb of the field before it grew: for the LORD God had not caused it to rain upon the earth, and there was not a man to till the ground. (6) But there went up a mist from the earth, and watered the whole face of the ground.

Here's another interesting thing. When Genesis speaks of the 7th day, it says the heavens and earth were created in generations, and made in a day. Remember we said in Genesis 1 there are the words "created" and "made". God created the heavens and the earth. This is to create something out of nothing. But he made the things in it. This is to make something out of already existing materials. And now in Genesis 2, we see God created them in generations and made them in a day. I don't believe we can fully understand this was time creatures.

Remember, Hebrews, when talking about rest, says the works were "finished from the foundation of the world." There is likely a "physics" explanation for some of this. But there is definitely a spiritual meaning. God created something (the heavens and the earth) and then He made something (the earth and the heavens). Then it says he created and made every plant and hebr of the field before it was in the earth and before it grew! When did it actually get put in the earth and begin to grow? From the plain reading of Genesis, it seems like the 7th day was the day of "manifestation."

The concept here is that in Genesis 1, God created everything, declared its existence, and affirmed its goodness. However, in Chapter 2, on the seventh day, everything starts to manifest. The blessing of everything God has ordained comes in the condition and day of rest, and Rest is where God reveals Himself in Christ.

Now we see the Lord God, Jehoavh Elohim for the first time:

Gen 2:7-9 And the LORD God formed man of the dust of the ground, and breathed into his nostrils the breath of life; and man became a living soul. (8) And the LORD God planted a garden eastward in Eden; and there he put the man whom he had formed. (9) And out of the ground made the LORD God to grow every tree that is pleasant to the sight, and good for food; the Tree of Life also in the midst of the garden, and the tree of knowledge of good and evil.

Many read this and interpret it as a second creation, but it's not. It's a zoomed-in view of the seventh day. During the six days of creation, God ordained everything and spoke it into existence. But the manifestation of the blessings, the positive aspects, occurs on the seventh day at least in type. I believe the 7th day overlaps the previous days and was "Today" then too. I believe the 7th day refers to the blessing of God manifested in Christ when all his decrees come forth for man's satisfaction. We covered this quite a bit in our pass through the Gospel of John, which will hopefully be a book soon.

As far as I know, the Bible does not mention the seas on the seventh day. We previously discussed that water was viewed as negative, and in the book of Revelation, it is written that in the new heavens and new earth, there will be "no more sea". This does not mean that there will not be bodies of water, rivers or lakes. However, the seas come from the abyss and the deep and were separated from the land when God brought it forth on the third day. It was only the land that was brought forth on the third day, which is also known as the day of resurrection.

In the state of rest, God brings man into existence, into his finished work. This is the emphasis of the seventh day, God's rest. God performs a creative act in rest. On one hand, the works were finished before the foundation of the world, but on the other, God is still active. This is what people often misunderstand about rest. They think it implies laziness or inactivity, but that's not the case.

Jesus, in resurrection, is the true embodiment of rest and is active. He is the *living* God. To enter into rest is to have your conscience purged from dead works to serve the living God. And yes, that service is a rest. We present ourselves to Him, but then He is active personally. This is the aspect that many fail to see or believe. They think that if they stop working, God won't work.

But it's actually when we cease our work that God begins His work. This intimate, personal fellowship can only be enjoyed in the "seventh day." It's when God becomes not just Elohim but Jehovah Elohim, and He creates you with His hands. It's incredibly intimate. Imagine Jesus himself, using His hands in the clay to form man.

Jehovah Elohim revealed Himself to man on the Sabbath, the day of rest. As we've said, this rest is pictured later by the Holy of Holies in the good land. It's a principle that runs through the entirety of Scripture. I'm using the law of first mention and expositional constancy to interpret this. I'm not making up my own ideas, but observing what the Scripture tells us about the Sabbath, why God instituted it, and what it depicts.

The Sabbath is a picture of God in Christ taking the burdens off of man, opening his eyes so that he can see Him, unveiling Him, bringing him into the Holy of Holies, and giving Himself to man as satisfaction. That's what the Sabbath is. You didn't have the reality of the Sabbath, you just had a picture unless you were in the Holy of Holies with the Shekinah. Now, the Shekinah glory and the face of Jesus Christ has been illuminated in our hearts. God's desire is to shepherd us into rest and bring us to a place where we're unveiled.

Creative Works on the 7th Day

This work of God is healing, but it's also creative. Remember the story at the Pool of Siloam if you need a visual representation of this. Jesus performed a creative act on the Sabbath. He made clay, put it on a man's eyes, and opened his eyes. The man said he saw men like trees, and then Jesus did it again, and then he saw clearly. The first thing that man ever saw was the face of Jesus Christ. That is the real significance. We don't see anything until we see Jesus Christ, and when we see Him, we are in the 7th day and living as a result of His creative work. (John 9:1-7)

This is probably what it was like for Adam to wake up when God breathed into Him. First, he saw trees, then he saw Jesus. It is a creative act, on one hand, to form man, but on the other hand, He's revealing himself. Elohim said "Let us create man" on the 6th day. But on the 7th day Jehovah Elohim formed Clay into a man, breathed into Him and woke Him up. (Genesis 2:7)

When He is healing you so you can see Him, He recreates you in His image. He's forming you in His image in the new creation. First the earthly, then the heavenly. We have the heavenly reality: God shone in our heart to illuminate the knowledge of the glory of God in the face of Jesus Christ in our heart, and to bring us into rest. He opened our eyes and healed us of our blindness, and in doing so, He recreated us in His image. (1 Corinthians 15:45, 2 Corinthians 4:6)

Now, we're not to be conformed to this world but be transformed by the renewing of the mind. We need to be renewed to enjoy the reality of rest, which is pictured as living water for us to drink. On the Sabbath day, the great day of the feast, Jesus said, "If anyone is thirsty, let him come to me and drink. Out of his innermost being shall flow rivers of living water" (John 7:36-38). The satisfaction is on the Sabbath when you have the reality which is Christ. Because we're in the new creation, this reality breaks us free from the seven-day pattern and brings us into the eighth day, the future day of the New Heavens and New Earth. But that is beyond what we can touch upon here.

The Lord God formed man of the dust of the ground and breathed into his nostrils, and man became a living soul. So, Jesus breathed into the first man and made an earthly man. But the last According to 1 Corinthians 15:45, Adam became a living soul, while Christ is the last Adam and a life-giving spirit. As the head of the human race, Christ inherited all of the titles, blessings, and covenants that God made with man, including the line of the tribe of Judah, the seed of David and Abraham. He went to the cross to destroy the old Adamic fallen human race and was made a life-giving spirit in resurrection.

When Jesus appeared in the upper room, he breathed into the disciples and said, 'Receive the Holy Spirit.' This is the "pneumatic" Christ, who is able to recreate people by breathing himself into them. He created the church through this creative act and is the transmittable, pneumatic, and life-giving spirit (John 20:22).

When we are regenerated and born of God, it means that Christ, the life-giving spirit, has joined himself to our spirit and made us part of a new creation in resurrection. As it says in 1 Corinthians 15, our body is sown in dishonor, raised in glory, sown in weakness, and raised in power. We have a natural body and a spiritual body (1 Corinthians 15:44).

However, that which is first is not spiritual but natural, and afterwards, that which is spiritual. The first man is of the earth, earthy. The second man is the Lord from heaven.

As of the earthy, such are they that are earthy. As is the heavenly, such are they that are heavenly. As we've borne the image of the earthly, we'll also bear the image of the heavenly (1 Corinthians 15:46-49).

Adam was created in the image of God, but it was an earthly image. Now, Christ, the last Adam, became the life-giving spirit. He's the Lord from heaven and he's remaking us in his image, not to bear the image of the earthly, but to bear the image of the heavenly. That's the trajectory of the church. We are going to be glorified, recreated in his heavenly, glorified image (1 Corinthians 15:45-49).

This is the Christ that appeared to John in Revelation. John fell at his feet as though dead. His eyes burned like a furnace, his skin was like bronze, and his face shone as the sun in its strength. We'll all be like that because we'll bear the image of the heavenly. But first, we had to be born of earth, then we had to be born of God. That's the pattern (Revelation 1:12-18).

So, the whole scripture, when we look at 'God created man in his own image, in his likeness, he formed him out of the dust of the earth,' it was Jehovah that did that on the Sabbath day, on the day of his rest, when all the works were accomplished. He breathed into him and made him a living soul. This man was created in his image.

But now, in the reality of the Sabbath, which is Christ and resurrection, after he's accomplished the work of redemption and finished our salvation work and the creative work of the new creation, he comes to us and breathes himself into us. This act reforms us in his image, in our spirit. We're to put on the new man who's created in the image of Christ, after true righteousness and holiness.

We're going to be transfigured into the likeness of His glory, to bear the image of the heavenly. First, we experience the earthly, then the heavenly; first the natural, then the spiritual. This is the principle. So, yes, this is a picture in the Old Testament of something that really did happen. Yet, it's also a picture of what God ultimately wants to accomplish.

That's why we say Jesus is on every page in Genesis. His redemption is on every page in Genesis because the whole Bible is encoded in Genesis. You can extrapolate all the major things that happen in the whole Bible by seeing them played out in the pictures in Genesis. I hope you're tracking with me.

The Tree of Life on the 7th Day

Genesis 2:7-9 And the LORD God formed man of the dust of the ground, and breathed into his nostrils the breath of life; and man became a living soul. (8) And the LORD God planted a garden eastward in Eden; and there he put the man whom he had formed. (9) And out of the ground made the LORD God to grow every tree that is pleasant to the sight, and good for food; the Tree of Life also in the midst of the garden, and the tree of knowledge of good and evil.

God created man, formed him on that blessed and sanctified day of rest. On the 7th day, God planted a garden eastward in Eden and put the man he'd formed there. So,

He didn't create him in Eden, He put him in Eden after he formed him.

So, that's the next step. Yes, God breathed into him, he became a living soul. That was the earthly, and he bore the image of the earthly. He was made of clay. But now, God wants to do something further, represented by the tree of Life. That represents God Himself, to become man's satisfaction forever. The eternal life, which is God in Christ, is presented as food, something you can take into yourself.

That's a theme that goes all the way through scripture too. God presents salvation in the light of eating and drinking. Sin had to do with eating and drinking from the very beginning. So, what we take in is very important because what you take in becomes a part of you. God's purpose is that God would be what you take in. Instead, man took something else into himself, represented by the tree of the knowledge of good and evil. The problem is no different today.

For instance, what does it mean that Jezebel is causing God's servants to eat things sacrificed to idols (Revelation 2:20)? In Corinthians, Paul had said that if you are in the marketplace, don't worry about what you eat. If you're invited to a party and the food was bought in the shambles, it doesn't matter. Although many of those foods were sacrificed to idols, he said not to worry about it, except for the sake of the person who is serving it and claims it was sacrificed to idols. If you know that it was sacrificed, don't eat it, not because of your own conscience, but because you could damage the conscience of the person serving it, who believes there is something behind it.

Well, if Paul said that, then what can Jesus mean when he says Jezebel causes my servants to eat things sacrificed to idols? It must be talking about something different, right? Well, what you eat becomes who you are, and God's intention is for us to eat Christ. "Unless you eat my flesh and drink my blood you have no life in you."

We're always taking something in, and whether we're pure or unclean has much to do with how and what we eat! We'llelaborate further in the next section.

Chapter 8
Spiritual Principles, Rest, 6th and 7th Day Overlap (Genesis 2)

Let's delve into a fascinating question: did God create man on the sixth day or on the seventh? My response would be both. I recall a college religion class where they dismissed Genesis as mere folklore, claiming it presented two creation accounts. Such an interpretation from a non-spiritual perspective seemed too simplistic to me.

The wording of Genesis itself suggests an overlap between the sixth and seventh days. Verse five of chapter two, presumably referring to the seventh day, asserts, "Every plant of the field before it was in the earth and every herb of the field before it grew," implying God had already created these elements.

The narrative states, "**These are the generations of the heavens and the earth in which they were created, in the day that the Lord God made the earth and the heavens.**" This raises questions about which day it refers to: the first or another?

When Genesis 1 discusses God "making" something, it suggests He was using existing materials, unlike when He created the universe by simply speaking. This distinction is particularly noticeable in the making of man, where it describes God forming man with His hands and breathing life into him.

This event is attributed to the sixth day, but when did we transition to the seventh? The second chapter seems to begin with the seventh day, but the creation of the heavens and the earth remains ambiguously timed.

The narrative circles back, stating, **"Thus the heavens and the earth were finished, and all the host of them. And on the seventh day, God ended His work which He had made. He rested on the seventh day from all His work, and He blessed the seventh day and sanctified it because He rested from all His work which God created and made."**

The phrase, "the generations of the heavens and the earth in the day that God made them," may seem strange at first glance. However, intentional confusion in the Bible's delivery often serves to encourage deeper contemplation. When we encounter a stumbling block, it may be God's way of urging us to slow down and reflect.

The Significance of the 7th Day

The significance of the 7th day is profound. It's a concept that often slows me down and prompts me to think deeply. Over my time studying scriptures, I've often found myself reading along smoothly until suddenly, I feel as though I'm wading through "molasses." Questions such as, "When did He create it? Did He finish it on the seventh day or the first day?" arise and leave me pondering. It's a strange and complex topic; I won't pretend to have all the answers.

I can say that the seventh day is somewhat of a mystery. It's associated with God's rest, as it symbolizes the completion of His work. It's the day when He acknowledges that all is finished, rests, and blesses and sanctifies the day. This is the first use of the word "sanctification" and the first introduction of the concept of holiness. This blessing and sanctification are reflected throughout the Levitical system, which God established to commemorate His rest. The strict observance of the Sabbath is tied to this spiritual principle God wants to illustrate.

Considering the whole of the Bible, I would say blessing is connected to inheritance, while holiness is linked to the divine nature or the priesthood. Maintaining the priesthood in the image of God relates to partaking in the divine nature. Being blessed, in turn, is associated with having dominion, which is a key aspect of the kingdom and priesthood. These are two vital elements for God to be represented by man, whom He created in His image and granted dominion.

When we look at the sixth day, we see that God created man in His image and gave him dominion. This is the blessing and the priesthood, or sanctification. However, God blessed and sanctified the seventh day, the day of His rest. The Sabbath, the seventh day, is where everything happens. The high priest enters the holy of holies on the Sabbath. It's a crucial day, a day when God manifests His blessing for His people based on all of His accomplished, and His people are brought into rest with Him. Rest is an enjoyment of the blessing of God's provision. Being fully satisfied with what God provides is the way for man to ultimately express God and live as His representative.

This is really something to think about. If, for example, we are not satisfied with God, perhaps based on ignorance of what He has done for us, how can we be expected to proclaim Glad Tidings about Him? How many people go on mission trips or door-knocking campaigns who think that this service is a way that they as a slave can put God in their debt so that He will bless them, or even worse, go for fear that if they don't, they will miss out on God's blessing or God will not be pleased with them? How "good" and attractive will their so-called Gospel preaching really be? I can tell you from personal experience that being completely dissatisfied with God, thinking He is displeased with you, that He will punish you or that you must earn some blessing from Him does not make for a good representative of the Gospel! I think many times we are afraid to tell people about Jesus because we are not actually enjoying anything about Him.

6th and 7th day Overlaps

When we see the numbers six and seven intersecting in scriptures, we often witness something supernatural. Take, for example, the story of David returning the ark to its rightful resting place from Obadiah's house. He was so thrilled to have the ark back in the tabernacle that he danced before it. However, it's noted that he took six steps before the ark and only broke into dance on the seventh (2 Samuel 6:14-16). From a charismatic perspective, it's as though God's power hit him on that seventh step, and he entered into something supernatural.

This pattern is repeated in the story of Jericho. The people marched around the city six times, and it was on the seventh time that something extraordinary happened (Joshua 6:3-4,15-16). They blew their trumpets, the seven, and the walls fell down. The 'seven' is when God manifests. That's the point.

In the Old Testament, the seventh day, or the Sabbath, was related to the Holy of Holies, the rest of God, and the good land as the inheritance. The Holy of Holies signifies the priesthood, sanctification, and everything that is holy. The good land signifies the blessing, the dominion, the kingdom, and everything God has for man as an inheritance.

Entering God's Rest

According to the Bible, the seventh day marks God's supernatural intervention in human affairs. This is why we are urged to strive diligently to enter into rest - not because we are attempting to do nothing, but because we desire God. We are presented with a choice between having ourselves and our own works, or God and His works. God's desire is to bring us into the manifestation of what He has ordained - His power and His work - which is the kingdom.

People who have a moralistic view of the Christian life look at it entirely in the light of six days, man's toil, his works, and keeping commandments. That's all related to being out in the Holy place, not having entered the land typologically. It's man's stuff. It's not God. It's related to

God because it seems religious, but it's not God Himself intervening.

On the seventh day, we assume that He's talking about events that happened. But from man's perspective, it could still be the six because we know that on the sixth day, God created man. He's talking about creating man, forming him. What's the difference, though?

Well, you see, Jehovah God, who is the God who reveals Himself and gives a name, set His name, the holiest places, where God set His name and manifested Himself. So this all corresponds to rest. When God reveals Himself, personally intervenes, and does something directly, you've got the seventh day intersecting with the sixth day again.

The way it's written, it's like molasses. It's hard to determine where the sixth day ends. Are we in the sixth day? We're still talking about the seventh day. What are we doing here? Well, it's a principle that God's rest is held out every day. It's always 'today'. The seventh day is always available today. You can either rest in God's work or keep trying to maintain your own. You can be in the sixth day or you can be in the seventh day, depending on whether you're in faith or unbelief. That's what Hebrews is about. It's about entering His rest, entering the seventh day today.

The reality of rest is Christ, seated at the right hand of God. He's got all authority in heaven and earth. He's purged our sin, He's made the one offering, He's forever sanctified those who He's forever perfected. He's there as the high priest according to the order of Melchizedek with bread and wine to minister Himself to us as life for our satisfaction and enjoyment. All of that is related to being in the seventh day. In principle, you've got no enjoyment, you've got no High Priest, you cannot find satisfaction with God, nor can you sense His presence unless you're in the holiest place on the Sabbath. This is where we're supposed to live.

The law of first mention is always vital. In the first mention of the seventh day, there's a sense of molasses, as you're trying to distinguish where the sixth day ends and the seventh day begins. Which part belongs to the sixth day, and which belongs to the seventh? It's not seemingly clear unless you have spiritual understanding.

The seventh day is God's day, and He comes to you from that day. Don't think of these as periods of time. That's the other problem. We assume that they're consecutive. God wants us to think of these as principles; the numbers have meanings. Six is related to man, and seven is related to God's creation and His fullness. There were in fact six consecutive days, but the spiritual principle is beyond time. Today is always the seventh day, and today is when God reveals Himself to the heart that's open to Him.

We see God, Jehovah Elohim, revealing Himself and intervening, personally forming man. You get the idea it's with His very hands, out of the dust, and then breathing into him the breath of life, like CPR. Jesus is personally, intimately intervening. He's right there, Jehovah Elohim, and He's the first thing Adam would have seen. It's presented as if it's on the seventh day, but we know from chapter one that it's the sixth day. Which is it? It's both. It's where God intervenes with man, into man's affairs, and that's what the kingdom is. The kingdom is God intervening. The kingdom of the heavens is God intervening in man's affairs.

This is how He brings the seventh day. God brings the seventh day with Him. The Day of the Lord is the Lord Himself. He's the day spring and the morning star. He brings the day. So, it's not meant to be super clear because it's not. There should be some molasses as you read through this, some ambiguity. It should make you feel like you don't quite understand because the natural man does not easily understand spiritual things (2 Corinthians 4:18).

Most people these days read the creation account according to their natural understanding. They think about disproving evolution, but that's natural thinking. I am not an evolutionist. God created everything. But the point is we are so carnally minded. If God is talking about the seventh day of blessing, sanctifying it, making it holy, and manifesting Himself in it, He's talking about spiritual things (Romans 8:5-7). He's talking about God Himself, and from His perspective and His position of rest, He created everything. He finished it, and then He blessed and sanctified that day (Genesis 2:2-3).

So, if you want to talk about holiness, if you want to talk about bearing the image of God and the kingdom, and His blessing, you need to understand it from this perspective. Most people these days read the creation account according to their natural understanding. They think about disproving evolution, but that's natural thinking. I am not an evolutionist. God created everything. But the point is we are so carnally minded. If God is talking about the seventh day of blessing, sanctifying it, making it holy, and manifesting Himself in it, He's talking about spiritual things. He's talking about God Himself, and He created everything from His perspective and His position of rest. He finished it, and then He blessed and sanctified that day.

So, if you want to talk about holiness and bearing the image of God, the kingdom, and His blessing, you need to understand it from this perspective.

The seventh day is when the blessing occurs, that's when God intervenes. Are we talking about a period of time? No, we're discussing entering in by faith. It's always today. If you're in unbelief, you're in the sixth day. If you are in faith, resting in God, resting in Christ in principle, you're partaking of the seventh day where God intervenes. This is what the Christian life is about. The Christian life is God intervening, not man doing something for God. God enters into your life. He didn't call you to do something, He called you so He could enter in. That's the point.

The Formation of Man

This brings us to the formation of man. We know from Chapter One, that man was created in His image and given dominion, the priesthood, and the blessing, the kingdom. As God's likeness and His representation, God's intention is that man would represent Him, bear His image, and reign with His authority. This is how God's authority is manifested on earth and is the reality of the "Kingdom of the Heavens."

Eden

Genesis 2:9-14 - And out of the ground made the Lord God to grow every tree that is pleasant to the sight, and good for food; the Tree of Life also in the midst of the garden, and the tree of knowledge of good and evil. And a river went out of Eden to water the garden; and from thence it was parted and became into four heads. The name of the first is Pison: that is it which compasseth the whole land of Havilah, where there is gold; And the gold of that land is good: there is bdellium and the onyx stone. And the name of the second river is Gihon: the same is it that compasseth the whole land of Ethiopia. And the name of the third river is Hiddekel: that is it which goeth toward the east of Assyria. And the fourth river is Euphrates.

But now, God is describing the garden He made. Is this on the seventh day or the sixth? I believe it's the seventh day. The seventh day is when God puts together all His finished works to be a blessing for man. He forms man, He personally intervenes, He reveals Himself to man, and He puts him in a garden called Eden, which is a paradise. There's the Tree of Life and the Tree of Knowledge of Good and Evil. Supernatural occurrences are happening on the seventh day.

We're not just talking about natural things, if you're discussing the Tree of Life and the Tree of the Knowledge of Good and Evil. We are victims of Renaissance art. We think of an apple tree. No, it's the Tree of the Knowledge of Good and Evil. We're talking about spiritual things versus the Tree of Life. Adam and Eve woke up to deal with spiritual things. They woke up in a spiritual environment, they woke up in the seventh day in Eden, in a paradise where everything had been provided. They were presented with the Tree of Life and the Tree of Knowledge of Good and Evil.

The Rivers of Eden

But it says a river went out of Eden to water the garden, and from there it parted into four heads. Their names are significant.

Pison: The name "Pison" is believed to be derived from the Hebrew word "Pishon," which means "increase" or "abundance." The river Pison is said to have encompassed the land of Havilah, known for its gold, bdellium, and onyx stones.

Gihon: The name "Gihon" is associated with the Hebrew word "Gichown," which means "bursting forth" or "gushing." The Gihon river is mentioned to have encompassed the whole land of Ethiopia.

Hiddekel: The name "Hiddekel" is thought to be derived from the Assyrian word "Idiklat," which means "Tigris." It is one of the four main rivers mentioned in the Bible and is described as flowing east of Assyria.

Euphrates: The name "Euphrates" is believed to have originated from the Greek word "Eu-phrates," which means "well-fruitful" or "well-watered." It is one of the most famous rivers in the world and is known for its historical significance.

Three rivers are rich in spiritual significance - Pison, Gihon, and Euphrates. Pison and Gihon are associated with abundance. Pison is linked with gold, bdellium (a type of pearl), and precious stones, and Gihon is associated with the gushing forth of blessings and provision. We know nothing about the locations or histories of these rivers. On the other hand, Euphrates is well-known in history; its name means "fruitful" and "well-watered," but that is the Greek word. The Hebrew word, Perath, is formed from the letters "Pey," "Resh," and "Tav," which all point to Christ. "Pey" conveys the concept of speech, speaking, and words. "Resh" is associated with leader, chief, and preeminence. "Tav" is associated with covenant, sign, seal, or markings.

These three rivers in Eden are associated with blessings, abundance, provision, and the rest of God on the seventh day with His man in His image and likeness. This man is appointed and marked to be God's spokesman, and his speaking is to be supplied by his enjoyment of the abundance and provision of God. This is how the Christian life and service work, by the way. When we are full of the knowledge and sense of everything we have in Christ, our real Sabbath rest, and are conscious of His riches and His presence, we are "watered" and renewed, which causes us to speak, and in this speaking, we represent Him. What is our speaking about? All of these things we have enjoyed in Him because of a covenant. I'm sure we're just scratching the surface of meaning here.

However, the other river, Hiddekel, is interesting in that it does not seem to be associated with any particular sense of blessing. Hiddekel is a transliteration of the word "Tigris," which is a river we know about. It is said in Genesis to be "east of Assyria." Historically it goes toward Iraq. Tigris can be translated as "swift as an arrow." We know that Assyria and Iraq are the places where two wicked cities emerged, one known for violence (Ninevah) and one for rebellion (Babel). A leader emerged from there, Nimrod, who was said to be "a hunter of the souls of men" in the book of Jasher, but in Genesis, he is called "a mighty hunter before the Lord" (but the Hebrew word for 'before' can mean in the sight of or also against or in opposition to.) It is interesting that the river that flowed in this direction, the Tigris, not openly associated with any blessing, is "swift as an arrow." The Hebrew word, had the Het pictured as a forbidding wall, which can mean separation and also hiding, the Dalet, which is "path or entrance," and the Qof, which can be associated with "revolution."

In Eden, two rivers represented blessing and provision, and we know nothing about them. They seem to have disappeared from the history along with the blessings of Eden. Another two rivers go out to the world, the Tigris and the Euphrates. The latter is associated with blessing, proper leadership, and speaking for God. The former the Tigris, seems to be associated with separation, rebellion, wickedness, Assyria, and nimrod. Man was also presented with the Tree of Life and the Tree of the Knowledge of good and evil. The man was given dominion, but was he going to be a priest or a rebel?

Nimrod and Babel become the root of the world system and represent, ultimately the beast system with the antichrist at the end. The man of sin who opposes God and exalts himself above all that is called God, the seed of the serpent, also referred to as the "Assyrian" in the Bible (2 Thessalonians 2:3-4, Revelation 13:1-18, Genesis 10:8-12).

I feel the path of Hiddekel and the tree of the Knowledge of Good and Evil go well together, as do the Tree of life and the Euphrates. Both flow out of Eden and into the world, both are paths "out." One is a path of destruction and rebellion, and the other a path of blessing and representation of God (Genesis 2:9-14, Revelation 21:1-27, Revelation 22:1-5).

The significance of gold, bdellium, and the precious stone onyx can be seen in the Bible. Bdellium is actually a type of pearl that grows in sea beds. As we continue to explore the Bible, we encounter the New Jerusalem at the end. This city is made from precious stones, gold, and features a river called the river of the water of life. The Tree of Life and gates made of pearl are also found within the city (Genesis 2:12, Revelation 21:1-27).

This pattern suggests a typological connection to God's building. First, the natural, then the spiritual. The place where Adam was put signifies the initiation of themes that point towards the New Jerusalem. This city is the ultimate consummation of God's work, which involves working himself into man. The river, the water of life, symbolizes God, flowing out of the throne of God and the Lamb. The Tree of Life, which grows along the river's banks, and the river itself, represent Christ as food and drink to sustain the city (Genesis 2:9, Revelation 21:6-7).

Living stones, which are people, construct this city. They've been transformed into precious materials for God's dwelling place. From its inception, the Bible is a narrative of life and building. Genesis 1 emphasizes life, whereas Genesis 2 points to the building material. On the seventh day, the building material - gold, pearl, and onyx, the precious stone - were presented. These are merely types; they were literally there but also serve as symbols (1 Peter 2:4-5, Revelation 21:18-21).

God's building always starts from a position of rest. For instance, the temple couldn't be built until they were in the good land and had rest from their enemies. Solomon was able to construct the temple after David had conquered all the enemies. It's not for wartime, but for peacetime, that the temple is built. God's authority steps in, the priesthood maintains its position, and God's blessing is there. The children of Israel were brought into the good land to establish the temple and the priesthood, to have dominion, the kingdom, and to have a holy man, represented by the priesthood. This process is mirrored in what God did with Adam (Exodus 23:20-31, 1 Kings 5:3-5, Genesis 1:26-28).

In the Old Testament, physical types are images of spiritual realities. There really was a temple in the good land, but it's not the real temple of God. The church is being built into a holy temple in the Lord. We're being built up to be a dwelling place of God in spirit. We are living stones that are being transformed and wrought within with gold (1 Corinthians 3:16, Ephesians 2:19-22, 1 Peter 2:5). In this, we have all the pictures. God laid it all out in pictures first to demonstrate the principles of what he was going to do. All the spiritual things that are ultimately fulfilled in Christ have analogs in the natural, in God's creation, in the stories in the Old Testament where he showed it all forth by pattern. So, it's just interesting to see how these principles arewoven into the fabric of the biblical narrative.

Chapter 9 What Rest Means (Genesis 3)

Rest in Eden

The seventh day of rest is reminiscent of Eden, the paradise of God, and the Tree of Life. These elements are positive, as are the building materials of gold, bedellium and onyx, and the river. All these features are prototypical of the new city, Jerusalem.

God gave the first humans commands, primarily related to what to eat. Interestingly, He did not explicitly command them to eat from the Tree of Life. Instead, He instructed them not to eat from the tree of the knowledge of good and evil, warning that they would die the "day" they ate from it. One might wonder, when exactly was that day? They lived for a thousand years before they physically died.

We often become fixated on aligning the Genesis account with our 24-hour day and night system in an attempt to disprove theories like evolution or an old Earth. However, this is not about supporting or refuting old Earth or evolution theories. Rather, we miss the spiritual significance when we take such a dogmatic and single-focused approach.

One person commented on my teachings about Genesis and said, "I know why you have a problem with Genesis...you don't realize that Darwin was a Jesuit, and those institutions you call 'schools' are brainwash centers."

Somehow, this person extracted from my teachings on Genesis that I have a problem with it and that I support evolution. This is an example of someone who is blinded by an ideological, dogmatic, and single-focused approach.

If I don't approach Genesis to prove that the Earth is flat or only a certain age, in this person's mind, it must be because I support the institutional education system and am an evolutionist myself. However, do you believe that Genesis was written to prove to Western European culture that the Earth is a certain shape? Is that really what this book is about? Spiritual principles are at play that require us to keep an open mind. And as we said, when we feel like we're wading through molasses, it's because we've encountered something of spiritual depth. This whole chapter is dense with such meaning

God told them they could freely eat from every tree, including the Tree of life, but forbade them from eating from the tree of the knowledge of good and evil.

The Tree of Life was certainly preferable. Had they eaten from it, they would have lived forever. The Tree of Life is what God intends for us to have. It's found in the new city, Jerusalem, in the paradise of God, and is entirely positive.

Then, why didn't God command them to eat from the Tree of life? Instead, He warned them not to eat from the tree of knowledge, threatening death. Why didn't He simply instruct them to eat from the Tree of life?

The answer lies in grace. Everything associated with absorbing God into our lives is due to grace and is freely chosen. The Bible says, "The spirit of the bride says come and let him who is thirsty come and drink freely of the water of life" (Revelation 22:17). There's no demand or command related to the good things God has prepared for us as an inheritance and blessing.

On the other hand, God does command us not to partake of the tree of knowledge of good and evil, warning that it will lead to death. Thus, they had two choices: to willingly partake of God's blessings or disobey His commands. Actually, we discover that if we are not satisfied with the Tree of Life, we have no strength not to disobey His restrictive commands.

God's commands are often restrictive, outlining what we should not do or have. They have a negative nature. To illustrate this, imagine a house with notes saying "pick up your trash," "leave the toilet seat up and wipe your poop off the sides when you're done," and "throw away used Kleenex instead of leaving them all over the room." Would you think this is a clean or messy house? The presence of negative commands indicates that something is wrong, not right. You don't tell an "A" student, "I'd better not hear you're cheating on your schoolwork and you better be getting it done." That's reserved for C, D, or F students. Commands are spiritual, good, holy, and right but point to something negative. In eternity, we will not live by commands, but rather by the incorruptible life of holiness that the law points to but does not provide. Adam and Eve were created in such a good situation that they should have desired the good things.

Temptation to Leave Rest and Work for What You Already Have

Unfortunately, Satan tempts us with evil things by presenting them as something good. Satan tempts us by presenting something evil, but he lies about it and dresses it up to make it look good. That's what religion is. It is sin cloaked in a beautiflu garment. You think you're doing something that's going to please God.

When Satan first tempts us, he uses the good thing but suggest we misunderstood it or misheard it. Eve thought, "This tree looks like it would make me wise and it'll make me like God." Did they really think they were disobeying God? I think down deep, they did. But Satan had turned Eve around so much that she had questioned what God said. Well, did God even really say that? Are you sure you got it right?

Satan presented this as something good for them and claimed God was withholding it. But if they had it, everything God wanted for them would be fulfilled. That's when Adam and Eve took of the tree of the knowledge of good and evil. They fell. That's when the curse, the toil, the labor, the burdens, death, and sin came. Everything came from leaving the position of rest by seeking to add something freely available to them in their situation.

They already had the Tree of Life. They were already in the image of God. They were already blessed. They'd already been given dominion. They had everything. They were in the garden, right? They had God Himself walking with them. They had everything.

That's the principle of rest. Everything is complete, everything is furnished. What did Satan do? He tempted them to exit rest and go back into their own thing. Their own works, their own knowledge of good and evil, their own judgment, their own discernment, their own provision for themselves.

God's only command that we really see is "You can't eat of the tree of the knowledge of good and evil." Again, it is restrictive. But as far as the rest of the trees, including the Tree of Life, they could have it whenever they wanted, and as much as they wanted. They could eat freely. That's how grace works.

Grace is an invitation to enjoy Christ, and it's freely given as a blessing. There's no sense of debt. There's no "I owe Him. I better eat 15 pounds from the Tree of Life today. I've got to eat this tree." No, that's not how it works. It's just there for you.

Christ is unassuming like that. He does not demand from you. The principle of rest is that it is the day no man can work. Nobody can do anything. It's all God. That's the point.

The Tree of Life symbolizes the essence of the Sabbath

The Tree of Life symbolizes the essence of the Sabbath and is considered the ultimate manifestation of God's divine revelation. When God created life during the process of creation, the Tree of Life marked the pinnacle of His work.

In the order of complexity, from the simplest and least conscious to the richest and most complex, one might think that it ends with man. Man, being the highest consciousness, the highest life. Yet, he is set before the Tree of life. If you observe the entirety of scripture, you'll see that the Tree of life represents God in Christ. It is meant to be man's food, his satisfaction, to take him in so that man may have his life. Man was created in the image of God to live God's life.

Consider the example of a glove. A glove without a hand in it is deflated. Yes, it's in the shape of a hand, but if it doesn't have the hand in it, it's going to be deflated. The fingers of a glove can be likened to our virtues. We do have an echo of God's virtues. We have the capacity to love, the capacity to be merciful, the capacity to be good, to do good, to be kind. All these things that God has are shaped in us. We're formed in that way.

However, if we are not filled, if the glove is not filled with the hand, then those finger shapes hang loosely. They deflate and deform. They don't hold their shape. That's what man is apart from God. Yes, we do have an echo of these virtues, but we can't sustain any of them. I can be kind in the morning and mean in the afternoon. My son can come to me wanting to play, but five minutes into it, it's getting old. He becomes more and more obnoxious, and I'm done. I want it to stop. I need my space. My kindness deflates. All of our virtues are like that. None of them are incorruptible.

We've been called to partake of the incorruptible virtues of the divine life. How do we do this? By taking them in as food, taking Christ in as food. Unless you eat my flesh and drink my blood, you have no life in you. We need to learn to partake of Christ so that he can fill us with himself and shape our virtues to be conformed to him. That's why it says we're predestined to be conformed to the image of the Son. That he might be the first order among many brethren. Conformed means my shape is being held by somebody else. My virtues are flaccid and deflate, but Christ's incorruptible virtues are imperishable. He's always merciful. He retains his form. He's God in man. God's life is the incorruptible life.

God's intention was that this life get into man as food. Yet, He did not make a demand on man to take this life. He made it freely available, and that's why the kingdom is taking forever to manifest. Because God made it a free gift and gave us the ability to freely choose. Since sin entered the picture, we don't choose Him. Eventually, He will put an end to all man's works and bring it in. But right now, He is saying look. That's why we don't have the authority to compel people to partake of Christ. He doesn't want to drag man to the Tree of life and make him eat of it. He wants man to understand that and freely choose based on an understanding.

Understanding that the Tree of life is everything man needs, God had to let man have the option to go another way. This is because, in going the other way, we've learned how much better it would have been.

The Purpose of Allowing Sin and Experiential Knowledge

Someone once asked me, "Why didn't God just kill Adam and Eve and be done with the whole creation? Then create one that would be right so we wouldn't have to have all this mess?"

Well, God is vindicating His righteousness and establishing the ground of trust so that in the ages to come, we'll never have a question of whether it could have been better another way. We got to experiment with it all. We know what the tree of the knowledge of good and evil produced, and what sin, death, and separation from God are. We've seen how our virtues deflated, how we destroyed the world and didn't maintain the image of God, losing His blessing.

When we get it all back in Christ and He brings us into the kingdom, we will freely love Him forever. We will know what perfect knowledge is and how good what we have is. Adam and Eve didn't know yet. This reminds me of what Paul said, "I pray that you love me more and more, and in all wisdom and understanding, that you may approve by testing the things which differ and are more excellent." There is an experiential knowledge that God wants us to have.

It's like a kid who was homeschooled and never went out of their house or to a party. They were raised in Christian homes, which is good, but then, all these options were available to them in college. They would backslide terribly, party, and act recklessly. After they had been dragged through the mud, many of them would hit rock bottom and return to the Lord, like the prodigal son. Now they knew how good it was in their father's house.

Until they've been dragged through the mud, sinned, and eaten the pig slop, they won't realize that The Father's

House is the best. That's what God wants. The Amish have a tradition where their kids are raised sheltered, then they let them go out and taste the world. God didn't withhold that from us.

Solomon, in the book of Ecclesiastes, led an experimentation in everything good and bad. It's astounding that he used all of God's wisdom to explore everything under the sun, only to find out that it was all vanity, both the good and the bad. Now, that doesn't mean it's a good thing. Evil is evil, sin is sin, and wickedness is wickedness.

In training my dogs or even my young child, I would allow them to make a mistake within certain limits. This way, they could face the consequence of their actions. The aim is to teach them - you give them a modicum of freedom, and as they approach something they shouldn't, you advise them not to. Essentially, you're teaching them to learn by feeling the boundaries. You're training them to respond appropriately, to understand that they don't want to engage in certain behaviors.

Consider this in the context of God, who had to let us go through all this mess so that we could appreciate the goodness we have in His house and understand what His Kingdom really is. He gives us a negative backdrop, and then His grace shines so brightly in contrast to that negative backdrop. Without experiencing anything negative, we might have just taken it for granted.

Sometimes, I say we should appreciate the time we live in. We're never going to have another opportunity in the ages to come to experience humiliation, insult, embarrassment, or failure. I'm not suggesting we pursue these things, but given that we're swimming in this toxic stew, it's unavoidable. However, we have the redemption of Christ and can freely come to Him and drink as much as we want. God knows how to arrange environments and allow situations that make us crave His presence intensely. He works with us, and never afbandons us. He allows us to go through things to train us to desire God over evil.

It's not about wanting good over evil, because then I'm still left to myself. I'm just a good version of myself, which is as empty as an evil version of myself. I want God. The Tree of Life is God himself to be your life and to sustain you by Himself. The tree of the knowledge of good and evil results in death, regardless of whether you choose good or evil. They're godless, devoid ofGod's presence.

Chapter 10 More on Christ a Rest and Enjoyment (Genesis 2-3)

Currently, we're examining Genesis 2, specifically the significance of the seventh day. The 'law of first mention' is at play here. As we saw in the introduction, this law suggests that when God first uses a word, it sets the context for its subsequent usage. In this case, God blessed and sanctified the day upon the completion of his works, signifying His entry into rest. This should be the framework for our understanding of "holiness." If we talk about holiness, we should be talking about rest!

The Three Types of Rest

At the beginning of Chapter 2, we have the establishment of the "Sabbath Day" - the 7th day set aside, sanctified and blessed. What is the purpose of the Sabbath in Hebrews? God's rest is portrayed in three ways in the Old Testament: Sabbath Day, the Good Land and the Holiest.

The Sabbath day symbolizes that God's rest is always available "today" for those who believe. When the "7th" day becomes our day, the past is gone, and we live in a state of " newness " created by God's finished work in Christ. Observing the Sabbath also signifies recognition of God's completed work and our ceasing from our own efforts. Rather than striving to change our condition or position, we acknowledge what God has done in Christ to bless us, regardless of our circumstances.

The Sabbath rest always being today means that every moment we can start fresh and new before God, and enjoy His provision and fellowship without requiring any work on our part to approach Him incrementally. Right now is the acceptable time, and today is always the day of salvation.

The Holy of Holies, the second type of rest, is where God is manifested and man can do nothing. While the sabbath day seems to represent the availability of the rest of God at any time, the Holiest represents His actual manifestation with His presence. Just as in the case of the Sabbath, there are no work of man in the holiest. The focus is on the completed work of Christ (represented by the ark of the testimony that was in the holiest with the propitiation lid and the blood that covered the broken law). All dead works are gone, which were represented by the priests with their services and sacrifices who maintained everything outside the holiest. They had no access to the holiest, and Hebrews 9:16 makes the point that as long as those works were going on, they just demonstrated that the way into the holiest had not yet been manifested. With the holiest, You are brought through the veil into the presence within and depicted as a living sacrifice (Rom 12:1-3). In this state, God must be the one to act next.

The Good Land is the third major type of "rest" in the Old Testament. The land is described as the "rest" for the children of God, but it also becomes the resting place for God's presence, represented by the temple, which is more permanent than the tabernacle in the wilderness. This land signifies their enjoyment of everything God has provided for them as an inheritance, without the need for toil. Since the curse, man has had to labor with the sweat of his brow to produce food from the cursed ground. However, in the good land, milk and honey flow freely (Hebrews 4:9-11). Everything is provided for you in the land, and you can find iron and ore just by putting your axe in the ground. The provision is abundant, symbolizing God's inexhaustible supply in his fullness, which is meant for your enjoyment, blessing, and inheritance. The enjoyment of the riches of their inheritance enabled the people to produce the Temple of God, which became God's rest as well. In the situation where God is resting in His building as the result of the people's enjoyment of their inheritance, God gains His inheritance - the people themselves (Deut 32:9). The people in the land, enjoying the riches that are freely provided by God become God's dwelling and inheritance. From the Garden to the Good Land, we have a unified picture of Sabbath Rest that prefigures the "Holy City, New Jerusalem." (Hebrews 4:9-11)

These three elements - the day, the Holy of Holies, and the good land - were all called rest, and all serve as metaphors to help us understand what rest and holiness truly mean. Rest is the present tense availability of Gods presence and blessing manifested because of His finished work in Christ, and this is the base and reality of holiness.

Rest and holiness are therefore intertwined. This rest is depicted by the day that we enter into rest, which is always 'today' if we believe. If we are in unbelief, we are not at rest. However, by faith in Christ, and exercising our faith in Him, we can enter into rest. We find rest in His finished work. In the holiest place, the rest is enjoyed in acknowledgment that Christ has already completed all the necessary offerings and preparations, making his own flesh a new and living way to bring us into the presence within the veil. There we have access to the "unsearchable riches of Christ" represented by the riches of the good land, to be our satisfaction and inheritance, and it is in this way that we are built up to become the habitation of God in spirit as Christ makes His home in our heart through faith.

In every type of rest, man is presented as totally dependent on God. God is manifested in the realm where we are powerless, and He does all. Rest, and holiness are dependent upon God bringing man into the enjoyment of Himself.

Man in a Garden of Rest

Now, God is placing man in a garden, called Eden, meaning pleasant, which can also be translated as "rest." Here, Every tree is available for him to eat freely. There all the pictures point to an inexhaustible supply, the trees, the food, the gold, bdellium, Onyx and the gushing rivers, as we saw in the last chapter. Furthermore, there is the Tree of Life, which symbolizes God's endless, incorruptible life. There is also a river with four heads, a foreshadow of the river of life that fills the New Jerusalem flowing out to all four sides of the square city.

First comes the natural, then the spiritual. This is a real event to which spiritual principles can be applied, but the literal should never be negated. A theologian named Origen erred in his excessive allegorization by dismissing the literal. He claimed that none of this happened and were merely allegories. He even fabricated what the allegories were. This was the beginning of the Catholic Church's allegorization of the Kingdom and the dismissal of the Kingdom by claiming that Israel would not literally inherit their land. They claimed all these promises were not literal and that they fell on the Church. They argued that the Church is spiritual Israel, and we are the Kingdom of God, and He reigns in our hearts. They dismissed the existence of David's throne.

It's important to remember that the literal comes first. Spiritual principles can be discerned by comparing the literal to themes that develop throughout the scripture. This is the correct approach. Paul allegorized in Galatians when he said that Hagar and Sarah were a picture of Sinai and the Jerusalem, which is above, and the law versus grace. He stated that Ishmael represents the flesh, while Isaac represents walking in the spirit by faith in the promise. He referred to this as an allegory but did not deny the literal events. He tied the metaphorical meaning to an actual reality that occurred.

This is an important distinction to remember when people start allegorically interpreting Genesis. We must be cautious. Are they negating the literal in their spiritual applications? Are they fabricating the allegorical from their own minds? This is a dangerous path. The Catholics, for instance, began making their own interpretations, leading to absurdity because they did not adhere to expositional constancy. Again, this principle, along with the law of first mention, dictates that God uses words and themes consistently throughout the scripture. These themes are seen repeatedly in the scripture, providing consistent illustrations.

When I use allegorical references like this, I'm not just conjuring them up from my own mind. I'm telling you what the word teaches on these things and referring to themes that you can confirm in the scriptures.

The Riches, the Inheritance and the Enjoyment

Rest is connected to the Sabbath day, the good land, and the holiest of all. Each has a different emphasis. When I read through the scriptures, I see that the good land is a picture of God's rest. When I return to Joshua and Numbers, I see what is said about the good land. The main feature is its riches, which are the people's inheritance and enjoyment. They enter for satisfaction, and it is there that God builds his temple and establishes his kingdom, using the freely available riches.

> **Numbers 14:7-8 "7 And they spake unto all the company of the children of Israel, saying, The land, which we passed through to search it, is an exceeding good land. 8 If the LORD delight in us, then he will bring us into this land, and give it us; a land which floweth with milk and honey."**

The good land is a picture of the unsearchable riches of Christ (Eph 3:8). Paul talked about how the blood of Jesus Christ has qualified us in (Colossians 1:12) to partake in the allotted portion of the saints in light, which is our inheritance. But it's a reference to the good land. It shows us that Christ is the good land.

After he speaks of the unsearchable riches of Christ in 3:8, Paul then prays that we will be strengthened according to the riches of his glory into our inner man. That Christ may make his home in our hearts through faith, that we be rooted and grounded in love, which are planting words.

Ephesians 3:16-19 That he would grant you, according to the riches of his glory, to be strengthened with might by his Spirit in the inner man; (17) That Christ may dwell in your hearts by faith; that ye, being rooted and grounded in love, (18) May be able to comprehend with all saints what is the breadth, and length, and depth, and height; (19) And to know the love of Christ, which passeth knowledge, that ye might be filled with all the fulness of God.

The fullness of God is a temple reference, an allusion to the temple where God is fully manifested. The height, breadth, length, and depth of the love of Christ, which passes knowledge, is another allusion to the good land. Abraham was told to walk the breadth and the length of the land that his children and his seed were to inherit. (Genesis 13:17)

In other words, consistent language throughout the scriptures connects these things. There are references to the good land that apply to Christ. The good land had so many riches which showed Christ as our enjoyment. He is the milk and honey, the rivers and the streams, the iron and the ore, the fig and the olive. He is all the things that abundantly flow out of God's inexhaustible supply for his children to be their inheritance and enjoyment.

Consider Christ. We know that Christ is the lamb and the manna. These are wilderness references and they are small things. They are types of Christ. When we compare the manna, the lamb, and the water from the rock in the wilderness to the good land, brimming with all its riches, we see a difference between seemingly "barely getting along" and enjoying God's inexhaustible supply as our enjoyment forever. You get a sense of the scale of what God's wanting to bring us into. Your enjoyment of the daily manna should eventually yield to a richer enjoyment of Christ, represented by the Good land. In this life we'll get richer tastes as we grow in the knowledge of Him but always greatly hampered by our flesh, and the world. However in the next age there will be no limit!

Through all these different types and pictures, which are literal realities but also spiritual principles fulfilled in Christ. In the account we see shadows, and in Christ we see the reality.

Sin and Righteousness Related to What We Consume

Notice that in all these types there are food references, and that's really important too. We saw with the tree of knowledge of good and evil and the Tree of Life that man's instructions were related to eating, and his options were related to eating from the beginning.Eating represents bringing something into you, something on the outside of you entered into you through digestion. The idea is that whatever you take in becomes a part of you, is assimilated by digestion so that it's metabolically part of who you are.

Eating and digestion make you become something. This is deeper than learning how to do something. The tree of the knowledge of good and evil wasn't an instruction manual that they read in order to study and learn how to become sin conscious and fallen. There were no instructions to be sin conscious and fallen. Rather they took the element of the tree of the knowledge of good and evil, whatever that is, into themselves and *became* sin conscious and fallen. They became what they ate.

It's important to understand that being sinners is a fundamental part of our nature, rather than something we do, because sin came into man through what he ate. Similarly, righteousness and holiness are also inherent qualities. The Tree of Life ultimately provides these found in God's garden, or in God's paradise on the seventh day of rest.

These things all go together. The Tree of Life is in the garden, where God put man after He sanctified the seventh day. After He finished all His works, He brought man into the provision and into the supply that was already there. That's the principle of rest. We're entering into someone else's work, we're not doing our work.

As Jesus said in the Church of Thyatira, "He that overcometh, and keepeth my works unto the end.." (Rev 2:26). That's what we're keeping, His work. We are believing in His work, we're entering into the fruit of His work. That's the Christian life. We're entering into something that's already there.

The Tree of Life as God's Life Given to Us

Amidst all of this, there is the provision of the Tree of Life. The Tree of Life represents the first type in scripture that reveals God in Christ for our satisfaction and even nourishment. On the other hand, there was the Tree of the Knowledge of Good and Evil, which led to death, produced sin and sin consciousness through the knowledge of good and evil.

From the entirety of scripture, we can see that the life of the Tree of Life must be God's life, the Divine Life in Christ. God's intention in creating man was for him to be formed in His image and likeness, to express Him. However, He also desired to infuse His life into us. Remember the analogy of the glove. A glove might be the perfect size to fit a hand, but the fingers are limp and lifeless if the hand does not fill it. Similarly, without the life of God to energize them, our nature and virtues can lack form and be flaccid.

God intended to create man in His image and form him in such a way that man would partake of His life and be shaped like His life. And yet this life is offered freely. We see no command or instruction to partake from the Tree of Life, even though it is the ultimate inheritance for man and is found in New Jerusalem. Man should have taken it, but after he sinned, the way to the Tree of Life was guarded, and he was barred from it. (Genesis 3:22-24)

Christ came to restore this access. He is the Tree of Life. This aspect of salvation is not just related to sin. The life was freely available whether man had sinned or not. This life had to be given. As Jesus said, "The Father loves me because I lay down my life for the sheep" (John 10:15). His intention, even apart from sin, was to give His life for us so that He would become our food and our supply.

Grace Without Compulsion

There is a positive element of death and resurrection of Christ that is not related to sin but is creative. As Jesus said in John 12, "unless a grain of wheat falls into the ground and dies, it abides alone. But if it dies, it bears much fruit." (John 12:24) This represents the positive intention behind death and resurrection, which is not related to sin but is creative, meant to produce a harvest. The Tree of Life is an aspect of salvation, the intrinsic essence of what salvation is. It is fully positive, apart from sin. There is no mention of sin with the Tree of Life and no instructions to partake of it.

I am unsure what this would have looked like if we had not sinned. However, we can see a type of this in the creation of Eve. God put Adam into a deep sleep, representing death, took a rib from his side, and built the woman. This process is seen as a type of the church, with Christ at its center. There is a positive element of death and resurrection in this that is not related to sin but is creative.

As Jesus said in John 12, "unless a grain of wheat falls into the ground and dies, it abides alone. But if it dies, it bears much fruit." This represents the positive intention behind death and resurrection, which is not related to sin but is creative, meant to produce a harvest. The Tree of Life is an aspect of salvation, the intrinsic essence of what salvation is. It is fully positive, apart from sin. There is no mention of sin with the Tree of Life and no instructions to partake of it.

There's no command that says, "you must take the Tree of Life". It is presented as available, and it is hoped that you would desire it. That's what salvation is. You definitely need it, and if you don't have it, you only face judgment and will not be able to maintain anything. But it's offered freely, with no price, producing no debt. That's grace. The Tree of Life produces no debt, but it's there, and man should have taken it. They needed to recognize its value, but Satan deceived them, leading them to believe that the tree of knowledge was more desirable.

Knowledge was highly valued, so much so that they mistook the Tree of Knowledge for the Tree of Life. By the time Satan was done manipulating them, they believed they would live forever. The Tree of Life, however, represents God's life as nourishment for man.

Between the tree of knowledge and the Tree of Life, we can also observe a difference between general knowledge and the wisdom that comes from God. Looking back, we know that the Tree of Life was essential. However, it likely did not have the attractive appearance that the Tree of Knowledge possessed. Genesis 3 describes the Tree of Knowledge as pleasant to behold and desirable. But what would have drawn Adam and Eve to the Tree of Life with no commands or warnings related to it? Perhaps it lacked the appealing features that the Tree of Knowledge had. Similarly, Christ has no form or comeliness that we should desire Him with our baser senses. To be drawn to Him requires wisdom, an entrance of light from God, spiritual understanding, and revelation.

As we see in Genesis 4, Abel was the next person to exhibit this kind of wisdom. As a prophet, he became a shepherd and offered the firstling of his flock and the fat portion to God without any outward command, instruction, or warning. He had wisdom. In contrast, Cain only had knowledge; he knew what God had said about toiling in the cursed ground to bring forth bread from the sweat of his brow, but he had no wisdom to understand that this was not something God desired. Instead, he tried to offer God the results of the fall and the curse.

Through grace, God gives freely without compelling us and desires that we would come to Him with an understanding of what He wants and who He is. He desires friends, not slaves. Jesus said, **"Henceforth, I call you not servants; for the servant knoweth not what his lord doeth: but I have called you friends; for all things that I have heard of my Father, I have made known unto you"** (John 15:15).

Eating as a Prominent Scriptural Theme

This concept is recurrent throughout the scriptures, where God often focuses on the theme of eating.

For instance, when God met with Abraham, they shared a fellowship meal (Genesis 18). Similarly, when he met with Abraham's descendants, the Children of Israel, he led them out of Egypt and immediately began teaching them about food and drink. They were instructed not to consume the leeks and onions of Egypt but to eat manna and drink water that flowed from a rock that was cleft in the side. These elements are symbolic of Christ. The rock is a representation of Christ, and Jesus himself tells us in John 6 that he is the bread from heaven, the real manna.

He also promised the overcomers in the letter to Pergamus that he will provide them with the hidden manna to eat. This referred to the manna that was stored in the golden pot in the Ark of the Covenant, located in the Holy of Holies in the temple. This symbolism represents the deepest aspects of God. Christ is the hidden wisdom of God, encapsulated in the golden pot, which typifies the Father, housed in the Ark, which typifies the Son. This is a picture of the Father in the Son and the Son in the Father, represented in the words, "Believest thou not that I am in the Father, and the Father in me?" (John 14:10) and "At that day ye shall know that I am in my Father, and ye in me, and I in you" (John 14:20). The hidden manna represents the profound depth of the relationship within the triune God, established in the holiest as the basis for holiness and rest.

The theme of food is pronounced in the books of Numbers and the Good Land. The day they entered the Good Land, the manna ceased. They stopped eating manna because the abundant riches of the Good Land now served as their sustenance.

From the beginning, God's intention has always been related to what we consume. Sin was associated with what Adam and Eve ate and took into themselves. Similarly, holiness and righteousness are related to what we consume, what we partake of, and what becomes a part of us.

Both the fall and its remedy involve what man "eats." The Tree of Knowledge of Good and Evil was not a manual on how to be evil or fallen. Rather, it was something they ingested and consequently became. It altered them, perhaps metabolically or genetically. Consequently, everything that came from Adam and Eve was ruled by sin and death, affecting the entire human race.

We know that the law of sin infiltrated the human race and death reigned through sin. In contrast, life is supposed to be something that enters us. We receive the divine, eternal life when we are regenerated. The Tree of Life truly resides within your spirit. It's Christ Himself. He is the food, the drink, and it's His life that He wants us to live. It's by consuming Him, by partaking of Him as our food and drink, that we truly live.

Consider what He did during the Last Supper: He presented Himself as food and drink. What do we commemorate at the Lord's table? Christ as our food and drink, symbolized by the cup and the bread (Luke 22:19-20). However, it's important to note that we're not talking about the literal elements here. We're talking about His word. Because as He said, "The flesh profits nothing, my word is spirit and life" (John 6:63). There's a certain way to handle the Word that is spirit and life.

Eating and Being Clean

Take, for example, Noah in Genesis 6. He was commanded to take seven of the clean animals and two of the unclean. He had to differentiate between clean and unclean. In Leviticus, we find out what that means. The clean animals are related to their digestion. Clean animals have multiple stomachs and chew the cud. This might sound gross, but it means they consume it, digest it, regurgitate it, chew it again, digest it again, and so on until they extract all the nutrients. Unclean animals don't chew the cud. The food just passes right through them. That's why dogs are considered unclean. I can attest to this, as just this morning, I had to clean up a mess from my dog.

Cleanliness and holiness are related to how you eat. An animal that chews the cud is a restful animal. Cows, for instance, just stand there, digesting, chewing, and re-digesting. They are not worried about anything but what they're digesting.

This reminds me of Mary and Martha. Martha was busy serving, while Mary sat at the feet of Jesus, absorbing every word. He commended her, saying, "She's chosen the better part." There wasn't a command for Mary to choose that. In the natural, it looked like she should have gotten up and helped Martha. But instead, she chose the Tree of Life, which are the words of Jesus.

God says, "Man shall not live by bread alone, but by every word that proceeds out of the mouth of God." (Matthew 4:4) And Jesus, referring to the living bread from heaven, said, "Unless you eat my flesh and drink my blood, you have no life in you." (John 6:53) He also said, "My words are spirit and life." (John 6:63)

So, the kind of person you are truly depends on what you're eating and how you're eating it. "Clean" and "unclean" are determined by what you consume and how you consume it.

Jesus warned us not to give our treasure to pigs or cast our pearls before swine or give our treasure to unclean animals. Why? Because they can't digest it, they can't appreciate it, and they will turn and attack you. An unclean person is someone who cannot understand spiritual things because he does not have the Spirit of God in him. (Matthew 7:6; 1 Corinthians 2:14)

Meditation and digestion of the word are crucial. That's why I recommend people to memorize the word. The point is not merely reading the word, but having the word within you, a word you've meditated on. Take for instance how I meditated on Romans 6 through 8 for years, endeavoring to understand what it meant that I died with Christ. I wasn't able to understand it until I believed it. I wasn't able to believe it until that word was so embedded in me that I was always meditating on it.

The word got into me as a kind of food, it sprung up within me, was assimilated into me, and washed me from within, and then the understanding comes. Many times, the light doesn't come until life comes. Until you're washed with it, you don't understand it. It's spiritual. The word is spiritual; the word is spirit and life. We're talking about the scriptures at this point.

All types of food in the wilderness and in the good land are Christ as our satisfaction (Jeremiah 15:16). But how is He made available? In the words. 'Your word was found, and I did eat it, and it was sweet to my taste.' (Psalm 119:103) Peter said, 'Desire the sincere milk of the word that you may grow by it, and if indeed you've tasted that

God is gracious.' (1 Peter 2:2-3) There's a taste. That's why I'm in the word so much: it has a satisfying taste. It's food.

Christ in the Food

I Feel sorry for people who have never experienced this kind of thing in the word. You can have the presence of Christ in the word. **He is the word** (John 1:1). Romans 10 talks about how righteousness which is of faith, doesn't say who shall ascend into heaven as if to take Christ down from heaven or who shall descend into the earth as to bring him up. But the word which we preach is in our hearts and in our mouths. What's he saying? He's saying Christ is in the word, and it's right here. (Romans 10:6-8)

"We're not going up to heaven to pull them down, we don't have to go down into the earth to pull them up. How do I bring Christ to me? Through the word. Jesus said, 'You search the scriptures daily thinking that in them you have life, but you won't come to me that you may have life.' So whether the word is food to you or not is whether it's Christ to you." (John 5:39-40)

For some people, it's just information. They try to understand it without eating it and get increasingly frustrated when they can't. It produces anger. The letter kills, but the spirit gives life. There's a dryness when you come to the word like a textbook of academia and try to read it like you would a social studies book. That's not how it's meant to be digested. It is meant to be ruminated on, and pondered. You're to chew the cud and think about it.

How many times have I been in Genesis? I don't know, 25 years I've been in Genesis, and yet I'm seeing things I've never seen before in this past. How is that possible? Well, it's because there's so much digestion that I've done that it all just comes up. (John 16:14) The Holy Spirit will reveal what is mine to you. He will also bring to remembrance whatever I have said to you.

When I talk about how to study the word, I often talk about building a reservoir of recognition" within you. The process is simple: you put the word in, and then, as you read other parts of the word, you begin to recognize themes. Things start popping out. For instance, while reading Genesis, you may suddenly think of Colossians. The concept of the seventh day, rest, the good land, the holiest - they're all related. I can see it all here - God's provision, His abundant supply.

Where is all this coming from? I hadn't thought of these connections before. Neither had I made these connections the last time I went through Genesis. I'm not reading from anyone's notes. This is how I teach - the Holy Spirit brings all these things to my mind as I go. In real time, images form. How did I make a connection to clean animals, Mary and Martha, the Tree of Life? It's the Holy Spirit showing it to me. It just comes up. This is how we fellowship with the Lord, through His word. That's how God always intended it.

Read Psalm 119, and you'll see that we are designed to delight in God's speaking, which is His Son, who is the Tree of Life. We come to Him for satisfaction, not to prove anything to Him. We are bankrupt, we have nothing. We are created in His image, and we're an empty vessel, a form to be filled with life. But He's the one with the inexhaustible supply of life. He wants to put that life on display in us by nourishing us with Himself. We are always in a position of receiving.

Ultimately, He wants us to come to Him for satisfaction. This is why we went through the Book of John. The Book of John is all about how Christ is our satisfaction as food and drink. He's the wine at the wedding feast. That's a picture of Christ. There were six vessels for purification, right? He filled them with water, which became wine. What is that? That's an intersection of the seventh and sixth day like we talked about yesterday. Yes, it's the sixth, but there's a seventh element, which is satisfaction from God's rest, to bring us into enjoyment at a feast.

Eating and Victory

Ultimately, the seventh day, the millennium, is a feast. That's what we're headed for. That's what God's been training us for - a feast. We learn to eat Christ today; we're going to feast on Him tomorrow. He's prepared a table for us in the presence of our enemies. That's an eating thing. Even spiritual warfare is about eating. I'm enjoying Christ. He's pouring His oil on my head, and I know I'm going to dwell in His house forever. I'm sitting and enjoying the feast. That's how I win the war.

What does it mean to win the war? It means that I'm full of Christ. You can say whatever you want about me, and the more you say, the more I eat, the more satisfaction I gain, and the more miserable you become because you're not eating. You're spitting out all the food all over the place.

You show that you don't understand spiritual things because you misapply every verse. You do not live by every word that proceeds from the mouth of God. You take the words not as life but as instruction. It's the letter that kills, and Paul makes that real clear in Corinthians 3. The word can be letter or it can be life. It's the spirit that gives life, and it all depends on what you're beholding.

We all, *with unveiled face* (2 Corinthians 3:18) - that's a Holy of Holies reference where we're in the Holy of Holies with the Shekinah Glory - are beholding as in a mirror the glory of the Lord. We're in rest, in the Sabbath, in God's Day, focused on what He has provided as an inheritance which is a person, Christ Himself. We all, with unveiled faces, beholding as in a mirror the glory of the Lord, are being transformed into the same image.

What's the mirror? It's the word. James shows us that there's a mirror. When James is talking about it, he's talking about looking at the law and looking at your natural face. He says he who's not a hearer of the word but not a doer is like someone looking at his natural face in the mirror, and he walks away and forgets what kind of person he saw.

We're not to look at the natural man through the mirror of the law unless we still haven't agreed that we are condemned and need to be crucified with Christ. If we're looking at the natural man, its because we still don't understand. We think we're righteous, we think we are good apart from God. The mirror is there to show us that that isn't the case. But we need to flip the mirror so that eventually I'm looking not at myself and how I'm doing and how I'm performing to try to copy or emulate, which is a work of the flesh. Emulation is a work of the flesh. Instead, I am focusing the mirror on Christ, whose image I hope to behold in the word.

As I behold Him, I'm transformed metabolically by what I assimilate. He becomes my life. He comes into me. That's what He wants through the word. His word is not to give you instructions of how to be something. His word is to present Himself as your food so that He will, you will become Christ on display. That's what He wants.

The church is for Christ, and Christ is for the church. His intention is to be so a part of you that He's been digested by you so that whatever you do is just Christ. Yes, it's you doing it. Yes, it's you choosing it. But you've been renewed. You're part of the new creation. Your mind is renewed. Your mind is life and peace. He's giving life to your mortal body. As you do what you want, it's actually Christ working with you as your life. This is the Christian life, which is supernatural, and demonstrated by the Tree of Life.

From the beginning, God intended to come into man and be man's life, live in man, and express himself in man. So, he formed man in his image, gave him dominion, and set him in a place where he had access to the Tree of Life. Man should have taken that life in so that he could hold that dominion and image in incorruptibility. However, our problem is that we have a reflection of the image of God, but it's corruptible. It dissolves at the slightest pressure unless we have his life in us. When we have his life in us, God delights in bringing us through pressure situations to show forth the virtues of his incorruptible life in us. This is discussed in 1st Peter; manifold trials are for proving our faith, which is more precious than gold because it's incorruptible and abounds to praise, honor, and glory at the revelation of Jesus Christ.

The Tree of Life represents eternal life, which is a gift that can be obtained without compulsion. You don't have to read the Bible, enjoy Christ, or understand spiritual things to be saved. You could be justified, believe he forgave your sins, and go on with your life, but you would be more miserable because you're poor and hungry. God wants to bring you into the house and feed you, which is the intention behind the Tree of Life and our salvation. Our enjoyment of salvation starts when we learn to feast on Christ, which is presented throughout scripture as the word.

God's intention is not for us to emulate or imitate Christ as awork of the flesh, but to assimilate Christ as a satisfying feast.

Chapter 11 A bride - Death and Resurrection as a Creative Act (Genesis 2)

A Bride from his side

We have learned a lot about Adam's peaceful circumstances. He is currently residing in the Garden on the seventh day, and all of his needs are met. He has been given a single restrictive command, which is not to eat from the tree of knowledge of good and evil. Other than that, he is free to enjoy everything else.

"The Lord God said, it is not good that man should be alone; for I will make a help meet for him." And out of the ground, the Lord God formed every beast of the field and every fowl of the air and brought them to Adam to see what he would call them. And whatever Adam called the living creature, that was the name thereof. Adam gave names to all cattle, to the fowl of the air, and every beast of the field. But for Adam, there was not found a help meet for him. The Lord God caused a deep sleep to fall upon Adam, and he slept. He took one of his ribs and closed up the flesh thereof. The rib, which the Lord God had taken from man, made he a woman and brought her to the man. Adam said, "This is now bone of my bones and flesh of my flesh. For she shall be called Woman, because she was taken out of Man. Therefore, shall a man leave his father and mother and shall cleave to his wife, and they shall be one flesh." They were both naked, the man and his wife, and were not ashamed. (Genesis 2:18-25)

Types and their Reality

There's a lot here. First of all, God says it's not good for man to be alone. Now, we have to understand that Adam is a type of Christ. We see that in Romans 5, that he is a figure of the one to come. In 1 Corinthians 15:45, Christ is referred to as the Last Adam and is also identified as the second man. The first man was earthy, but the second man is the Lord from heaven. The first man is natural; the second man is spiritual.

Everything that God did, including the temple, the tabernacle, the feasts, and the law, were all shadows. Christ is the reality. Everything that He does, He perfects in a figure first. The figure is modeled after the heavenly reality.

For example, God said to Moses, "see that you make [the tabernacle] according to the pattern which you saw on the mount." There's a heavenly tabernacle, which is the real thing after which the patterns were made. The reality just Christ Himself, presented in signs that point to aspects of His Person and work.

Adam is also a type of Christ in the sense that God intended for Christ the image of God and has authority over all things and is the true Heir. However, just as with Adam, it was not good for Christ to be alone. God's intention was for Christ to have a helpmate, and this is His Bride, the Church. Paul makes this connection for us in Ephesians 5, where Genesis 2:23 is quoted,

> **Ephesians 5:28-32 So ought men to love their wives as their own bodies. He that loveth his wife loveth himself. (29) For no man ever yet hated his own flesh; but nourisheth and cherisheth it, even as the Lord the church: (30) For we are members of his body, of his flesh, and of his bones. (31) For this cause shall a man leave his father and mother, and shall be joined unto his wife, and they two shall be one flesh. (32) This is a great mystery: but I speak concerning Christ and the church.**

Paul is quoting Genesis 2 where Adam said, "This is now bone of my bones, and flesh of my flesh: she shall be called Woman, because she was taken out of Man."

In Paul's revelation of what he calls "the mystery of Christ", it is revealed there is a counterpart for Christ. All of this literally happened in Genesis with Adam and Eve. Yet, it's also a figure of God's ultimate intention. Remember, we're on the seventh day, we're in the paradise of God, the garden. The building materials for the new city, Jerusalem, are there in a figure. The Tree of Life there, the river, the water of life, is there in type as well as the Gold, silver and precious stone that represents the incorruptible material of God's building. Everything related to the consummation of all the positive themes in scripture, which is called the New Jerusalem, is here in type, in the natural. Now Adam has a helpmeet, just as the city is called the bride, the wife of the lamb.

It seems that Genesis 2 and Revelation 19 through 21 have a lot in common. They both mention the new city of Jerusalem and the fulfillment of God's plan as described in scripture. There are many positive themes that tie the two together. However, one thing that seems to be missing in the depiction of the New Jerusalem is the tree of the knowledge of good and evil, which will be present in the lake of fire. It's important to keep this in mind when examining these passages.

The first couple of chapters in Genesis set up all the themes of scripture and what happened. They're spoken to us in stories that are true in a sense. They're literal, but there's probably more to the story than we can understand. Chuck Missler said there's no reason to believe that Adam and Eve were limited to the dimensionality and the physics we have today. This is creation before the fall. Jesus was able to appear in the midst of the upper room without going through a door. We don't know what things were like before the fall. The point is, this is a radically different situation than what we can comprehend based on our observation of the present fallen universe.

The garden contains two trees that are not of the natural variety that we typically associate with trees. The Tree of Knowledge of Good and Evil is not an apple tree, nor is the Tree of Life. Ultimately, both are representative of a person, serving as symbolic figures. These trees are examples of types and signs, much like the symbolism present throughout the book of Revelation. The various signs and symbols present in scripture embody themes that span the entirety of the text. While these signs are literal in one sense, their visual aspects are crafted to embody a multitude of meanings.We cannot void the literal. There really was a garden, they really were created there.

There really was a Tree of Life and the tree of the knowledge of good and evil. All the trees were for their food. But that's about the extent of what we can understand. When you search for trees in scripture, you see that people are likened to trees, angels are likened to trees . There's a lot going on in Eden.

Consider the fact that Eve spoke to a cherub. Anytime you see a cherub in scripture, you see people falling on their faces, saying, 'Woe is me, I'm undone.' Yet, Eve conversed with the chief of the cherubim as if he was just another figure she was acquainted with." Remember how Ezekiel described, and Isaiah responded to, visions of cherubim.

Ezekiel 1:5-14 - "And in the fire was what looked like four living creatures. In appearance their form was human, but each of them had four faces and four wings. Their legs were straight; their feet were like those of a calf and gleamed like burnished bronze. Under their wings on their

four sides, they had human hands. All four of them had faces and wings, and the wings of one touched the wings of another. Each one went straight ahead; they did not turn as they moved. Their faces looked like this: Each of the four had the face of a human being, and on the right side each had the face of a lion, and on the left the face of an ox; each also had the face of an eagle. Such were their faces. They each had two wings spreading out upward, each wing touching that of the creature on either side; and each had two other wings covering its body. Each one went straight ahead. Wherever the spirit would go, they would go, without turning as they went. The appearance of the living creatures was like burning coals of fire or like torches. Fire moved back and forth among the creatures; it was bright, and lightning flashed out of it."

Isaiah 6:5 Then said I, Woe is me! for I am undone; because I am a man of unclean lips, and I dwell in the midst of a people of unclean lips: for mine eyes have seen the King, the LORD of hosts.

With Eve, we don't see a detailed description full of wonder and awe. Since the fall, we don't have encounters with the glory without dramatic responses of fear and awe from men. However, in the account in Eden, these things are normalized. There was no fear, no terror, no wonder from Eve. We can't fully understand what this is like. We know that in the end, God has human beings who can stand before Him without falling down, except to worship in thanksgiving.

God's Intention foreshadowed – Not Good for Christ to Be Alone

It was not good for man to be alone. Man, as a type of Christ, and God's intention throughout the whole of scripture is summed up in Ephesians. God had an eternal purpose, the good pleasure of His will. This was a mystery hidden in His heart, never revealed to the angels, men, or even the prophets. It's related to the church as the counterpart of Christ. The intrinsic mystery of the church is this: She does not exist as one separate from Him, she is someone that springs from His resurrection life. She springs out of Christ Himself, just as Eve was built from Adam's rib.

There is a group of people who were foreknown in Christ, chosen by Him, accepted in Him (Eph 1:4-6), reconciled through Him, raised up together with Him, seated in the heavens with Him, built in Him to be the habitation of God, and crowned with Him (Eph 2:6-8, 2:22). They are called the masterpiece of God (Ephesians 2:10, Colossians 1:27).

According to Ephesians 3:10, God will make known His multifarious wisdom to the angels through the church, which is the mystery of Christ. This hidden wisdom of God that He had in His heart is the purpose of God. The purpose involves the church as the Counterpart of Christ (Ephesians 5:31-32).

We see with Adam and Eve, again the type of Christ and the church, His bride, is that God didn't intend for man to be alone. Then God brought all the beasts to Adam to see what he would name them. When Adam named all the animals, it demonstrated his dominion and participation in the course of things. God had entrusted everything to him, and he named all the animals. However, "not one was found that was a suitable companion for him."

I remember Chuck Missler said, "Think about his mental capacity. He was able to categorize and name all these animals that had never been seen before and didn't have names." This means nobody had ever classified, designated, or identified them. Scientists take years to agree on names of different classifications of species. Adam was able to do it as they walked by.

I believe that's true. There's something significant about his mental capacity before the fall. He was able to think at that level. This topic calls for a deep dive into the theological narrative. The timeframe of creation is not the focus. Whether it happened in five seconds, seven days, or 30 years is irrelevant. God's seventh day was not about time spans. He was in his rest. We don't know how long Adam was in this situation, but we do know that no suitable helper was found for Adam. None of these animals were a match for him. They were all formed from the ground and were all alien to him.

Adam was totally unique. He was created in the image of God and he was alone. This uniqueness is mirrored in Christ. Christ is unique as the only begotten Son of God. He dwelt among all the creatures that had been formed, all the men, the apostles, the Pharisees, his parents, his friends, childhood friends, and yet he was alone. They were there, but could any of them understand his heart? Could any of them match him? Could any of them understand the fellowship he had with the Father? No, they couldn't.

When Christ spoke about the things that were truly on his heart, none of them could match him. There was no one fit, no one qualified to be his companion. Because of that, He was a man of suffering, he was alone, a man of sorrows acquainted with grief, and he had no place to lay his head (Matthew 8:20). This is mirrored in Adam's situation. Adam was alone in a sense. I believe God wants us to feel a pang of loneliness when we read this. Even though everything is beautiful, it's not complete.

This narrative is a picture of God's heart. God had the angels, He created the universe, everything in it, and yet He was still alone. There was no one suitable to be His help meet or match Him. All the creatures were created, formed, and inferior. Yet, according to the mystery of God and His eternal purpose, there is a people who God foreknew in Christ, who eventually become a suitable help meet for God to share His seventh day or forever with. This is the wife of the Lamb, the New Jerusalem.

Death and Resurrection – a Creative Act

We see the Lord God caused a deep sleep to fall on Adam. In the scripture, sleep is symbolic of death. First Corinthians 15 and Thessalonians talk about those who are asleep in Christ, that He's going to raise them together. So falling asleep is a type of death. This is because you are no longer active; it's passive.

God took out one of Adam's ribs and closed the flesh thereof. The rib which the Lord had taken out of man, He made a woman.

The word for 'made' is 'built'. Remember that the body of Christ, as the Bride of Christ, is "built." Everything else was created from the ground, but this woman was made from Adam, from a piece of Adam. She came out from him.

Then God woke Adam up and brought the woman to him. Adam declared, "This is now bone of my bone and flesh of my flesh; she shall be called Woman." Why? Because she was taken out of the man, and that is the type that the church comes out of Christ. I often think of myself as having lived on this earth for twenty-something years before I was saved. I tend to think that, when I got saved, I was brought into a relationship with Christ. We automatically assume that there are terms on us and terms on Him. We think He's going to be the husband and we're going to be the counterpart, or He's going to be the Lord and we're going to be the servants. But that's not it.

We were baptized into His death, and the old person that we were, connected to Adam, was terminated; crucified (Romans 6:3-4, Galatians 2:20). We died with Christ, and God does not deal with us based on any history that we have apart from Christ. We are not formed from the earth, coming to Him like one of the animals to be named and ruled over. Instead, God put Adam to sleep, opened up his side, took a rib out, and built the woman. God said, 'This is a woman, she's bone of my bone and flesh of my flesh. She was taken out of me.'

A woman is called 'woman' because she's taken out of a man, just as the church comes out of Christ. In type, the blood and water flowed out from the side of Jesus and we were created by what flowed out. The Spirit and life of Christ (1 John 5:8). We were not only reconciled through the blood, it was not only a restorative, reconciling act, but when it comes to the church, the death and resurrection of Christ was a *creative act.*

Yes, the blood obtained forgiveness for the sins of all mankind. For those who believed, we were chosen to be part of something. As members of the Church, we are members of the body of Christ. As a believer, you were born again in time, saved and came to know Christ during this time of the body of Christ being built up. But from God's point of view you were foreknown in Christ, chosen in Him, and predestined with Him to be an heir with Him in this unique entity called the Bride of Christ, which was a mystery.

The rules governing the body of Christ cannot be found in any other place in Scripture except for the Epistles of the Apostles, as it was a mystery. The identity of the Bride, Christ's counterpart, cannot be deduced by examining the words of the Old Testament prophets. Instead, one must look to the death and resurrection of Christ and what was created there. Paul first revealed this doctrine, stating that we were baptized into His death and then raised up together with Him. This is evident in Ephesians, Colossians, and Romans (Ephesians 1:4-6, 2:6-8, 2:10, Colossians 1:27, Romans 6:3-4, Galatians 2:20).

We are Not Apart from Him (Our Identity in Christ)

We are His counterpart not because of what we were apart from Him, but because of who we are out of Him. God knows there is a 'you' that you have not discovered yet. It's called the new creation. God has already spent, in Christ, the ages to come with you, lavishing the riches of His grace and kindness on you towards you in Christ Jesus. As Ephesians says, 'He raised us up and seated us with Him in the heavens, that in the ages to come He might show forth the exceeding riches of His grace in kindness towards us in Christ' (Ephesians 1:7-8, 2:6-7).

This is a bridal kindness. Christ loved the church and gave Himself for her, and that's because He knew her. We don't know our future; we haven't experienced it yet. But for God, everything that's future has already happened. He's the 'I Am,' right? The lamb was slain before the foundation of the world. He foreknew us in Him, predestinated us in Him, chose us in Him, accepted us in Him. He knows us because we are in Christ, and He knows us as members of the body of Christ.

How intimately does God love you? Well, He loves you with the love of Christ. Jesus said that the love that you have for me may be in them and I in them, and that the world may know that you have loved them even as you love me. This is an eternal love, an everlasting love that God knows you with, and it's because of who you are in Christ. (John 17:23, Ephesians 3:19)

We only look at Adam when we think of who I am. We look at our history in Adam. Now, that was terminated at the cross, and now there's something new coming forth out of Christ, and this is who you are. It's Christ in you. There are ages to come, exploits to come, time to come, affections to come, love to come that you have not been made aware of yet. God knows you according to the history He's already had with you, and He's coming to you to bring you up to speed, so to speak. (1 Corinthians 15:45, Ephesians 2:7)

He did it in the death and resurrection of Christ. He produced this bride, the glorious church. This is a type for us to see that God had no counterpart to match Him. Christ had no counterpart to match Him. None was suitable. Everybody was alien, and everything was alien. It was all created, but Christ is the uncreated, incorruptible, imperishable, eternal One. In order to bring forth something that matched Him so that He wouldn't be alone, God creates the church through the death and resurrection of Christ.

This is a picture again of an aspect of our salvation that is not related to sin at all. This is related to Christ and His life and God building something from Him that comes out of Him and then is presented to Him to match Him. That's what the bride is. Christ is unsearchably rich in who He is, and only this kind of building work of God, this masterpiece of God, presented to the Son as an inheritance, can match Him. That's who we are.

You have no idea how spectacularly you'll be arrayed. You have no idea how spectacularly you are fitted for Him because you came out from Him. Because you barely know Him, because all you have is your history in Adam, which is terminated. So, we take it by faith. We just wonder at the word and say, "Thank you, Jesus," and what else can you say?

Christ loved the church and gave Himself for her. We know God loved the world and so that He gave His only begotten Son, whoever believed in Him would not perish but have everlasting life. That's some kind of love. God loved me, and the life I now live in the flesh, I live by the faith of the Son of God who loved me and gave Himself for me. That's a redemptive love. But then there's this: "Christ loved the church and gave Himself for her."

He gave Himself for her, that He may sanctify her, washing her by the water of the word, to present her to Himself a glorious bride, without spot. This is the New Jerusalem. This is the building of God. This is the eternal purpose of God. This is why everything was created in the first place. It was not good for Christ to be alone.

The heir of all things needed a cohort to share it with, who could match and understand Him. Eventually, we're going to be transfigured by His life and glorified by His life to match Him. We will be conformed to the image of the Son and we will be as He is. We will know as He knows. You just can't even imagine what's ahead of us, but we have the first fruits and the spirit now.

We get a taste of His love. He's shed abroad His love in our heart by the Holy Spirit, which He's given to us. He is betrothed to us. He is making Himself known and purifying us by getting our eyes off everything else and onto Him. We're starting to learn a little bit about this glorious destiny that we are positioned to inherit.

This garden God created, with the Tree of life and all the things in it that we can't really even imagine, would have been meaningless if Adam was alone. God created all these creatures for Adam. He named them, and he had dominion over them, but none of them matched him. It would have been a sad story if he had no one to share this with. The purpose of God's creation is to share. That's why He created everything.

We got this picture with Adam and Eve. The idea is that there is an earthly type. The natural comes first, then the spiritual. There's this garden on the seventh day, and God's resting from all His works. Then He brings forth this man, created in His image, with His likeness, gives him dominion, sets before him the Tree of Life and all the other trees, makes everything freely available to him.

Yet, it wasn't good that man was alone. Everything He'd done so far, He said was good. God did this and it was good. But when it came to man, it was not good that he was alone. That's the 'not good', the incompleteness that motivated God to create the universe. It's not that He's lonely because He has the fellowship of the Triune God. But still, it's not good until He wants to share it. That's the good.

That sharing is called the good pleasure of His will (Eph 1:5;1:9). The reason He created everything was to be able to bring forth a bride for His Son, who are also the many sons of God, and His inheritance. That's us. We have an inheritance. He prepared the heavens and the earth, created the angels, and everything in it for us to inherit with Christ. It's beautiful.

A Marriage of Creative Union

Eve was created from Adam in his deep sleep and presented to him when he woke. This is a type of death and resurrection. The next time we see God putting someone to sleep will be Abraham. That's when He will make or confirm the everlasting covenant with the Son. That is not a covenant with Abraham, but ultimately with his seed, Christ. A deep sleep, which is a type of death, fell upon Abraham. Then the oven and the torch, the Father and the Son, passed through the pieces of the sacrifice and made a covenant. This is really where God, Christ, confirmed that He would give His life for the sheep, and that He would do everything to secure us. (Genesis 2:21-25, Genesis 15:12-17, John 10:11; Heb 13:21)

Adam, in a sense, sacrificed for Eve to be produced. Adam had never been asleep before; perhaps it was scary, we don't know, but he paid a price for Eve. Something came out of him to create her. She was not created from the dust of the ground, but from him. Similarly, Christ paid a price to produce us. Creating us cost Him something.

Yes, He redeemed us with His blood. As sons of Adam, we needed to be redeemed to even be qualified to have anything to do with Him, but then this special group were baptized into His death. Our starting place was while He was asleep and God built something out from Christ. In resurrection, we are that building, we are the creative work of God. We are what God produced and brought to Christ. He loves us.

There is no covenant between the original man and woman. There doesn't need to be because they're one party.

There's no sense of separateness, no contractual stipulations of 'I'll be your husband if you do this, and you be my wife if I do that.' There's no idea of a dissolution because it's your own flesh. No one hates his own flesh but nourishes and cherishes it. This is speaking of Christ and the church.

The first marriage was indissolvable and inseparable and what God joined, no man could separate. This is a picture again of Christ and the church. However, 'Therefore shall a man leave his father and his mother and cleave to his wife, and they shall be one flesh.' On one hand, this is a type of Christ in the church, but on the other hand, it's a picture for marriage on the earth.

Remember, Genesis was written by God through Moses. Moses is recounting all this and writing it down according to God's commandment while giving the law. I believe he wrote all this while he was up in the mountain. He also came down with the law. The law was a covenant God made with the nation of Israel because they existed apart from Him. They were not from His side, so to speak, and He was dealing with them as a nation and as individuals (Gal 3:19-20).

He gave them this covenant called marriage for two parties to come together, who are not from each other, who are not part of each other. That's what marriage in the world is, and it's a picture, but it's not the reality. We are not literally one flesh with our spouse, but marriage kind of makes it so. Marriage, in that sense, in the natural realm, is like a covenant. Yes, God has a covenant with Israel to betroth her to Himself, but it's not the same kind of marriage that we see in the beginning as God intended.

When the Jews asked Jesus about marriage and divorce, He said, "Moses permitted you to divorce your wives because of the hardness of your hearts, but it was not this way from the beginning" (Matthew 19:8). From the beginning, the type of marriage we have is meant to be like that of Christ and the church. This is what God is referring to.

Between Christ and the church, it is not a matter of two parties with obligations. It is one party, Adam, and this woman drawn from his side. He is irrevocably identified with her, and she with him. When she eats from the tree of knowledge of good and evil, the account says, 'and her husband with her'

> **Gen_3:6 And when the woman saw that the tree was good for food, and that it was pleasant to the eyes, and a tree to be desired to make one wise, she took of the fruit thereof, and did eat, and gave also unto her husband with her; and he did eat.**

He follows her wherever she goes. If she falls into sin, he follows her into sin. Didn't Christ do the same for us? He became sin for us. Whatever we went through, he had to take upon himself. However, whatever he has, we take upon it, it's bestowed on us. He took our sin, but we became His righteousness. He took our death, but we took His life because he's the eternal one and death can't hold him. Today He goes with us. Remember what Paul said in 1 Corinthians 6?

> **1 Corinthians 6:15-17 Know ye not that your bodies are the members of Christ? shall I then take the members of Christ, and make them the members of an harlot? God**

forbid. (16) What? know ye not that he which is joined to an harlot is one body? for two, saith he, shall be one flesh. (17) But he that is joined unto the Lord is one spirit.

When Paul deals with the matter of fornication in Corinth he deals with it by pointing them to their union with Christ and its implications. Not only are they sinning, but they are bringing Christ with them, as members of Him, joining Christ to a harlot. That's heavy, like "Eve ate, and her husband with her."

In a positive since, because we come from Him, death cannot hold us either. Even though He was identified with us in sin, we have been identified with Him in life to reign with Him, through grace.

Naked and Unashamed

They were both naked, the man and his wife, and they were not ashamed. Nakedness means no clothes, but the point of the shame is that they had no consciousness of the fact that they were naked. It was God's design that they were naked. There was nothing shameful about it.

Nakedness is the ability to stand God's inspection close up without hiding anything. That's what real nakedness is. The word is sharper than any two-edged sword, able to divide between soul and spirit and pierce even to the thoughts and intentions of the heart. There is nothing hidden from the eyes of God, with whom we have to do (Heb 4:12).

God's intention is to present us without spot before Him, so we can stand His inspection without shrinking back. Eventually, He'll find no spot in us because we're in Christ.

God has arranged redemption, the court, the blood, everything so that we are without spot before Him. We are holy and without blemish before Him. We are presented in the body of Christ, flesh through death, without spot before God. We are holy and without blemish before Him, with no blame. (Ephesians 5:27, Colossians 1:22, Hebrews 9:14, 1 Peter 1:19, 1 John 1:7)

In that sense, we are both clothed and naked. We are arrayed with Christ, He is our garment, yet we can stand the inspection of God without shame. This is difficult for us to understand because we have sin in our members. We still have this connection to Adam as long as we're in this vessel. Until transfiguring, we may not fully comprehend what it means to be free in God's presence, bold, confident, and unashamed.

The apostles taught that we could be without spot when He appears. Through the work of the Gospel, God completes a perfecting work in our conscience to perfect us in His love and to make us confident in the day of judgment. John said, "Abide in Him, little children, so that when He comes, you may have confidence in His coming and not shrink back in shame." (1 John 2:28, 4:17).

Shame started in the next chapter in Genesis. After they ate from the tree of the knowledge of good and evil, they realized they were naked. They attempted to cover themselves, and when that failed, they tried to hide themselves in the presence of God. This tendency in man is what we call shame.

Many Christians who get saved don't start dealing with shame until after they're saved. It's because God has been brought into their being and now they're dealing directly with Him. There is a tendency in the flesh to hide from that. I didn't deal with all kinds of condemnation until after I got saved, because my being was awakened to the presence of God. I didn't know how to put on my clothing, how to put on what He had provided.

Being unashamed before God and naked is the best place to be because it means that you are not self-conscious. There's nothing in you that needs to hide from His gaze. We have to understand that Christ became like us in every point, tempted in every point as we are, yet without sin. He's touched with the feelings of our infirmities and He's our high priest to make intercession for us. He knows all about your secret sin, the secret thoughts of your heart that you haven't been able to purge. Yet, it says He's not ashamed to call us brethren.

He wants us to be able to stand before Him without shame. There are so many concepts in religion that make that hard. When you preach the Gospel, there's always someone ready to say, "Yeah, but what about God's discipline? What about overcoming sin?" No, let's first learn to stand in the presence of God. That's what discipline is for. Discipline is to teach you how to put on your Christ as your clothing, so that you can stand freely in God's presence and not be ashamed.

It doesn't talk about shame and nakedness until after Eve is there. Adam didn't have a problem, but now there's this woman out of his side and he's charged with caring for her. Now there's an issue. She wasn't there when the command was given to eat from the tree of the knowledge of good and evil. In a sense, he's responsible for her stand and she doesn't have a stand before God apart from him. He's identified with her - whatever she's going to go through, he's going to go through. That's the way it is and that is what Christ took on himself for us.

Christ says, "Whatever she goes through, I'll go through. Whatever she endures, I'll endure. I will cover her, and I will be her covering. I'll stand before God on her behalf." So, it's all good news for us.

Here in Eden, we encounter a full type within the seventh day rest - holiness, the Tree of Life, the garden, gold bdellium, which is a type of pearl, onyx, precious stones, and the river. These elements are all prototypes or building materials for the New Jerusalem. Then we have a type of Christ and His bride, the Church, which isn't produced independently of Him, but comes out of His side. It is Him, and is composed of the incorruptible materials of His life, built to be His counterpart.

Chapter 12 Departing from Rest – (Genesis 3)

The Introduction of Shame

Gen 2:25 And they were both naked, the man and his wife, and were not ashamed.

Gen 3:1-8 Now the serpent was more subtil than any beast of the field which the LORD God had made. And he said unto the woman, Yea, hath God said, Ye shall not eat of every tree of the garden? (2) And the woman said unto the serpent, We may eat of the fruit of the trees of the garden: (3) But of the fruit of the tree which is in the midst of the garden, God hath said, Ye shall not eat of it, neither shall ye touch it, lest ye die. (4) And the serpent said unto the woman, Ye shall not surely die: (5) For God doth know that in the day ye eat thereof, then your eyes shall be opened, and ye shall be as gods, knowing good and evil. (6) And when the woman saw that the tree was good for food, and that it was pleasant to the eyes, and a tree to be desired to make one wise, she took of the fruit thereof, and did eat, and gave also unto her husband with her; and he did eat. (7) And the eyes of them both were opened, and they knew that they were naked; and they sewed fig leaves together, and made themselves aprons. (8) And they heard Chapter

Chapter three begins with a reflection on the previous events in chapter two. As we recall, at the conclusion of chapter two, Adam and Eve were described as being "naked and unashamed" (Genesis 2:25). This notion of nakedness extends beyond the physical aspect; it represents a state of complete transparency and openness. Unlike the tendency to wear masks and manage perceptions that come with clothing and fashion, nakedness in this context signifies authenticity and a lack of hidden agendas (Genesis 2:24).

In contrast to this authenticity, we encounter the serpent, who is described as "more subtle than any beast of the field" (Genesis 3:1). Subtlety here refers to the cunning ability to manipulate perceptions and situations, akin to a form of sorcery. The serpent's approach contrasts with the openness and honesty displayed in the state of nakedness. This subtlety is emblematic of the serpent's nature and intentions, as later revealed to be the devil or Satan (Revelation 12:9). It's important to note that the serpent isn't merely a literal snake but represents a fallen cherub, a celestial being associated with God's glory and righteousness.

Cherubim as Witnesses

These cherubim, including the serpent, serve as witnesses to God's glory and holiness (Psalm 99:1). They also symbolize God's righteousness, as seen in the Ark of the Covenant, where the blood on the mercy seat represents Christ's propitiation and is witnessed by the cherubim (Romans 3:25). This imagery conveys the profound connection between God's righteousness, Christ's sacrifice, and the angelic witnesses in the heavenly realms.

Satan—though he is eventually cast down—is in a position where he accuses us day and night. He still maintains this role of getting close enough to God to make accusations against us. Christ is being put on display, and God's righteousness is being vindicated in dealing with us.

It's rather interesting to consider who this serpent is. He was a cherub, and I believe that among the four known cherubim with the faces of an ox, an eagle, a man, and a lion, there was a fifth cherub. These winged creatures are described as incredible; there's lightning going up and down their bodies, they're very large, and they have wings and eyes within and all around. They are the closest beings to the glory of God, besides the church, which is ultimately brought even closer.

The anointed cherub that covered was Lucifer, possibly having the face of a dragon. He was the most beautiful thing in God's creation and was super wise and intelligent. At some point, we know he fell and now approaches Eve, who is, until this point, naked, unashamed, guileless, and transparent. This reminds us of Nathanael, who Jesus described as an "Israelite indeed, in whom there is no guile" (John 1:47). It means he was sincere, honest, and not trying to control or manage himself; he simply said what was on his mind.

Satan's Subtlety and Eve's Response

But here comes the serpent, full of subtlety, approaching the guileless woman. He would have been manifested as an angel of light, looking beautiful. It's interesting that he just talks to her, and she talks to him without any sign of fear. The pre-fall condition of Adam and Eve was glorious; they could stand in the presence of angels and God unashamed.

The serpent, described as "more subtle than any beast of the field which the Lord God had made" (Genesis 3:1), begins his conversation with the woman by questioning God's command: "Yea, hath God said, You shall not eat of every tree in the garden?" His subtlety is evident; he says very little, yet his words have the power to disrupt destiny and create chaos. The enemy does not have to say much to turn us around; sometimes, one whisper is enough. He is a master of psychology, knowing how to trip us up, make us second-guess ourselves, and bring us into a place of defeat.

The serpent cleverly begins by questioning God's command, asking, "Has God said, 'You shall not eat of every tree of the garden?'" Yet, God had indeed said they could freely eat from all the trees of the garden except for the tree of the knowledge of good and evil. There was only one tree that they weren't supposed to eat from, but the way the serpent framed his question made that one restriction seem more significant. This tactic illuminates the nature of the enemy, focusing attention on the only restrictive thing, even though it shouldn't have been that attractive.

The woman, in response, insists that they may eat the fruit of the trees of the garden, emphasizing that everything is available to them. However, she goes on to say, "But of the fruit of the tree which is in the midst of the garden, God says, 'You shall not eat of it, neither should you touch it, lest you die.'" Interestingly, she added a word, claiming they shouldn't touch the tree, something God never said. This addition reflects a problem with interpretation and marks the beginning of legalism. It's like she made a Talmud out of God's word adding conditions to make sure they were safe from it.

Capitalizing on Ignorance

Once the serpent realized that the woman had added to God's command, he knew he could capitalize on her misunderstanding. The enemy had baited her with a leading question, just as he often baits people into responding to engage them and provoke them into fleshly reactions.

The woman's addition to God's word demonstrated that she wasn't clear about it, possibly because she received the information second-hand from Adam since she wasn't there when God gave the command. The serpent seized on this ignorance, saying, "You shall not surely die; for God does know that in the day you eat of it, your eyes will be opened, and you shall be as gods, knowing good and evil." This was all the enemy had to say to entrap her.

This interaction illustrates how the enemy uses diversionary tactics to put people on the defensive, just as he did with Eve. By asking a question that wasn't fully truthful and making her defend the truth, he led her to a place of uncertainty. Once he saw that she was not completely clear on God's word, he knew he had her. It's a profound lesson in how easily humans can be led astray by subtle deceptions and how careful we must be in understanding God's words as they are, without adding or subtracting from them (Deuteronomy 4:2; Revelation 22:18-19).

The serpent, having placed the woman on the defensive, now injects a doubt about God's character. He insinuates that not everything is freely given and questions whether they really have everything they need. He then lies to her, saying that God knows that the day they eat of the tree, they will be like gods, knowing good and evil.

This promise of knowledge carries with it an imagery reminiscent of the Kundalini serpent force in mystical religions like Hinduism. It's depicted as a serpent that moves through a person's seven chakras or points of light, emerging from the third eye as illumination and enlightenment. The enemy was promising her something that seemed greater than what she already had, being created in the image of God, having dominion over everything, even the serpent, if she had known.

Corruption from Simplicity

The woman then saw that the tree was good for food, pleasant to the eyes, and desired to make one wise. These three things correspond to what makes up the world, as described in 1 John: the lust of the flesh (it's good for food), the lust of the eyes (it's pleasant to the eyes), and the pride of life (the desire to be wise) (1 John 2:16).

The serpent temptation of Eve is a corruption from the simplicity that is in Christ. (2 Corinthians 11:3) Remember that Paul warns of being seduced from the simplicity in the Gospel unto another gospel, another spirit, or another Jesus. (Galatians 1:6-7) The tree of the knowledge of good and evil becomes a substitute for the things already available in Christ, represented by the tree of life. (Revelation 2:7) The enemy corrupted her mind, got her attention off what she had, made her second guess what God said, and offered an alternative.

She took it and gave it to her husband, Adam, who ate as well. Though the Bible says that Adam was not deceived, he partook of the forbidden fruit with her. In this act, Adam can be seen as a type of Christ. On one hand, he sinned, but on the other, he identified himself with Eve, something he didn't have to do.

After eating the forbidden fruit, their eyes were opened, and they knew they were naked, leading them to sew fig leaves together to make aprons. This newfound awareness of nakedness reflects a loss of innocence and a realization of their disobedience. They were now separated from God, not just physically but spiritually, marking a significant turning point in the narrative.

Upon realizing their nakedness, Adam and Eve sought to cover themselves. Was there a problem with them being naked? No, but now they've acquired guile and subtlety in their character. This newfound self-consciousness and shame become the foundation of their interactions with God and everything else. It marks the fallen human personality, constructed largely from shame and defense mechanisms that people use to navigate the world and cover their nakedness.

This lack of transparency is something that God aims to undo once a person is saved, taking off those layers and reducing us to a state where we can stand in His presence again without the tendency to hide. This process involves perfecting our conscience, something that has become warped in Adam and Eve. They became ashamed of themselves, something God created and declared good, and began to see it as something to hide.

Hostility

They sewed fig leaves together to make aprons, but the word "apron" in the Hebrew Scriptures is almost always translated as "armor" or a "girdle for war." This is a telling choice, as it reveals an awareness of rebellion and a preparation to fight (Ephesians 6:14). A similar sentiment is found in the story of the Tower of Babel, where people attempted to storm the heavens and cast God off His throne, and in the Book of Revelation, where the armies of the world try to overthrow the Lamb (Revelation 19:19).

This moment marks the beginning of mankind's fall and a war with God, a theme that runs through the Scriptures. Colossians tells us that the fallen mind is at enmity with God, alienated through wicked works, hostile and full of wrath (Colossians 1:21). The atheistic mind or the mind that rejects God becomes a blaspheming mind full of accusations towards God. Adam and Eve's transformation here signifies that they were ready to go to war; they were at odds with their Creator. But along with this rebellion, they were also covering their nakedness in shame and fear, introducing a complex andprofound change in their relationship with God and themselves.

Chapter 13 The Result of Falling From Grace (Genesis 3)

Sin Consciousness and Alienation - The Fall of Man and

Our previous discourse introduced the concept of shame as a foundational issue within the human condition. This shame serves as a delineating factor, setting individuals apart. With opened eyes, they recognized their own nakedness. Though they anticipated that their eyes would open and they would become akin to God, discerning good and evil, they were ensnared by falsehood. Their newfound understanding of good and evil prompted self-judgment, leading to self-condemnation. I firmly believe this aligns with the principles of law, fleshly thinking, mirroring carnality, legalism, and condemnation.

Initially, they perceived their nakedness and hastily sewed fig leaves, fashioning makeshift aprons for themselves. This shame arose from a misjudgment of something inherently good, prompting them to conceal and protect themselves. Upon hearing the voice of the Lord God as He walked through the garden in the cool of the day, Adam and his wife sought refuge among the trees, hiding from God's presence. Adam's fearful response, "Where are you?" was met by God's inquiry, detailing his awareness of his nakedness and consequent hiding. Created by God to be unashamed in his nakedness, Adam's reaction highlights a broader context that transcends mere physical apparel. They are now misjudging because they consumed the forbidden fruit of the tree of the knowledge of good and evil, misunderstanding even what God might find displeasing, and hiding for incorrect reasons (Genesis 3:6-10).

Despite God's clear command and warning of death, their transgression in eating from the prohibited tree was undoubtedly sin. However, their hiding was instigated not by this disobedience but by their state of nakedness, a condition bestowed upon them by God. This shame, based on a misapprehension of their situation, represents a profound misjudgment. Stemming from consciousness of sin, shame, and law, this flawed perception paves the way to death by fostering a spirit of bondage, terror, and an oppressive sense of condemnation.

I find myself reflecting on Romans 8 in this scenario. The law engenders consciousness of sin. As Paul articulated in Romans 7, "I was alive once until the law came, but when the law came, sin revived, and I died" (Romans 7:9). The injunction "thou shalt not covet" allowed the law of sin within Paul's being to provoke covetousness, leading him to that which he abhorred. The law, paired with consciousness of sin, awakened the emotions of sin, yielding shame and fear. In Romans 8, this pathway culminates in death, as the carnal mind or mindset of the flesh is synonymous with death (Romans 8:6).

Contrastingly, the focus on the spirit equates to life and peace. The spiritual mindset in Romans 8 aligns with the spirit of sonship, corroborating with our inner spirit that we are indeed children of God and co-heirs with Christ, compelling us to exclaim, "Abba, Father." This intimacy, which regenerated believers experience as sons of God, stands in stark opposition to the spirit of bondage and fear arising from a perspective rooted in sin-consciousness, shame, law, and slavery. One path leads to life; the other leads to death.

Life is embodied in Christ Himself, residing within us, nurturing a connection with God wherein we can voice the affectionate cry of "Abba, Father." This utterance is a pure, intimate, and sincere call, unburdened by self-awareness, instead filled with a consciousness of God's manifold blessings. Acknowledging Him as the Father of Jesus Christ, our own Father, and recognizing ourselves as His heirs with the Spirit's testimony within us, gives rise to life and peace. This awareness stands in direct contrast to the mindset of the flesh, leading to death and condemnation (Romans 8:1-2). The Lord desires to liberate us from this condemning mindset, reinforcing the glorious truth that in Christ Jesus, condemnation has no hold on us.

Dead and Dying

From our own experiences with condemnation, we can discern the shame that gave rise to the spiritual death that Adam and Eve endured. Though their physical demise would come later, they were, from that moment, dwelling in a state of death, encumbered by a spirit of bondage and terror. Consequently, when the presence of God approached, they sought refuge, concealing themselves. Even in God's absence, the thought of Him compelled them to cover their nakedness with fig leaves. This self-imposed concealment serves as both a symbol of preparation for conflict (as the word used can also mean armor) and an expression of a sorrowful disposition toward God. Adorning themselves as if in sackcloth, they felt an intrinsic wrongness. This condemnation could either be specific or vague, as the tree of the knowledge of good and evil bequeathed just that: an understanding of good and evil (Genesis 2:17).

Their downfall lay in self-judgment; they erred in their assessment of themselves. They presumed their nakedness to be the issue, but the true fault lay in partaking of the forbidden tree of the knowledge of good and evil. What escapes the comprehension of the legalist is that the continued engagement with the law is the very catalyst for this death. By setting oneself as both judge and jury, the outcome inevitably leads to self-righteousness or shame. Either path culminates in death; whether viewed as good or evil, it results in demise, for humans were not designed to function as their own arbiters. We were shaped to live in Christ and partake of the tree of life. In Eden's Garden, the absence of restrictive commands emphasized life, which naturally bore fruit if nourished correctly (Genesis 2:16-17).

The sole exception was the tree of the knowledge of good and evil, accompanied by a restrictive commandment—a commandment so misunderstood that the woman believed they were forbidden even to touch it. This association with the law breeds confusion, not because the law itself is malignant, but because we were not created to be governed by it. Our design is aligned with God; the law is but a shadow, with Christ as the true substance. A shadow can never yield reality; only Christ can forge the genuine life we were designed for.

Adam and Eve's actions at this juncture can be described as misdirected. Legalism, with its fixation on good and evil and a desire to please God, leads to a misjudgment of right and wrong. It manifests from a shameful attire, a figurative girdle of sackcloth. Even this armor, meant to protect, can metamorphose into overt defiance against God, instigating wrath, as the law itself incites wrath. Yet, beneath this wrath lies shame (Romans 4:15). A shame stemming from a self-image that ought not to be there, yet persists due to misjudgment. The tree of the knowledge of good and evil imparted no subtlety or nuance, only a generalized sense of shame. They were unable to coherently express why they were hiding, a quintessential illustration of the bewildering power of condemnation.

Sin Consciousness

Indeed, I firmly contend that this concept is intrinsically connected to the law and the consciousness of sin. The death that invaded Adam and Eve instilled fear towards their friend, with whom they had previously walked in the garden during the cool of the day, hearing His voice—a scenario that appears anything but frightening. In the Hebrew, when they hear the voice of the Lord walking in the cool of the day, the word for "cool" is wind or "ruach," signifying spirit. This is something more than just the God walking. This is His glory approaching. Yet, His voice resonated differently to them. The voice that once comforted them now bore an unfamiliar atmosphere, one that would be recognized by slaves in bondage and fear—an atmosphere akin to that of Sinai.

Consider the appearance of God on Mount Sinai, where He manifested as a smoking fire atop the mountain, and His voice struck terror into the hearts of those present. Moses himself declared, "I exceedingly fear and quake" (Hebrews 12:21). The writings of Romans 7 and 8, 2 Corinthians 3, and Galatians 4 draw a vivid contrast between the voice of God upon that mount and the voice of God within our spirit. This disparity marks the difference between the voice of the law, engendering a spirit of bondage and fear, and the voice of our Shepherd within us—the spirit of sonship that cries, "Abba, Father" (Romans 8:15), with the Spirit affirming that we are indeed the children of God (Romans 8:16).

These two voices signify opposing realities: one brings life and death. This distinction lay at the heart of what the tree of the knowledge of good and evil accomplished. The emergence of shame set them at odds with God and fundamentally altered their perception of Him. Henceforth, His voice likely sounded absolutely terrifying to them, akin to the blast of a trumpet. When God proclaimed the Ten Commandments on the mount, a trumpet-like sound grew in intensity as He spoke, leaving the children of Israel trembling and pleading, "We cannot hear this voice anymore" (Exodus 19:19). On that momentous day, three thousand lives were lost, and the people recoiled from ever hearing God's voice again.

Was this reaction sparked by God's anger? Certainly not. Rather, it stemmed from their flawed relationship with Him. From that point forward, God concealed Himself, either within the tabernacle or the temple, necessitating a complex priesthood to act as a mediator between His direct presence and the people. This arrangement endured until He donned His tabernacle—the flesh of Jesus Christ (John 1:14)—a divine suit that enabled Him to interact with humanity, whose nature cannot withstand the glory of God. This profound alteration originated from the tree of the knowledge of good and evil, marking the moment when sin infiltrated the human race, bringing with it the shadow of death (Romans 5:12).

Legalism

Death pertains profoundly to how one relates to God: how God is perceived, how His voice is heard. This is why the Gospel reaching one's conscience is the singular pathway to God's presence. It's the revelation that confirms peace with God. Once this peace is solidified in the conscience, the voice of the Father and the Son, the spirit of sonship, and the affirmation of being God's child can be discerned. Through this realization, one can know God's love, which banishes fear (1 John 4:18). It is for this reason that God seeks to address sin and conscience, to heal the fear and shame that have defined our relationship with Him for much of our lives, until our salvation.

However, even as saved individuals, if we fail to transcend the legalistic approach to God, if we do not learn to align with the Spirit by accepting what the Gospel declares about God's reconciliation with us, we will remain hidden. As John warns, "Abide in Him, so that when He appears, you may have confidence at His coming and not shrink back in shame" (1 John 2:28). This image recalls the Garden of Eden, evoking empathy and even anger towards Christians who claim justification by faith yet persist in approaching God through law, shackled by fear and bondage.

Tragically, many are oblivious to this, and one cannot liberate oneself from it; only God can. But when you become a teacher and now you're introducing others to it, that's the problem, and that's where I get mad. This, I believe, is a manifestation of what truly invaded humanity in the Garden. Romans 5 illustrates that sin was present from Adam to Moses, even before the law was given (Romans 5:12-14). An overwhelming fear of God existed even before the law was delivered because they were already sinners, death was reigning, and they were incapable of relating to God.

This disconnection was never God's intent; He desired to walk with Adam in the day's cool breeze, but the consumption of the forbidden fruit altered their entire consciousness. Many misjudge the problem, failing to recognize that their relationship with the knowledge of good and evil is the root of their shame, not their nakedness (Genesis 3:7-10). Religion often misleads, making one believe that God demands something from them. However, God's desire is to provide covering, and His next action demonstrates this: He will declare His plan for redemption, then slay an animal to replace their fig leaves with its skin—a garment, a covering.

God's intention to be our covering is what enables us to stand in His presence with boldness. This covering is now Christ, symbolized beautifully by the ultimate sacrifice of Christ as the Lamb of God, who takes away the world's sin (John 1:29). Our righteousness and covering are found in Him alone.

Before their sin, Adam and Eve were encompassed by the entire Garden, a glory and covering filled with symbols of Christ. The river, the tree of life, the fruit, the serenity—all were emblematic of Christ. Adam represented Christ, his wife symbolized the Church, and together they painted a picture of the New Jerusalem (Revelation 21:2).

However, their compliance with the serpent brought sin and death into the world (Genesis 3:1-6). We may not sin as Adam did, but we die because of his sin. Even without sin, we would face death, as Romans 5 explains, for death arrived through one man's transgression (Romans 5:12). In this, Adam typifies Christ: his sin ushered all into sin and death.

Now, Christ comes as the second Adam, and His singular act of obedience in offering His life for us brings righteousness to many (Romans 5:19). As sin once reigned in death, now grace reigns through righteousness unto eternal life, allowing us to reign through Jesus Christ (Romans 5:21).

Jesus, thus, is the solution and the fulfillment of this picture—an anti-type, where Adam's negative fall contrasts with Christ's redemption. As the new head of humanity and the righteous inheritor of all promises, Christ has performed the obedient act that brings us all to life through faith in Him. This striking contrast between Adam's failure and Christ's redemption unveils the profound Gospel truth and vividly portrays how Christ mends what was lost in the Garden, becoming the ultimate source of our redemption

Chapter 14 Grace In Promise (Genesis 3)

God Intervenes with Grace

Gen 3:8-21 And they heard the voice of the LORD God walking in the garden in the cool of the day: and Adam and his wife hid themselves from the presence of the LORD God amongst the trees of the garden. (9) And the LORD God called unto Adam, and said unto him, Where art thou? (10) And he said, I heard thy voice in the garden, and I was afraid, because I was naked; and I hid myself. (11) And he said, Who told thee that thou wast naked? Hast thou eaten of the tree, whereof I commanded thee that thou shouldest not eat? (12) And the man said, The woman whom thou gavest to be with me, she gave me of the tree, and I did eat. (13) And the LORD God said unto the woman, What is this that thou hast done? And the woman said, The serpent beguiled me, and I did eat. (14) And the LORD God said unto the serpent, Because thou hast done this, thou art cursed above all cattle, and above every beast of the field; upon thy belly shalt thou go, and dust shalt thou eat all the days of thy life: (15) And I will put enmity between thee and the woman, and between thy seed and her seed; it shall bruise thy head, and thou shalt bruise his heel. (16) Unto the woman he said, I will greatly multiply thy sorrow and thy conception; in sorrow thou shalt bring forth children; and thy desire shall be to thy husband, and he shall rule over thee. (17) And unto Adam he said, Because thou hast hearkened unto the voice of thy wife, and hast eaten of the tree, of which I commanded

thee, saying, Thou shalt not eat of it: cursed is the ground for thy sake; in sorrow shalt thou eat of it all the days of thy life; (18) Thorns also and thistles shall it bring forth to thee; and thou shalt eat the herb of the field; (19) In the sweat of thy face shalt thou eat bread, till thou return unto the ground; for out of it wast thou taken: for dust thou art, and unto dust shalt thou return. (20) And Adam called his wife's name Eve; because she was the mother of all living. (21) Unto Adam also and to his wife did the LORD God make coats of skins, and clothed them.

This section is quite familiar, and sometimes such familiarity can numb us, rendering us unable to see anything new or gain any inspiration. Man's perception, due to his fall, has now altered. His condition has changed, especially his relationship with God. We've discussed how ever since the fall, man has been hiding in fear when it comes to the presence of God. I believe even the tone of God's voice sounded different. When Adam heard the voice of his friend walking in the garden, he hid himself. Considering what I know about Mount Sinai, and how God appeared in His glory, and how terrifying that was for the people of Israel, I believe that because man is gripped with a spirit of bondage, fear, condemnation, weakness, death, mortality, and corruption, he cannot bear the presence of God. It's a terrifying thing.

However, it's God who took all the steps to rectify this. There is nothing man can do to deal with God. God had to intervene. In the Old Testament we see Him do this in dramatic ways. for example, he instituted the priesthood and the tabernacle, which served as a buffer between Him and the people He wanted to interact with. In this way, He could still make a way to bless fallen people. God's intention is still to bless man. God did not revoke the blessing, nor did He retract the fact that creating man was good. He created man in His image and likeness, and He wants man to have dominion.

Death entered the picture due to the Tree of the Knowledge of Good and Evil. There is nothing man can do to rectify this situation by himself; he is dead. It is all up to God to intervene now. The next move has to be God's.

Returning to the aftermath of Adam and Eve's actions, their perspective underwent a drastic transformation. Once accustomed to walking alongside God in the serene coolness of the day, now they cowered in terror, dreading His voice and concealing themselves in fear. It's likely that the sight of God's presence has historically evoked such profound reactions. Think of the prophets like Ezekiel, Jeremiah, or Isaiah – when faced with God's presence, they fell prostrate as if lifeless, only to gather strength to stand once again. As to whether God manifested His glory or appeared in human form during this incident, the specifics remain uncertain, though my inclination leans toward His glory.

Reflecting on my past encounter with a Hebrew-English Bible, its words conveyed an extraordinary potency. The sound of God's voice echoed through the ruach, akin to a majestic passage of glory. The Hebrew language captures this image in a more vibrant manner. As they discerned His approach, an overwhelming terror enveloped them. Their future was shrouded in uncertainty, fear casting a long shadow. Their experience seemed akin to standing before the awe-inspiring judgment seat. Remarkably, even in the midst of their trepidation, God extended His grace.

Let's consider this analogy: envision yourself on death row, acutely aware that your execution date approaches. Suddenly, a reprieve arrives – the death sentence commuted to a lifetime behind bars. Relief surges unless an inexplicable desire for death persists. Such a parallel could be drawn to our human existence, a mortal coil akin to a prison term, replete with life's sorrow, afflictions, suffering, and groaning.

God subjected the entire creation to a state of futility, resulting in pervasive sorrow (Romans 8:20-22). Nonetheless, even within sorrow, lies the potential for solace (2 Corinthians 1:3-4). God assumes the role of comforter, a compassionate Father and the source of all mercies (Psalm 86:15, 2 Corinthians 1:3-4). Jesus fulfills the role of comforter (John 14:16), joined by the Holy Spirit as another advocate of solace (John 14:26). Throughout history, God's prevailing intention has been one of grace. Despite the tumultuous events that have unfolded, His overarching plan for humankind remains intact (Ephesians 1:9-10).

Progressing in the narrative, the subsequent act of God is one of grace. We may be too familiar with this story. But our familiarity is with the retelling of it rather than the details of the account itself. We've encountered images from art of Adam and Eve, bearing the weight of a curse, departing the sanctuary of the garden for a cursed, desolate expanse. We've been told that this was where divine judgment was pronounced upon them. Yet, this portrayal is only partial.

The story divulges a nuance often overlooked – despite the proclamation that death would befall them on the very day they consumed the forbidden fruit, they didn't die. Moreover, God was attuned to their vulnerability, their nakedness shrouded in shame; and so, He provided cover. By doing so, He sanctioned taking an animal's life (the first death) to drape them in its skin. This event serves as a visual embodiment of substitutionary atonement, memorialized shortly after in Abel's role as a shepherd, which foreshadowed the Levitical sacrificial framework. Amidst disclosing the curse that loomed, God also imparted a promise – that of the Gospel, the Seed destined to crush the serpent's head. A cherub was placed, not to irrevocably bar access to the Tree of Life, but to "watch over the path to the Tree of Life." Following their expulsion from Eden, Adam and his partner, now named Eve (meaning "mother of all living"), bore fruit. Upon the birth of their first son, she announced that she had begotten him of the Lord. Within them resided a sense of vitality and even blessing. Recall that within Eden, they were blessed and instructed to multiply. Clearly, some blessing remained.

In reflection, "while we were yet sinners, Christ died for us" (Romans 5:8). In due course, God dispatched His son to perish for the ungodly, during a time when we were utterly feeble (Romans 5:6). This encapsulates God's move in grace – instantaneously bestowing the gospel, proffering an unwavering hope, and bestowing eternal life (Titus 1:2, 3:7). Their solitary task is to embrace God's promise through faith. To assert that grace is absent from the Old Testament is be a fallacy. Here in the first pages of the Bible grace resounds loud and clear.

God first gave Adam and Eve the gospel to hold on to. That started the whole program of grace that we are now standing in. God has become a man. He died, resurrected, became the Spirit, or sent the Spirit. He became a life-giving spirit according to First Corinthians 15:45 and breathed Himself into us. Now He's our life and He says, "Abide in me." His life is in us. He's in charge of the life. We are to abide. But even that, we're weak. We tend to drift, we tend to get distracted through immaturity, lack of understanding, through deception, and all kinds of stuff. We have a High Priest who intercedes for us. We have the body of Christ and the ministry of the New Testament. He's given us all kinds of things. He intercedes for us and He shepherds us. So even the abiding eventually comes from Him.

Knowledge of Good Evil and Self Justification

. (11) And he said, Who told thee that thou wast naked? Hast thou eaten of the tree, whereof I commanded thee that thou shouldest not eat?

God asked them, "Who told you you were naked? Have you eaten from the tree?" Their concepts were skewed, their view of right and wrong was off. They felt shame because they were naked, yet that's how God had created them. What they should have judged themselves for was eating from the tree, but they didn't even mention that in their self-justifying answers before God. Their view of things was skewed.

The knowledge of good and evil didn't help man. Man is not equipped to judge correctly by himself, nor was he intended to be. He was intended to be vessel for God, living by Him and receiving everything from Him. Through redemption, God has brought us back to a state of total dependence on Him. He's to be our life. He has brought us back to the Tree of life, giving Himself to us as our food and drink. This is how we are to live. They saw that they were naked, becoming conscious of their own state and perceiving it as lack, and then moved to provide for themselves where no provision was needed. This is self-justification. As we learn to rest in Christ and live by His supply, we will find that this tendency to justify and provide for ourselves is an inconvenience and an obstacle to our fellowship with God. He desires us to just live before Him as we are and acknowledge His supply by faith.

We are brought back to Christ, the Tree of Life. and He is our food and drink. We come to Him, and He sees everything about us. Though we are naked, there is not a single thing in our hearts that He does not see, and He accepts us. His intention is not for us to deal with our hearts, but for Him to deal with our hearts. Our role is simply to believe. You believe in the blood, come near by faith in the blood, and are washed.

That washing is God in Christ, as the Spirit, cascading over you as life, renewing and refreshing you, and then living out of you. He changes your nature. It's still you living, but it's Christ in you. That's what He wants. What you spontaneously desire and want freely is what He wants and what you do is what He does. We're just one. He's our life, and we're the vessel. He doesn't obliterate us, He moves in!

What you eat becomes what you express. This kind of assimilation is unconscious. It's like grafting a peach tree branch into an apple tree. The life from the apple tree will eventually produce fruit through the peach branch. This doesn't happen by giving an instruction manual to the peach branch on how to produce fruit! If there were any instructions for the peach branch, they would be very simple: "hold onto the trunk. Just stay in me and then I'll produce my life in you. Don't focus on how. Focus on me and holding on to me." We do that through the gospel.

God's Pronouncement of Judgment Reveals His Grace

God asked them, "Who told you that you were naked?" The man responded, "The woman you gave to me." He was now blaming God. The man continued, "She gave me the tree and I ate from it." The Lord then asked the woman, "What have you done?" She replied, "The serpent deceived me, and I ate from the tree." Neither of them took responsibility for their actions. As a result, the Lord cursed the serpent, saying, "Because you have done this, you are cursed more than any livestock and more than any wild animal. You will crawl on your belly and eat dust all the days of your life."

We know that Adam and Eve came from the dust, or that Adam came from the dust and into dust he will return. Dust is the serpent's food, so the enemy comes to devour and somehow eats the energy of man. Man living in shame and condemnation is Satan's food. This was a curse to Satan. We tend to picture Satan as delighting in man's suffering, but I don't think that's entirely true. I believe Satan must feed on man's death, and as he does, just as Adam and Eve became what they ate, he becomes what he ingests. Somehow all of the ugliness in us becomes his constitution as well.

He becomes even more depraved as we are depraved because he must "eat it!" We saw that Satan and some of the angels were appalled that God would create man in His image and give him dominion - this man of clay - when angels, greater in power, glory, wisdom, and beauty, should have had that dominion (in their minds). God chose the foolish things, so Satan sought to bring man into depravity. By making Satan "eat" the residue of the fallen man he slew (dust), God brings Satan into the very depravity that Satan projected onto man. He becomes what he despises, and even worse! He loses all his glory.

Here is the Gospel: "**I will put enmity between you and the woman, and between your seed and her seed. It shall bruise your head and you shall bruise his heel**" (Genesis 3:15). Here we have Satan, the woman, and her offspring, which is the seed that will bruise Satan's head. Satan also desires to have offspring.

The serpent also has seed. What is the seed of the serpent? Ultimately this is Antichrist. But John says, "there are many antichrists" (1 John 2:18). The serpent's seed represents the final antichrist, but many who come in Christ's name reveal themselves to be tares. They hate

Christ, His witnesses, His people, His testimony, and His word. This speaks not just of the world in general but of people who received Satan's bad seed sown into the field (Matthew 13:38-39).

In the parable of the wheat and the tares, God sowed a good seed: which is the Word of the kingdom, which produced the wheat. Then the servants slept, and Satan sowed seed, which produced tares in the field, which is the world. Therefore, the tares and the wheat are not humanity in general. This is speaking of those who received good or bad seed sown into the heart. The good seed was the Gospel, the word of the Kingdom, and it produced wheat. The evil seed from Satan is a counterfeit of the Gospel that produces something that looks just like wheat and is almost indistinguishable from it. Only the servants of the Lord initially discern it. That means that whatever the seed was, it must have been very close to the gospel, and people received it and were, in a sense, begotten of Satan and became active enemies of God's plan in and among the wheat (Matthew 13:3-30).

Christianity, in its outward form, is mostly populated with tares. False prophets seem to be on the rise, to the point where even media outlets like CNN, Newsweek, Washington Post, and New York Times have written articles about false prophets and the Trump Christian right. They have made so many outlandish predictions and claims.

Millions of people watch and donate money to networks like TBN without realizing that they don't even have the gospel or anything close to it. Just because a message mentions Jesus and contains numerous Bible verses doesn't necessarily mean it's authentic. This misrepresentation has been going on for a long time. Sadly, the visible aspect of the Kingdom, the part that the world can see, is primarily represented by the tares. The wheat, the true believers who know how to abide in Christ have always been hard to find.

There are many people who call themselves Christians, but they oppose God's Kingdom. They resist His testimony, the Gospel, and the people who bear witness to it. They actively campaign against the wheat and against the doctrine of Christ. This will all be dealt with eventually. The tares will be thrown into the lake of fire.

Bitter with the Sweet

The promise of the Gospel in Genesis 3 is the promise of the seed that will crush the head of the serpent. Remember that they thought they were about to die when God spoke to them. What a relief to hear, "your seed!" She's going to have a seed, she's going to live, and her seed is going to defeat Satan. They realized they would not only live but also come out ahead.

There is also sorrow. God said to the woman, 'I will greatly multiply your sorrow at conception. In sorrow, you will bring forth children, and your desire shall be to your husband, and he shall rule over you.' The desire here is a grasping desire for position, and the man is now set to be somewhat of a tyrant. In the human race, by default, there is an enmity between the man and the woman related to authority.

When we come into the body of Christ, we recognize that Christ is the head, the man is the head of the woman. But this is not according to the curse, where the male is an abusive party and the woman is trying to usurp him through whatever means she has at her disposal. We'll see this enmity played out dramatically when we come to Genesis 10 with Semaramis, the wife of Nimrod. She ultimately killed him, created a religion in his name, and exercised authority on his behalf to rule over the people and launch her attacks against the seed.

God said to Adam, **"Because you have listened to your wife and have eaten from the tree of which I commanded you, 'You shall not eat of it,' cursed is the ground because of you. In toil you shall eat of it all the days of your life. Thorns and thistles it shall bring forth for you, and you shall eat the plants of the field. By the sweat of your face you shall eat bread until you return to the ground, for out of it you were taken; for you are dust, and to dust you shall return."**

Adam's fate was pretty grim, on the surface. As a result of his actions, the ground was cursed. This brought disharmony to the relationship between man and everything else. It's unclear whether the earth was the direct object of the curse, but it's certain that man's dominion was no longer present. When there is God's blessing, like when Isaac sowed in a famine and reaped a hundredfold (Gen 26:12), it doesn't matter where the people go, the earth yields. However, this blessing was no longer present. Now, everything is going to be much harder. There will be sorrow, toil, and sweat. "In sorrow, you shall eat of it all the days of your life. Thorns and thistles it shall bring forth for you, and you shall eat the plants of the field. By the sweat of your face you shall eat bread until you return to the ground, for out of it you were taken; for you are dust, and to dust you shall return."

There isn't much to say about this; it's not profound. It is what it is. This is life. Since then, everything that humanity has done has been an attempt to mitigate the effects of the curse. All technological advancements that support the current world system have been made to protect us from the curse. We have epidurals for pregnancies, hospitals, entertainment, air conditioning, and comfort. All of these things are meant to shield us from the elements, but they demonstrate how weak we are. We had to create a system, and now that system entirely consumes us. Every thought of humanity is about how to toil in sorrow for bread. Yes, we eat, but there's a sense of futility and gloom about it all. That's the state of fallen humanity.

So, Adam called his wife's name Eve because she was the "mother of all living". That's Adam's response to what God said. The timing of this is very interesting in the narrative. God finishes speaking about the curse, and Adam's response was to call his wife's name Eve!

"...**In the sweat of thy face shalt thou eat bread, till thou return unto the ground; for out of it wast thou taken: for dust thou art, and unto dust shalt thou return. (20) *And Adam called his wife's name Eve; because she was the mother of all living. (21) Unto Adam also and to his wife did the LORD God make coats of skins, and clothed them.*

That's why I said they must have been elated, even though God said all these horrible things about how their life will be. Adam heard, "we're not going to die. We're going to live!" There's a gospel promise. It was after this that God clothed them with skins. Adam's statement revealed he believed the Gospel, and the skins were a sign of the righteousness he had by faith when he believed.

The Elements, Titles and Covenants of a Glorious Heir

Christ is the seed of the woman, and that represents the promise for him to crush the head of the serpent, to deal with the original effects of the fall. As such, He's the second man and the last Adam. He's also called the seed of Abraham and the seed of David, which represents further promises that God made to the seed that would eventually give him the land, the kingdom, and the blessing.

The elements that make our future glorious in Christ come through these titles and covenants. The woman's seed, or the "seed of the woman" is the first title God gave mankind concerning Christ. This implies that the woman and the man must live to bear seed. I learned from the commentaries that it is significant because it is the "seed of the woman." In the Old Testament, when dealing with genealogies, it is always the seed of the male. The reference to the seed of the woman is an early allusion to the virgin birth. We know that God was the one who overshadowed Mary and produced the seed.

Moving on, the Lord made coats of skins for Adam and his wife and clothed them. They were already clothed supposedly with fig leaves, but this act of God is highly significant. God gave them the promise of the gospel, and they believed it and would have been justified by it. Everything we know from Scripture about justification shows us that they were justified when they believed. For example, he was justified when Abraham believed the promise given to him, which Galatians 3:8 says was the gospel. It was reckoned to him as righteousness. This applies to those who work not but believe in Him who justifies the ungodly (Romans 4:5). Their faith is counted as righteousness, and it has always been like this, even with Adam and Eve.

I believe Adam and Eve were justified. God revealed that a person is coming, and they believed in the promise of the seed. He also showed them a method to deal with sin. He killed an animal, a substitutionary death, as they were supposed to die but didn't. This was the first death they witnessed, with God shedding blood right in front of them and covering them with the animal's skins. This is a significant moment when God sacrifices an animal right in front of Adam and Eve, covering them with its skins. This act signifies an acknowledgment that they now need to be covered to stand before God. Before, they were nake,d but it was God covering them. I mentioned that the Garden of Eden was their covering. It's not that they were uncovered but God's provision was their covering. They need to be covered again, which will require another provision - providing a life through death.

The garments made by God through the sacrifice of a lamb would have held significant value and were given to Adam and Eve. They would have served as a constant reminder of God's act, and, as their descendants multiplied, there would have been some sort of recognition of those garments. According to Jewish mythology, Elijah's mantle may have been made of these skins, passed on to Elisha, and later worn by John the Baptist. Whether this is true or not, it is a fascinating thought.

This picture accompanies the promise of the seed and the offering. It must have made quite an impression, Abel became a shepherd just so he could offer the first thing of the flock, along with the fat portion. This is how we know they understood the significance of the sacrifice. Jesus grouped Abel with the prophets in Luke 11:50-51, meaning he had Christ's testimony. The spirit of Christ is the testimony of Jesus Christ, which is the spirit of prophecy (Rev 19:10).

According to apocryphal Old Testament Jewish books, an altar was also there. Jesus said that the blood of all the prophets, from righteous Abel to Zechariah whom was slain between the altar and the temple, would be required of the generation. With Abel, you have an altar and with Zechariah, you had the temple. All the prophets were martyred. Abel was a martyr, a prophet, a shepherd, and he understood the significance of these garments and what they meant in relation to the promise of the seed. This was the gospel at their time that justified them.

Our gospel is the same; but the events are past tense. Back then, they looked forward to it. All the prophets knew about the sufferings of Christ and the glories to follow. They knew there would be a seed that would deal with the situation. They knew that there would be a substitutionary death and a resurrection which we'll see when we get to Abraham.

It's important to know that the gospel is there from the beginning. This is God responding to the situation and He does it entirely in grace. He doesn't do it based on their repentance, sorrow, or anything other than His sovereignty and purpose to step in and continue to fulfill His desire with man.

We continue to live and are saved, regenerated, and destined for glory because of God's good pleasure, not because of something in us (Philippians 2:13, Ephesians 2:8-9). All we did was believe. We believe what God said. That's the only quality we have that recommends us to God and it's not really even ours. What would we believe if God hadn't said anything? Faith comes by hearing and hearing by the word (Romans 10:17). How will they believe without a preacher? (Romans 10:14) God is the one who spoke this whole thing forth (Genesis 1:1, John 1:1-3).

The program was not devised by us, but by him. Even Adam did not come to the Lord and confess his wrongdoing, saying, "We are truly sorry and repent. I cannot believe we did this, and I beg for your mercy." Instead, they justified themselves from the beginning and blamed each other. Adam blamed God, saying, "It was the woman you gave me."

As previously mentioned, the aprons they wore were a form of protective armor. This was complete rebellion. They believed that God was withholding something from them and did not want them to be like Him. Consider the implications of that rebellion. When you say that God does not want us to be like Him and that He is withholding from us, it reveals a root desire: "I want to be like God, and I think I can match Him. I will be like He is." This is similar to what Satan said, "I will ascend to the mount and receive worship in the great congregation" (Isaiah 14:13-14).

I believe there is more to the story than the simplistic narrative we are told. When examining the details of the Tree of the Knowledge of Good and Evil, and how it is portrayed in world religions, it represents mystical knowledge and power. The goal is to open your eyes so that you can become like God. Jehovah is merely a fragment of the Godhead who has been deceived in the mystery religions that spring from this tree and celebrate it. He believes he is the "I Am," but there is actually a God beyond him. This philosophy is known as the Perennial Philosophy and is the root of all world religions.

They were initiated into mysteries when they ate that tree. But then, when God came around, it was all undone and they were exposed as just being slaves and in bondage. Man loves to think he's something because he has mystical knowledge, but when God comes around, he's undone. That's what it will be like for many of these Illuminati folks when they meet God. They're going to be "shaking in their boots." But while they were on Earth, they thought they were "big stuff" and spent their whole life preparing their armor to meet God in opposition.

Adam and Eve sort of did that with those fig leaves, and God just removed them and covered them with skins. I'm making a point that God sovereignly intervened while man was at the height of ungodliness and rebellion, and offered the Gospel and a way. Adam and Eve could have rejected it, and said, 'No, we don't want anything to do with you. We don't believe you.' But they didn't. They believed, and Adam, based on God's promise, called Eve the mother of living.

Justification and Covering with Witnesses

Now, let us consider Adam and Eve, covered in these skins. A sacrifice has been made, and they've been given the promise of the Seed. They've received the Gospel and are justified by faith. How do I know they're justified by faith? I have to examine the entirety of the Bible. How do I know a lamb was involved? Again, I have to refer to the whole Bible. While there may be some ambiguity, the Bible is consistent within itself. According to Romans 4, justification has always been by faith, apart from works. For those who believe in Him who justifies the ungodly, their faith is considered righteousness. The Gospel they believe involves the Seed, which is Christ, and the covering with these sacrifices involves a prophecy of his death for sin.

Because Christ is the Seed, he has the right to deal with Satan and receive the kingdom by inheritance. However, we are not entitled to enter into it righteously unless he pays for our sin. That's what the covering represents. God provided them with "Gospel t-shirts", and they went forth and preached to their children.

Genesis 3:22-24 (KJV)
"And the Lord God said, Behold, the man is become as one of us, to know good and evil: and now, lest he put forth his

hand, and take also of the tree of life, and eat, and live for ever: Therefore the Lord God sent him forth from the garden of Eden, to till the ground from whence he was taken. So he drove out the man; and he placed at the east of the garden of Eden Cherubims, and a flaming sword which turned every way, to keep the way of the tree of life."

Some may say this was to keep them away from the Tree of life, but it was also to protect the way to the Tree of Life. God's intention was to restore it. The Cherubim are known to be witnesses to God's holiness (Revelation 4:8). They surround the throne of God, proclaiming, "Holy, holy, holy," and they praise the Lamb, as recorded in Revelation 5. One might think they're looking at God, but according to the design of the Tabernacle, which was made according to the heavenly pattern, the Cherubim statues on the Ark of the Covenant were facing inward, gazing down at the blood on the propitiation. The "mercy seat" which covered the law is found in the holiest part of the ark, within the tabernacle. This is where God's presence resided. The only person permitted to enter this sacred space was the high priest, and only with the sacrificial blood. This represents Christ as the propitiation - the satisfaction of God's righteous claims (Hebrews 9:7-8, 11-12, 24-26).

According to Romans 3, God is vindicated as righteous in passing over sins. He is declared to be both just and the justifier of those who believe in Jesus. (Romans 3:25-26) This vindication of God answers a critical question posed by man and Satan alike. Man often questions how a loving God can send people to hell, while Satan's query is the opposite. He asks how a righteous God can allow sinful man access to paradise and the tree of life. (Genesis 3:22)

Satan, a cherub, continuously accuses us before God. (Job 1:6-12, Revelation 12:10) The answer to both these questions is the same: Christ, the propitiation. Christ is set forth as a propitiation through faith in His blood, a justification freely given by God's grace through the redemption that is in Christ Jesus. (Romans 3:24-25) God sent Him to be a propitiation through faith in His blood, to declare His righteousness for the remission of sins that are passed through the forbearance of God. (Romans 3:25)

God is put on trial, forced to answer the question: how can He permit man back into paradise? The response is the propitiation, Christ. He was publicly manifested as God's righteousness. (Romans 3:21) Through faith in His blood, God's righteousness is declared, allowing Him to forgive sins. God can be just and the justifier of those who believe in Jesus. (Romans 3:26)

Who bears witness to this? The cherubim. The propitiation refers to the lid on the ark of the covenant in the holy of holies. In the past, only the high priest could access God's presence. (Hebrews 9:7) Now, because Christ has come and done what no man could do, He has entered into the heavens with His own blood. (Hebrews 9:12) He presents it as a manifestation of God's righteousness, proving that God can be just and the justifier of those who believe in Jesus.

His righteousness is vindicated in front of the cherubim, including Satan. This was the purpose of God's establishment at the gate of Eden. The gate of Eden is the barrier to the tree of life, located in the midst of the paradise of God. Jesus promised the thief on the cross that he would be with Him in paradise. He also promised the overcomer in the letter to the church of Ephesus access to the tree of life in the midst of God's paradise. This access, this ability to partake of the tree of life, is the same as entering into communion with God.

Coming forward to the Holy of Holies, we find our path through the blood. We come forward by faith, cleansed and washed, and gain access to the tree of life. This act takes place right in front of the cherubim, who surround God's throne, saying, "holy, holy, holy". They praise God, magnifying His holiness and righteousness. This is put on display in the propitiation that grants us access, as God promised. All of this was put in place, right in front of Adam and Eve, and right in front of Satan at the Garden of Eden.

The cherubim, with the two-headed sword or the sword that goes back and forth to guard the way of the tree of life, are present. I believe this sword represents the word and the testimony. The cherubim, the witnesses of the lamb, have eyes all over them. They are there to witness the glory of God and that witness is the word.

We know that there are four Gospels. There's the lion, which represents the lion of the tribe of Judah, Matthew, focusing on the kingship of Jesus. Mark represents the ox, the servant who went serving. Luke represents His humanity. The genealogy comes all the way back to Adam, tracing the blood, and is full of His compassion and feeling as a man. In John, we find references to the wilderness where He was likened to an eagle that bore the children of Israel.

We know that the cherubim with the forms of lion, an ox, a man, and an eagle surround the throne of God, saying "holy, holy, holy", and witness this propitiation. I believe that the two-edged sword represents the witness of the testimony of Christ. The angels saw it first and then God gave that testimony to men as well. At Eden, God and Man were both vindicated in front of the angels (in type), just as in the heavens, God and justified men are vinidicated before the principalities!

Chapter 15 A Legalist and a Prophet - Two ways of Responding to God (Genesis 4)

Gen 4:1-15 And Adam knew Eve his wife; and she conceived, and bare Cain, and said, I have gotten a man from the LORD. (2) And she again bare his brother Abel. And Abel was a keeper of sheep, but Cain was a tiller of the ground. (3) And in process of time it came to pass, that Cain brought of the fruit of the ground an offering unto the LORD. (4) And Abel, he also brought of the firstlings of his flock and of the fat thereof. And the LORD had respect unto Abel and to his offering: (5) But unto Cain and to his offering he had not respect. And Cain was very wroth, and his countenance fell. (6) And the LORD said unto Cain, Why art thou wroth? and why is thy countenance fallen? (7) If thou doest well, shalt thou not be accepted? and if thou doest not well, sin lieth at the door. And unto thee shall be his desire, and thou shalt rule over him. (8) And Cain talked with Abel his brother: and it came to pass, when they were in the field, that Cain rose up against Abel his brother, and slew him. (9) And the LORD said unto Cain, Where is Abel thy brother? And he said, I know not: Am I my brother's keeper? (10) And he said, What hast thou done? the voice of thy brother's blood crieth unto me from the ground. (11) And now art thou cursed from the earth, which hath opened her mouth to receive thy brother's blood from thy hand; (12) When thou tillest the ground, it shall not henceforth yield unto thee her strength; a fugitive and a vagabond shalt thou be in

the earth. **(13) And Cain said unto the LORD, My punishment is greater than I can bear. (14) Behold, thou hast driven me out this day from the face of the earth; and from thy face shall I be hid; and I shall be a fugitive and a vagabond in the earth; and it shall come to pass, that every one that findeth me shall slay me. (15) And the LORD said unto him, Therefore whosoever slayeth Cain, vengeance shall be taken on him sevenfold. And the LORD set a mark upon Cain, lest any finding him should kill him.**

I view chapter 4 and 5 as pair, showing two manners of living with respect to God. Therefore I've grouped them in the same section.

Coming back to Genesis, Chapter Four, we're now in a post-fall world. God has already intervened with grace and given them the promise of the seed, the Gospel. The Gospel has two aspects: the "positive" which focuses on inheritance, and the "negative" aspect of dealing with sin.

Salvation in its Positive and Negative aspects.

Let's delve into the positive aspect first. This focuses on the inheritance, which is all tied up in the seed of the woman, who is also the seed of Abraham, the seed of David, the last Adam, Christ. He inherits what we could not but does it on our behalf. He became like us to represent us and inherit for us what we could not. This is fully positive and focused on inheritance. The destiny of this seed focuses on sonship, and glorification. Everything we receive in salvation are tied up in this Person and his inheritance. He is the heir, and He makes us His fellow heirs. As members of the body of Christ, we are co-heirs with Christ. It is His inheritance that we are entering into.

Then, there is the "negative" aspect of dealing with sin, which was represented by the fact that God killed the lamb, or the animal, right in front of Adam and Eve and clothed them with the skins. This shows that the way back to the tree of life is going to take God intervening and doing something. We know that this act is a picture of the sacrificial system, which was prefigured by God showing us that this seed, Christ, would also die for our sins and be resurrected. He alone could deal with sin. God killed an animal, setting forth the pattern according to the law of first mention in the scripture. The first death was at God's hand, and it stood as a figure of Christ. "No one takes it from me, but I lay it down of my own accord. I have authority to lay it down and authority to take it up again. This command I received from my Father." (John 10:18). God gave His only begotten Son.

On one hand, the Gospel deals with inheritance, restoration of everything, Satan, and sin. On the other hand, it also describes the consequences of sin, such as sorrow. Man will eat bread in sorrow and toil, sweating from his face. For the woman, childbirth will be laborious. The ground is cursed for their sake, producing thorns and thistles. These things are significant and were all foretold.

Cain and Abel

In Chapters Four and Five, two genealogies are presented that represent two distinct ways of life resulting from what man heard in God's speaking. Both Cain and

Abel received the stories of what God said to Adam and Eve, but they each took away very different messages from it. These differences reveal two approaches to God: one is accepted, and the other is rejected. They also reveal two kinds of life: one is approved, and the other is disapproved. The story of Cain and Abel is fundamental to understanding the conflict between the people of God and their enemies.

Cain becomes a figure of the Antichrist, as we learn from the First John. Peter and Jude referred to the 'way of Cain', but it was John who discussed what the 'way of Cain' truly meant. The 'way of Cain' is to reject the blood as the means to be justified before God, to reject the propitiation, and to reject those who seek refuge in the blood. They reject the testimony of Christ and are therefore Antichrist. They hate their brethren and are murderers.

1Jn 3:11-16 For this is the message that ye heard from the beginning, that we should love one another. (12) Not as Cain, who was of that wicked one, and slew his brother. And wherefore slew he him? Because his own works were evil, and his brother's righteous. (13) Marvel not, my brethren, if the world hate you. (14) We know that we have passed from death unto life, because we love the brethren. He that loveth not his brother abideth in death. (15) Whosoever hateth his brother is a murderer: and ye know that no murderer hath eternal life abiding in him. (16) Hereby perceive we the love of God, because he laid down his life for us: and we ought to lay down our lives for the brethren.

As stated in First John 3, the crux of the matter is that we should love one another, not as Cain did. He was of the wicked one and slew his brother. Why? Because his brother's deeds were righteous and his were evil. The record of these deeds is here in Genesis 4. All we know about Abel is that he became a shepherd to offer the firstling of the flock with the fat portion. According to First John, this was his righteousness. This is what it means to practice righteousness. Cain's rejection of this way of righteousness and his hatred for Abel was his practice of evil.

Cain's actions were a reflection of his walking in darkness, his abiding in death, his committing the sin unto death. It was a prefigure of the Antichrist, a definition of what it means to be of the world. The world came from Cain. First John warns us not to marvel that the world hates us. Cain hated Abel, and his descendants formed the world. We see a lifestyle emerging from Cain, which is negatively referred to as the world.

God loved the world so much that He gave His only begotten Son, so that whoever believed in Him may not perish but have everlasting life. But there's also the world as a system, and there's a god of this world, which is Satan. John said that if you have love for this world, which is characterized by the pride of life, the lust of the eyes, and the lust of the flesh, then the love of the Father is not in you (1 John 2:15-16). As believers, we are in the world but not of it. We don't love it (John 15:19).

The world is tied up in the Tree of Knowledge of Good and Evil and the desire to "be" something, the desire for vain glory, the desire to be respected. It's a religious desire at the root. Cain's problem was a religious problem. He wanted to be approved by God for his works. Genesis 4 mentions that God respected Abel's offering but did not respect Cain's offering. This respect is tied to honor. Cain is the first fruit of what the Tree of Knowledge of Good and Evil looked like flowering in humanity.

Cain and Abel had very different responses to God, based on two different perceptions of who He is, which led to totally different interpretations of His word. The same is true of those today who read the Bible. Who we think God is is definitely going to impact what we see in the word and how we respond. Paul distinguishes between the letter that kills and the spirit that gives life (2 Corinthians 3:6). Those who read Moses without seeing Christ, but only taking the law, are blinded by a veil, resulting in ignorance, a hardened heart, wrath, enmity, and persecution of the children of the promise (Galatians 4:29).

Then there are the children of the promise, resting in faith in who God has revealed Himself to be in Christ and what He has said. This disposition can be characterized this way: "God has to do everything, and I can do nothing. I'm not qualified to do anything for God. I'm not seeking my own religious glory. I know I'm a sinner, and I know the only way I can approach God is through the offering."

When you come to understand that God has given you a way to approach Him, not based on your own righteousness but on His righteousness manifested through Jesus Christ, it changes your perspective. By accepting Jesus Christ as the propitiation for your sins - the righteous one, as John calls him - you are placed in a different position. The word becomes spirit and life to you, and what you focus on is very different from before (Romans 3:21-22, 1 John 2:1-2).

This disposition can be characterized this way: "God has to do everything, and I can do nothing. I'm not qualified to do anything for God. I'm not seeking my own religious glory. I know I'm a sinner, and I know the only way I can approach God is through the offering." The gospel promise is God intervening to say, "I'm taking care of everything".

So we see that there are two very different ways to read the Bible. You can either go to the Bible and read the law, which is the diagnosis of what you are, (Romans 3:19-20) or go to the Bible and read the gospel promise, which is God intervening to say, "I'm taking care of everything."

Martin Luther said, "The true doctor of theology is the person who knows how to distinguish between law and gospel." (Lutheran Quarterly, Vol. 1, No. 1, Spring 1987) . Throughout the scripture, there is a consistent presence of both law and gospel. Law was added for transgression and it is because of a negative environment, a negative situation due to sin. Some people only see law when they read the Bible. Law was introduced not because God desired it, but because of sin. It diagnoses the problems in man. On the other hand, the promise of the gospel is that God intervenes to say, "I'm taking care of everything." You can either read the law in the Bible, which diagnoses what you are. If you accept that diagnosis, then eventually, you will look to the gospel. It will produce a crisis where you ask, "What is God's remedy? I can't remedy my situation." The remedy is the gospel.

Adam and Eve were standing there, knowing that the next thing that came out of God's mouth would determine their fate. However, instead of condemning them, God offered them the gospel - the promise of the seed of the woman. To cover their nakedness, He killed an animal and used its skin. God provided the way and guarded the tree of life with the cherubim..

Yes, they were cast out, but there's evidence that even though they were cast out of Eden and even though they were proclaimed to be full of sorrow and the ground would be cursed for them, there's evidence that God blessed them anyway. They were fruitful to multiply. The human race came from them. Hundreds of billions of lives, destinies, and futures came from them!

Cursed Line

> **And now art thou cursed from the earth, which hath opened her mouth to receive thy brother's blood from thy hand; (12) When thou tillest the ground, it shall not henceforth yield unto thee her strength; a fugitive and a vagabond shalt thou be in the earth.**

In Cain's downfall, God cursed the ground, which raises the question: "Wasn't the Ground already cursed?" Didn't God say the ground was cursed when Adam fell? (Gen 3:18). However, for God's people who believe the Gospel, there is a persistent blessing. For instance, Isaac sowed during a famine and still reaped a hundredfold. Regardless of the global situation, if God blesses you, you can live independently of the world's circumstances. As Christians, we should remember that we are not removed from the world situation, but rather here as ambassadors from a heavenly, blessed, and rich country. We experience and sympathize with others, share the comforts of God, and proclaim His Kingdom. This is what Christ did.

According to God's words, Cain bore the brunt of the curse, and it wasn't just that the ground was cursed. The wording of the scripture says that Cain was cursed from the earth. This means that our traditional understanding of the curse is wrong according to the law of first mention. Until now, I had always thought that the curse came upon Adam and Eve and upon the earth when they fell, but that's not what the scripture says.

God had told Adam and Eve that the ground would bear thistles and thorns. However, the first use of the word "cursed" is actually in reference to Satan. **"And the LORD God said unto the serpent, Because thou hast done this, thou art cursed above all cattle, and above every beast of the field; upon thy belly shalt thou go, and dust shalt thou eat all the days of thy life"** (Gen 3:14). The next time we see the word "cursed" is with Cain. He was "cursed from the earth." Later we will see that Noah was named prophetically because he would bring comfort to men concerning the toil of their hands for whom the ground was cursed (Gen 5:29.) So the ground was indeed cursed, but it seems that the strength of that curse is applied to those that are hostile and alienated to God. Meanwhile, God's people, though living in an environment impacted by the curse, who toil because of the curse and experience its effects, realize that they are still blessed in spite of it. The disposition of cursed people and blessed people is very different.

The next pronouncement of cursing we will see is after the flood with the cursing of Ham's 4th son, called Canaan (sounds a little like Cain!) and he was the grandfather of Nimrod. From Canaan's line came a city built in opposition to God, in opposition to His judgments, as a symbol of vanity and man's exaltation of himself, denying that he is cursed. As we will see in this chapter, from Cain came a city, named after his son (vanity) and Cain's line came the rudiments of what we know to be the "world system," all of man's building work to stave off the effects of the curse and fight it.

The present world comes from Babel, and Babel ultimately comes from Cain. It comes from man fighting against the curse, denying the curse, denying God's judgment, and fighting to vainly establish himself in God's place. These are the truly cursed people.

The blessed people of God are also impacted by the curse, and groan and long for God's deliverance, acknowledging God's judgment and living by faith in Him. They are "in the world but not of it."

Abel and Cain perceived different things than what God said. Cain's focus was on the sorrow, work, and toil. He believed that's what God wanted, so he offered the fruit of his labor. God didn't respect his offering. Cain assumed this is what pleases God. This is similar to the legalist, who believes that the law pleases God and that our attempts to keep it, and even our sorrow, are commendable.

This is similar to Cain's perspective. He didn't focus on why we aren't in Eden. Instead, he focused on our present state of toiling. Perhaps he thought, 'I'm going to sweat harder than everybody else,' he said. 'We'll eat bread from the sweat of our face and toil in the ground. I intend to do it better than anyone else.' In sorrow, he resolved to wear sackcloth and ashes, to show his remorse. He saw himself as the most mournful worshiper of God, believing that this was what God desired. After all, he offered the fruit of his toil from the ground.

Let's shift our focus to Abel. What did he see? He saw that God had promised the seed. We We know that Abel believed in God's promise of the seed because Jesus called him a prophet. He referred to him as "righteous Abel" and linked him with the prophets. Jesus said that the blood of all the prophets, from righteous Abel (Matthew 23:35) to Zechariah who was slain between the altar and the temple (Luke 11:51), would fall upon the generation living during their judgment. Therefore, Abel was a prophet.

According to the scriptures, the spirit of prophecy is the testimony of Jesus Christ (Revelation 19:10). The prophets inquired into what manner or time the spirit of Christ in them was testifying concerning the sufferings of Christ and the glories to follow (1 Peter 1:10-11). The gospel was always present in the scripture. It always focused on the seed and consistently illustrated his death and resurrection for sin. This is something all the prophets knew (Acts 10:43). Not everyone understood it, but the believers did, and so did the prophets. This is evident throughout scripture.

Abel didn't focus on the sorrow. Instead, he focused on God's provision and became a shepherd. This was an "impractical" choice at the time since they weren't eating meat. Perhaps it was for clothing, but being a shepherd didn't make much sense unless you understand that he offered the firstling of the flock, with the fat portion. This implies a pre-Levitical understanding that the fragrance from the burnt offering goes up as a pleasing sacrifice to God, satisfying Him. (Genesis 4:4)

According to the book of Jasher, Jewish history, and Jesus, there was an altar at the gate. How do we know that Abel's offering was accepted and Cain's wasn't? They put their offerings on the altar, and fire would have signified that God respected an offering. Apparently, there was no fire for Cain. (Genesis 4:3-5)

Let's read further. 'And Adam knew Eve, his wife, and she conceived and bore Cain, the firstborn.' She said, 'I've gotten a man from the Lord.' Some translations say, 'I've got the man, even the Lord.' They would have thought that this is the seed that God had promised that would crush the head of the serpent. Perhaps even Cain thought of himself in that way! The mighty sent one of God!

That's something you might want to do. In the process of time, it came to pass that Cain brought the fruit of the ground as an offering to the Lord. Remember, the ground is cursed, and Cain is offering the fruit of this cursed ground. The ground bearing thorns is a picture of our flesh; we're cursed in the flesh. Jesus became a curse for us and bore the crown of thorns, representing that curse.

Cain offered the works of his flesh, the works of his toil, the sweat of his bw, because he thought that's what pleased God. That's warped because it's not what pleases God. It was never God's good pleasure to put man in sorrow. That's not how God created man in the beginning. This world and the conditions we live in are not representative of God's will. Living by sight and not by faith, and then trying to respond to God according to the senses, is misguided.

Cain was what we would typically think of as ann unbeliever." He was a religious person, the firstborn, a leader. He would have considered himself honorable. He would have been expecting an honorable response to his offering, made in front of the whole family. But his offering was a vainglorious show of the flesh. It was an offensive offering. It might as well have been a pig in the holy of holies, like Antiochus Epiphanes. I think of it as the first foreshadowing of the abomination of desolation.

I wonder what Adam and Eve thought when Cain offered the fruit of the ground. I've heard many people teach that Cain was rejected because He didn't offer his "best" to God. I've heard pastors say that, and I think it shows that they don't understand justification by faith. This misunderstanding likely means they won't understand the whole Bible. Everyone I've ever encountered who taught that way ended up being a legalist. They didn't see Abel as a prefiguration of the sacrificial system, the Lamb of God, Christ. They don't see Christ when they read this, and so it's meaningless. The Bible is meaningless apart from Christ.

The story of Cain and Abel is often misinterpreted, with people assuming that Cain didn't work hard enough or love

God as much as Abel did. However, I believe that Cain actually worked harder than Abel. He toiled in the ground, while Abel, much like Jacob in the story of Jacob and Esau. Jacob was a shepherd too, seen as "lazy" by the mighty hunter, Esau. Cain was definitely angered when his offering wasn't accepted, and Abel's was. He hated Abel, as stated in 1 John 3:12, because Abel's deeds were righteous meaning God accepted his offering.

The practice of righteousness means to be credited with righteousness through faith. It means acceptance of one's "offering." We have one offering that has already been accepted: Jesus Christ. We are accepted based on our faith in Him, and nothing else. Abel brought the firstling of his flock and the fat thereof. God respected his offering but did not respect Cain's. This rejection angered Cain and caused his "countenance to fall."

I believe that this phrase, "his countenance fell," suggests that sin had gripped him. In the early days of humanity, there was a certain innocence in their faces, but when a countenance falls, it signifies the disposition that has been set in sin, hardness, and rebellion.

This sin-stained face and falling countenance often occur when people get offended. It's one thing not to understand the way of righteousness and feel condemned as if you need to offer something more to God. It's another thing when they get angry at the righteous and start to hate them. This hatred hardens one's heart and sets them on a path of self-righteousness, often leading to a works campaign against the grace of God and those who stand for the testimony of Christ.

This falling countenance is evident in the modern world, with people doubling down on their self-righteousness and expressing hatred towards the brethren. According to First John, Cain hated his brother and committed a sin unto death. He walked in darkness, was of the wicked one, and slew his brother. No one who hates their brother has eternal life in them. This hatred is a murderous one, motivated by resentment for someone being accepted by God.

The Sin unto Death

Think about this. Why did Cain hate Abel? It was because God accepted Abel's offering. Abel's deed was righteous. Abel was respected, and Cain was looking for honor. He was vainglorious and believed he should have been honored and respected for his offering. When he wasn't, and Abel was, his response was hatred and his countenance fell.

That's a sin a believer cannot commit. This is what is referred to as the sin unto death. When First John talks about the sin you can't commit, he says there's a seed that abides in him, and you can't sin. Many people think this means that my spirit man doesn't sin, that I cannot sin. But this is not true because First John already told us that if any man sins, we have an advocate with the Father, Jesus Christ the righteous.

He wrote these things to us so that we could understand sin. But if anyone sins, as stated in First John 5, and you see a brother commit a sin that is not unto death, pray for him and God will give him life. Brothers can sin, but there is a sin that leads to death. John also said, "I'm not saying you should pray for that." The sin that leads to death is the sin that the antichrists commit, who take the way of Cain, who hates his brother because his deeds are righteous.

This individual hates the propitiation and rejects God's way of justifying sinners. At the root, they do not believe the gospel. A believer can't commit the sin of Cain, because it would mean rejecting, not believing. You don't believe that God's way of justifying sinners is right, but you oppose it. You call it a license to sin. That's what Satan does. Satan accuses us night and day.

God, in the way He dealt with our sins, is said to have vindicated His righteousness. That's why we have an advocate with the Father, Jesus Christ the righteous. He himself is the propitiation for our sins and not only ours but also the sins of the whole world (1 John 2:1-2). Romans 3 shows us that the propitiation is Jesus Christ, set forth as the righteousness of God apart from the law.

The law and the prophets witness to manifest His righteousness and declare that He is just and the justifier of those who believe in Jesus, even though they work not but believe on Him. He justifies the ungodly. He justifies sinners and He's declared righteous in doing so by setting forth Jesus Christ as the propitiation to manifest His righteousness. (Romans 3:1-26)

We talked about how the cherubim are witnessing this. They surround the propitiation, the Ark of the Covenant, and say "holy, holy, holy". as the blood is sprinkled. They declare God's holiness in dealing with sin. It is righteous through and through. The accusation against people who say, "You're just looking for a license to sin," is not an accusation against you. Don't take it personally. They're accusing God. He's the one who came up with the method of justification. He's the one who slew the animal in front of the cherubim He set at the gate.

"God covered Adam and Eve with skins and promised the seed, saying, 'This seed is going to destroy the serpent.' This wasn't humanity's idea, rather, it was God's. Our obedience is to believe. Cain's offering was disobedient, representing his unbelief. Abel's was obedient, representing his faith. Both were responses to something God said.

Seeing and Truly Hearing vs Hearing but Not Seeing

What do you see? Do you see the word as the letter, or do you see it as spirit and life? Do you focus on the sorrow and the toil, thinking that must be what God wants? Or do you look at the big picture and see that God created Adam and Eve, put them in the garden, and gave them access to everything? The tree of life, all the trees in the garden - they had this glorious situation.

Yes, they fell, but then God immediately intervened. He gave them the gospel concerning the seed, offered up an animal for them, covered them with its skins, and blessed them. They didn't die. God's intention is life, His desire for man is good.

It all comes down to what you think is the nature of God. Is He for you or against you? What you offer will be based on what you see. All Cain could see was that God wants the works of our hands, our toil and sweat, something from this ground. He didn't even acknowledge that the ground is cursed. Abel, on the other hand, chose to be a shepherd so he could offer the first leg of the flock with the fat portion. He knew God's heart.

It all comes down to a spirit of wisdom and revelation. What do you see? People read Colossians and Ephesians looking for marriage advice and instructions to follow. But these books offer heavenly views of God's heart, His desires in creating the universe, and what He's accomplishing in Christ.

The works person is just looking at themselves, searching for something to do to make themselves righteous. The root of this is vain glory. It's not even a desire to please God; it's rooted in an accusation of God's character. The tree of the knowledge of good and evil was based on an accusation that God was withholding from them because He didn't want them to be like Him and live forever.

This was based on a vainglorious desire to be like God, which was the root of the sin, an accusation of God's character. This is the fruit of the tree of the knowledge of good and evil, which is religion. Religious people don't love God, they want to love God. They want to be the kind of person that loves God, but their very desire is worldly.

It's the lust of the eyes, the lust of the flesh, the pride of life. It is vain glory. This is proved when their offering is rejected and they see a righteous person who's blessed by God, even though they're a sinner. They double down and hate him, their countenance falls, and they're full of wrath. That's what Cain did. He revealed what was really motivating him when his countenance fell. He is motivated by vainglory. He doesn't love God, he thinks God is a hard taskmaster. This lazy shepherd offers up a firstling of a flock and he's accepted. I worked, I toiled, just like God told us to. They were both responding to things God said.

What's interesting is, God didn't say anything when he killed the animal. He acted it out as a picture and covered them, but he didn't really explain the significance, at least in the record we have. Whereas Cain, his response was based on what God literally said: "In sorrow you're going to be toiling and eating bread from the sweat of your face."

So Abel had revelation. His decision to become a shepherd and offer the firstling of the flock was based on a vision of watching what God does and looking into his character and understanding why he did it. It's a big picture kind of view of God. Whereas Cain just blindly followed the letter of what God said. Now, I'm not saying we should dismiss the literal in the scriptures, but there's a fundamentalist way to read them which is hard-hearted and obstinate, that doesn't see God, it only sees letters on the page.

The Word as a Mirror

You're looking at yourself, not God. The word is a mirror: you either see your face and your natural state, looking for something to do so you can be blessed, or the mirror is flipped and you're beholding Christ(James 1:23 vs 2 Cor 3:16-18). James talks about this, if you're a doer of the word and not just a hearer, you are like a person looking at his own natural face in the mirror. He walks away and forgets what kind of person he was. He's looking at the law and his own natural face, he's not seeing Christ, he's seeing himself. The root of that is vainglory.

Even though you think it's a love for God, it's actually an accusation against God's character. You think that God gave the law for you to keep because he's a hard taskmaster. No, God gave the law as a diagnosis of sin, like a physician's diagnosis of a patient's cancer. He doesn't expect you to be able to keep it, he's telling you what you are. If you don't listen to that judgment and you walk away thinking you can keep the law, you're deceiving yourself.

The law should have brought you into crisis. Until you say, "Okay Lord, what is your way of deliverance?" That's when you see another mirror in 2 Corinthians 3:

When the heart is turned to the Lord, the veil should be taken away. We all, with unveiled faith, behold ourselves in a mirror reflecting the glory of the Lord. We are being transformed into that same image, from glory to glory.

The natural man seeks to "obey" not out of love for God, but because of a desire for glory and honour. This is rooted in the knowledge of good and evil. It's rooted in Satan's desire to exalt himself. Indeed, religion can be terrible in this way, forming the root of the world system, particularly its religious aspect.

Abel offered the firstling of the flock with the fat portion, which is associated with the burnt offering and is for an aroma that is pleasing to God (Genesis 4:4). This aroma is called a "sweet savor" to God (Leviticus 1:9). When Paul talks about how we are a fragrance of Christ unto God, he is referring to the burnt offering (2

Corinthians 2:15). The burnt offering was the basis of all the offerings and was offered first. Its blood was sprinkled over the altar seven times, making the altar most holy (Leviticus 8:11). All other offerings were accepted on the altar because of the burnt offering.

That burnt offering represented Christ for God's satisfaction. Christ lived entirely for the Father, seeking not his own glory, but the Father's. The burnt offering symbolizes this: "I come not to do my own will but the will of Him who sent me. I seek not my own glory, but I receive glory from the One who sent me. I seek only my Father's glory" (John 6:38, John 8:50, John 7:18).

Every motive of Christ, from the depths of his heart, sprang from a desire for his Father to be glorified. We are not like that at all, and so we need an offering. We have the burnt offering, which is Christ in that way, the perfectly obedient one satisfying the Father. That's a fragrance in us to God. Christ is in us with that fragrance and that's why God loves to be near us. The burnt offering caused God to draw near.

This is a picture of Christ as God's satisfaction. Abel lived for God's satisfaction, while Cain lived for his own. However, Cain cloaked his selfish pursuit of his own glory in a religious facade and tried to offer it up for God. That's why it's so disgusting. Self-righteous Pharisees are the most repugnant, obnoxious people in the world. God detests it.

A self-righteous Pharisee is different than a legalist. A legalist is just someone who struggles in their conscience and is not perfected. I believe you can be a legalist and still be a saved Christian. A self-righteous Pharisee, on the other hand, has a fallen countenance set against God's way.

Sin Crouches and Waits

The Lord asked Cain, **"Why are you angry, and why has your countenance fallen? If you do well, will you not be accepted? If you do not do well, sin lies at the door."** All Cain had to do was grab a sheep and offer it. God didn't kill him! He had an opportunity to rectify his situation, but he was hardened in his trajectory by his anger, his hatred, and his fallen countenance.

This is the first appearance of the word 'sin' in the Bible. We've discussed how the law of first mention describes the principles that surround any major theme that starts in the scripture. Here, sin is presented as something outside of Cain's control. It's crucial to understand that there are sins, and then there is sin. Sin is the root principle, while sins are the individual things that you commit in response.

You can transgress, or "commit a sin", like cursing or whatever you did. However, that came from a source called sin. You may be able to stop sinning for a while, but you can't stop sin. Sin deals with the heart. The commandment "Thou shalt not covet" fully exposes it (Romans 7:8). Paul discussed this in Romans 7. The law said, "Thou shalt not covet," and sin took occasion by the commandment and worked all manner of covetousness in him (Romans 7:7-8).

The thing that he wanted to do, "Thou shalt not covet," he couldn't do. But the thing which he hated, he coveted all over the place. This covetousness, for Paul and for Cain pre-salvation, was for religious glory. Covetousness is an inward desire of your heart that operates beyond your control when your pride is hurt and you are still resting in your own righteousness. You can't let it go. (Romans 7:15)

Pride isn't the only sin. Lust is another. Jesus' entire Sermon on the Mount was based on the command, "Thou shalt not covet." It's not about the individual sins you commit; it's about the fact that the desire is there in the first place. If you look at a woman with lust in your heart, you've committed adultery. If you've fantasized about her, that's also a sin. If you hate your brother, you're a murderer in your heart, which John applies to Cain.

Sin is a deeper principle. It is presented as something more powerful than you in the scripture. That's why we had to die. It wasn't that God could rectify our nature, but that our nature was fallen.

God's answer to our sin is to crucify us with Christ because He is done with the flesh. The imaginations of our hearts are only evil continually, and these imaginations come out of our hearts spontaneously without even trying. The law makes it worse. The very knowledge that I shouldn't do it actually stirs it up in me. We learn this from Romans 7. This is what the tree and knowledge of good and evil is about.

That's why knowing good and evil and judging yourself in that way is the path of death. God wants to deliver us from that and let us learn to live by faith in Christ. But that's another topic I can't get into too much now. "Sin is crouching at the door," it says. It's like a tiger, stronger than you, ready to overtake you.

I don't know if Cain necessarily understood that. He thought he could control himself. A self-righteous person thinks he can control himself. "I can master this," they say. But they don't realize what's operating in them. It's interesting to watch when someone's countenance falls, which means they've decided to hate a brother because of their testimony of Christ and thunto thee shall be his desire' is a phrase I understand. However, 'but you shall rule over him' is difficult to comprehend. I believe the original Hebrew might translate slightly differently, but as I don't have multiple translations in front of me right now, I'll leave it as it is.

The story continues with Cain talking to his brother Abel. In the field, Cain rose up against his brother and killed him. This act of rising up was sin manifesting within Cain. He let the lion, symbolizing sin, jump through the door in their conversation.

This is why it's dangerous to engage with a 'Cain'. Some people might argue that we should show compassion and keep the door open. However, John warned against even allowing them into your house if they deviate from the doctrine of Christ. If they don't bring the doctrine of Christ, don't let them in unless you want to partake in their sin. Don't bless them or pray for them if you see them committing a sin unto death. Why? Because they are dangerous.

These individuals could kill you if given the opportunity, mostly if it makes them look good. Consider those self-righteous, philanthropic, benevolent, prayerful individuals who cried, 'Crucify Him! Give us Barabbas instead of this one! We have no king but Caesar!' This sentiment was always in their hearts; it just took time to surface and be revealed.

Once the countenance falls, Satan is already present, biding his time to express himself. This expression occurs through the ignorance of the person who doesn't understand what sin is. If they did understand, they would grasp the necessity of an offering. They think they can control sin, which might be what God is saying here: sin's desires can be for you, and you shall rule over it.

There seems to be a cooperation between Cain and sin. However, sin broke out in Cain, leading him to murder Abel. I believe this was a surprise to Cain because God didn't execute him; instead, He marked him for protection so that anyone who harmed Cain would suffer sevenfold vengeance.

Cain's conversation with Abel led to Abel's murder. What was their conversation about? Likely the offerings. But note that Abel's response isn't recorded. The text says Cain talked 'with' Abel, implying a dialogue. Abel probably referred to his testimony, stating that he offered what he believed God desired, and this was his only way to justification. He might have expressed regret and claimed his blessings were a result of his faithfulness. Whatever he said was likely related to the offerings."

Jesus proclaimed Himself a prophet, and this is the only conversation we have a record of Abel having. I'm sure he spoke other things in his life, but this is the significant one that sets the tone for everything. Jesus called him a prophet, so I guarantee whatever he spoke was the testimony of

Christ. He was slain; he was martyred as a result. Jesus counted his blood among the testimony of the prophets, among the blood of the prophets that would be required of that generation.

In avenging Abel, his blood cried out from the ground. The Lord said to Cain, "Where is your brother?" Cain responded, "I know not. Am I my brother's keeper?" The Lord then said, "*What have you done? The voice of your brother's blood cries to me from the ground.*" This is the blood that speaks better things of age than that of Abel. Jesus' blood says, "forgive them", it's a propitiation, but Abel's blood cries out for vengeance against the Cain persecutors.

Not everyone is a Cain. The way of Cain is a path where unbelief, denial of Christ's testimony, wrath, anger, self-seeking, self-righteousness, and the seeking for vain glory all come together in a religiously toxic stew. This proves someone is a tare and a son of the evil one, a seed of Satan. First John said that Cain was of the devil; he was the seed of the devil. Remember, there's enmity between Satan's seed and the seed of the woman. This is the first fulfillment of that prophecy. It's Satan directly working against the Adamic human race to try to thwart redemption and steer people away from the testimony of Christ, the Gospel.

God said to Cain, "You are cursed from the earth, which has opened her mouth to receive your brother's blood from your hand." Weren't they already cursed? This is why I believe there was some blessing when they were covered and walking justified. There was a partial lifting of the curse so they could be blessed even in that situation. They were blessed, Adam and Eve. That's my belief.

God continued, "When you till the ground, it shall not henceforth yield unto you her strength. A fugitive and a vagabond shall you be in the earth." Cain responded, "My punishment is greater than I can bear. You have driven me out this day from the face of the earth." Cain could have repented. I still think there was an opportunity at any point for him to realize and repent, but he couldn't. His sin took him over.

Cain went on, "From your face I shall be hid. I'll be a fugitive and a vagabond in the earth, and everyone that finds me will slay me." This is a religious person taking what God says literally without seeing any of the hope or mercy in the nature of God, which is often revealed in what He doesn't say or do. God is still speaking with him and hasn't killed him. The last people that God spoke to and then killed were those who waited for God's intervention, received the Gospel, and were given the covering. Cain, however, did not."

I should have learned from my past experiences and realized that if I remain quiet, God may provide me with hope. All God desires from us is to place our hope in Him and His mercy. Unfortunately, Cain couldn't do this because his heart was hardened. Therefore, the Lord spoke. Cain, despite his hardened heart, echoed God's words verbatim. As a stickler for the Word, I find this peculiar. What I'm implying is, Cain failed to see the person behind the words. He failed to understand God's nature.

One might wonder why God hasn't already passed judgement on Cain. In fact, His restraint is an act of mercy. The Lord declared to him, 'Therefore, whoever slays Cain, vengeance shall be taken on him sevenfold.' The Lord then placed a mark upon Cain to prevent others from killing him. This is yet another act of mercy.

Why would God show mercy? Because God desires that all men be saved and come to the knowledge of the truth. Could Cain have come to this knowledge, changed his ways, and perhaps one day brought a lamb as an offering? Could he have confessed, 'I am a sinner. I'm undone. Who will deliver me from this body of death?'

Paul did. Before his conversion, Paul was as misguided as Cain, persecuting Christians in his ignorance. He didn't understand the force at work within him and was thus no different from Cain. However, unlike Paul, Cain continued to harden his heart, taking God's words literally with no hope of redemption. He then turned his back on God, ceasing to seek Him.

In our next message, we will discuss the two genealogies. Cain's genealogy reveals the works of iniquity and the pursuit of vainglory that builds the worldly system. In contrast, the genealogy of the righteous places little emphasis on activity, focusing instead on multiplication and life to bring forth the seed. These two genealogies present two distinct ways of livingbefore God.

Chapter 16 The Line of Cain (Genesis 4)

The Strong Distinction Between the Line of Cain and the Line of Life

Genesis 4:16-26 KJV And Cain went out from the presence of the LORD, and dwelt in the land of Nod, on the east of Eden. (17) And Cain knew his wife; and she conceived, and bare Enoch: and he builded a city, and called the name of the city, after the name of his son, Enoch. (18) And unto Enoch was born Irad: and Irad begat Mehujael: and Mehujael begat Methusael: and Methusael begat Lamech. (19) And Lamech took unto him two wives: the name of the one was Adah, and the name of the other Zillah. (20) And Adah bare Jabal: he was the father of such as dwell in tents, and of such as have cattle. (21) And his brother's name was Jubal: he was the father of all such as handle the harp and organ. (22) And Zillah, she also bare Tubalcain, an instructer of every artificer in brass and iron: and the sister of Tubalcain was Naamah. (23) And Lamech said unto his wives, Adah and Zillah, Hear my voice; ye wives of Lamech, hearken unto my speech: for I have slain a man to my wounding, and a young man to my hurt. (24) If Cain shall be avenged sevenfold, truly Lamech seventy and sevenfold. (25) And Adam knew his wife again; and she bare a son, and called his name Seth: For God, said she, hath appointed me another seed instead of Abel, whom Cain slew. (26) And to Seth, to him also there was born a son; and he called his name Enos: then began men to call upon the name of the LORD.

The Word is not here to fill you with knowledge that you have to remember. That doesn't work. The Word is to wash you. That's why we need to focus so much on grace . Anything I teach, I want it to be a washing where we are renewed in our appreciation of Christ. Not because of facts we remember alone, because we'll forget the facts. You'll forget what this message says. But through the washing, there's an impression of Christ conveyed.

Actually, He imparts Himself and deposits Himself into you, a little more each time through these impressions. This is how transformation works. Growth in the Christian life is transformation. Transformation comes by renewing. "Be not conformed to this world but be transformed by the renewing of your mind." Renewing is a washing, and the washing comes from the Word. It's the washing of the water of the Word. But the Word is spirit and life, and the Word is Christ Himself.

That's why focusing on Christ when you read the scriptures is so important. You're looking for Christ. You want an impression of Christ. You want to have your concept changed about Christ and see something of His nature. That's what we were talking about in the last message. Cain couldn't see the nature of the One who was speaking. He only looked at the words God had spoken but understood none of the significance of what God had done or who God was.

The purpose of the Word is to convey a vision of Christ that washes and renews your perception of Him. You see something of His nature in grace, and that becomes a permanent part of you that no one can take away. I've looked up the names and academically researched some of the things in this chapter about the genealogy of Cain. I've done this before, which means I've forgotten it, and I'm likely to forget it again. However, as I talk about it, I pray that we won't get so bogged down with the fact that we miss the "forest for the trees." Instead, we're going to gain an impression of Christ, an impression of grace. Through this, we'll be renewed, and refreshed, and He will impart Himself to us. That's what growth is - a washing over time.

Think of it like this: You put a basket in water not to hold the water, but for the water to flow through the basket and clean it. With time, people can transform too. I find this process beautiful because I receive emails almost every other day from individuals who've been quiet on my page for a long time. They'll say they've been watching my videos and now, they can see how real Christ is. They understand that everything is about Jesus Christ, and they've found inner peace. It's not because of me; it's because of the sowing of the word with a focus on grace, and a desire to impress us with Christ.

Cain Exposed, the Cloak Removed

We're in Genesis, but I'm not looking at it as a history book. I'm looking at it as a Christ book, a gospel book, and a book about God's grace. It is designed to convey the impression of God and Christ, to wash and renew people. I know that this is the true sowing of the word, that's our "work." Legalists, on the other hand, focus on work as a measure of productivity for God. It's about commandment-keeping, stewarding their resources, and what they can achieve in their lives.

However, the grace builder - not worker, but builder - because we are building the habitation of God, understands that we are not working with our own materials. We're working with Christ. We know that the material we use is not the letter but the Spirit, which gives life. Our hope is to convey something of Christ Himself that washes over people and renews them so that they know Christ. That's the difference between actual ministry and vain jangling and clanging cymbals.

There are many people who seem to have a lot of Bible knowledge, yet no Christ is conveyed. It's just vanity. If we are not conveying Christ, we don't have a ministry; we're not building. However, conveying Christ is far easier than the laborious work the legalists want us to do. They toil away, thinking they'll be rewarded for it, and they consider us lazy because we're like Mary, not Martha. We're just sitting at the feet of Jesus, appreciating His word, and sharing that appreciation with others. Nothing could be more relaxing, edifying, enjoyable, and satisfying. And because we're satisfied, at rest, and not "freaked out," worried, and under condemnation, they accuse us of being lazy. They think that work means toil and sorrow, and pleasing God means bringing the fruit of the cursed ground that you sweat and toiled over. This is like Cain; this is the flesh.

We do want to serve God, but we understand that we are co-laborers with God, and God does the real work. As Paul said, 'one planted, one watered, but God gave the increase.'

(1 Corinthians 3:6) He does all the work. All we're doing is sowing the seed. We're just speaking the word. Sometimes it's a seed, the first time they've heard it, other times it's a watering of what they've heard. It's not just about the facts. The power is the life in the Word, which is Christ Himself. Only He has the authority to give his life. Ministry is about Christ being conveyed, the life being conveyed, and this is beyond us.

Usually, "workers" are individuals who meddle in other people's affairs, attempting to control them under the guise of "discipleship," all while building their own vain religious kingdoms. Unfortunately, this behavior is becoming more and more prevalent on YouTube but this is already the way it is in institutional churches. There is a clear distinction between these individuals the true "colaborers" with God; genuine New Testament ministers.

As we've been seeing, there are two ways of living a religious life, represented by Cain and Abel - two different perceptions of God, both based on what God said and did. One was erroneous, not seeing His character because the heart of the person is full of pride and vanity. This was Cain. On the other hand, Abel saw what God did and had a humble heart. He recognized he was a sinner, realized how God justifies sinners through blood and approved of it. He said 'amen' to it and then set his seal on it by offering up the firstling of the flock, which showed he agreed with how God justified sinners.

Cain did not agree with God's way. It made Cain mad. The way I know when I'm dealing with an enemy of the truth and a wolf is when they get angry that their "righteousness" is rejected and they reveal the doctrine of justification actually angers them. It's one thing to be confused and feel condemned, thinking, "I just don't believe God can forgive me; I've done too much." That's a humble heart struggling to understand justification. God invites us to come and reason with Him, so that we may be justified (Isaiah 1:18, Romans 4:5).

But Cain hates the brethren. He is full of his own self-importance and vain glory. He wants to be honored for his work and his toil. He's furious when his offering is not respected and then he turns and hates the ungodly sinner who's justified by faith alone. That's the chief characteristic that tells you that you're dealing with a wolf.

To a bystander, Cain and Abel may have appeared the same. They both looked religious and offered something to God. They were both dealing with God, working for God, serving God, and speaking about God at first. Many Christians and ministries appear to be similar on the surface until we gain knowledge and discernment. It all "sounds like Bible" to us, making it difficult to distinguish the difference.

Cain wasn't originally exposed. Everything seemed fine. Who knows how many years they lived, maybe a hundred years before the offering mentioned in Genesis 4. Eventually, what Cain really believed came out and he was exposed.

A religious person can hide behind their countenance. This is what the Pharisees did. They believed they were righteous, and so did all the people. Jesus came to take away the cloak from their sin. He said, "Now that I've been among them, they have no cloak for their sin." (John 15:22) This was their fig leaves. They had covered themselves in their religion and the pretense of having these nice virtues. They pretended to be loving and to love God. However, they secretly thought of God as a hard taskmaster. Inwardly, they hated Him and didn't even know it. They were unknowingly siding with the devil (John 8:44).

Jesus came and exposed them. Their offense at Him, and the fact that He was justifying sinners and friends with sinners, led them to label Him Beelzebub, an unclean spirit, and other derogatory terms. Their hearts were revealed. The cloak was taken away from their sin. Their countenance fell. This is what happened with Cain. He was wrathful and "his countenance fell." The cloak was taken away from the sin in his heart (John 15:22, John 8:44, Gen 4:4-5).

There is not much surface difference between Cain and Abel. They looked the same. They both approached the altar. They both offered something. They both seemed religious. They both appeared to be serving God in their own way. But when Cain's offering was not respected, he became wrathful and his countenance fell. There was no recovering from that. The falling of countenance is a serious thing.

I'm talking about YouTube channels that start out seeming to be going in the way of grace. They seem to be going the way of God, so to speak. They're talking about prophecy, the rapture, the gospel. They even say you can't lose your salvation. But at some point, they start to get angry that sinners are being justified. Ungodly sinners who "work not but believe on Him who justifies the ungodly."

The 'Cain channels' start saying you can't just let these sinners continue sinning. Their countenance falls and the cloak for their sin dissipates. They display their anger and defense at the way that God justifies sinners. That's really the root of their problem. They may seem to argue for justification, but why is it that every single one of their messages is about law? Why do they say you can't let these sinners go running around, and that they need to be disciplined, or that God is going to punish them?

This is the cloak starting to come off their sin. Eventually, they start making accusations that go beyond just, "You can't let these sinners go around." They start looking for people's sin to accuse them. They want to find a way to exclude you and say you're not a believer. That's when you know that they don't believe the gospel.

This is why 1 John was written, centered on Cain and Abel. John's epistle was not written to instruct us on fellowship but rather to differentiate between an antichrist and a son of God. The sons of God are recognized as sinners. They are not yet what they will eventually become, but they are still considered sons of God (1 John 3:2). Even though they are imperfect, they hold the hope that when they see Him, they will become like Him. This hope purifies them. They have an advocate with God, Jesus Christ the Righteous, who is the propitiation for their sin (1 John 2:1-2). They have faith and confess that Jesus came in the flesh (1 John 4:2-3). He came by blood and water as the propitiation for sins (1 John 5:6-7).

They acknowledge their sins and their propitiation, meaning they are in the light, which is the truth (1 John 1:7). This is how we identify them as the sons of God. However, those like Cain, who walk in darkness and hate their brethren, reject this path of propitiation for sins. They deny having sin (1 John 1:8), claim they love God, and insist they have fellowship with God. Yet, their hatred for their brethren reveals their religion as a lie (1 John 2:9-11).

If you hate your brother, whom you can see, you cannot love God, whom you cannot see. These individuals demonstrate love in word only, not in truth or action. They are exposed as those who hate the brethren. This is what John discusses. They may depart from us, but just like Cain, they cannot remain in fellowship when their countenance falls.

The Root of the World System - the Way of Cain

Immediately, they begin constructing a system to include or exclude people. This also occurred with first John. They leave us in one sense, but remain zealously building. Cain was the first to build a city, and his lineage is all about productivity, constructing a world system. World systems are primarily about inclusion and exclusion.

Seduction and Exclusion: First John's Warning

Who would have been excluded? Likely those on the line of life in Genesis 5, such as Seth, Adam and Eve's replacement for Abel, and their descendants who walked with God. They were not of this world. They were strangers and pilgrims not recognized by Cain. Their righteousness, which is Christ Himself, was rejected. Their profession was scoffed at. Abel was murdered. This is the true nature of Cain.

First John discusses the same thing (1 John 2:19). They may leave us, but they are attempting to seduce you and exclude you. Diotrephes wants preeminence among the brethren, rejects the apostles, and even casts people out of the fellowship (3 John 9-10). This was a novel occurrence in the church during the time of first John. Someone was exercising lordly authority in the church, casting people out of the fellowship for receiving the apostles. This was within 30 years of the Lord's resurrection. The Church life is a brand-new situation, and yet this kind of thing was already happening. I'm referring to 1 John quite a bit here because that doctrine really shines light on the significance of Cain, and Cain shines a light on the darkness spoken of in 1 John. It all boils down to this - it's crucial to understand Cain and Abel in the light of their perception of God, which significantly controlled their destiny and their response to God.

Then, we see the lines that this produced. In Genesis 4, we have the line of Cain, and in Genesis 5, we have the line of Seth, who replaced Abel. Seth can be viewed as Abel, resurrected from the dead if you will. But these lines are very different. In Cain's line, there is no mention of the passage of time, which is quite interesting. Cain's line is all about building, building, building! The strangers and pilgrims not recognized by Cain. Their righteousness, which is Christ Himself, was rejected. Their profession was scoffed at. Abel was murdered. This is the true nature of Cain.

First, John discusses the same thing. Although they may leave us, they are attempting to seduce and exclude you. Diotrephes desires preeminence among the brethren, rejects the apostles, and even casts people out of the fellowship. This was a novel occurrence in the church during the time of First John. Someone was exercising lordly authority in the church, casting people out of the fellowship for receiving the apostles, within 50 years of the Lord's resurrection. It's a brand-new situation, but it was already happening.

Throughout these chapters, I refer to First John often because its doctrine illuminates Cain and highlights its significance. In First through Third John, everything John is referring to centers on the story of Cain and Abel. It all boils down to this - it's crucial to understand Cain and Abel in the light of their perception of God, which significantly controlled their destiny and their response to God.

Worldly Building vs. Life Viewpoints

Now in Genesis in Genesis 4, we have the line of Cain, and in Genesis 5, we have the line of Seth, who replaced Abel. Seth can be viewed as Abel, resurrected from the dead if you will. But these lines are very different. In Cain's line, there is no mention of the passage of time, which is quite interesting. There is much activity, as we will see. Cain's line is all about building, building, building. But no record of lifespan. In Seth's lineage, as we will see in Genesis 5, we don't see a lot of "activity" (from the world's perspective), but we see a meticulous record of time marked by the births and deaths of the people in the line.

How does God view time? He dwells in eternity. A thousand years is as a "day." Ages can pass in an "instant." It's all present with Him, and it is all "now." Does that mean He is disinterested? No, David said, "Your thoughts towards me, if I could number them, would be more than the sands of the sea." (Psalm 139:17-18) God's view of time and its measurement is all about the life of His people before Him. Recently, my wife asked how long we had lived in our house. The way I recollected it was to say, "Well, our son was born 10 years ago, and we were pregnant with him the year after we moved in." I anchored my sense of time by connecting it to something I love. I'm created in the image of God. I'm sure He does the same thing!

You would think that when Cain went out from the presence of God, he would have disappeared from the narrative. But this is not the case! The "Cain's" never go away. John said, "They went out from us, showing that they were never of us," (1 John 2:19) and yet he said, "I write these things concerning those who seduce you." (1 John 2:26) They separate themselves and call themselves part of something that you do not belong to, that you are excluded from, and try to seduce you to want to be a part of it. They stick around, but they're not "of us."

Cain went out and built a city, and his descendants were the pioneers of agriculture, weaponry, entertainment, music, and more. Everything they did was an effort to mitigate the curse and its effects.

This is what we call the world system - an attempt to make life palatable and livable. It is associated with Cain. This line is the one that the world recognizes. When the world thinks of its history, it thinks in terms of the world empires. Interestingly, these empires are all rooted in a religion that celebrates the pre-flood days and the line of Cain. Tubal Cain, for instance, is worshipped as a god in Masonry and other world religions. The major architectural wonders of the world are attributed to him and dedicated to him.

The world chooses the line of Cain because that's where we have the mighty works and civilization. But all that building work is just a response to not having God. They've gone out from the presence of God and now they have to fend for themselves. There's no mention of the passage of time with them, which I think is significant because God doesn't remember their works or regard them at all. All their work is in vain. It's all going to be burned up. There's no reason to record their generations, so there's no time.

But with the line of life in Genesis 5, it talks about how each person lived for a certain time, then had the next person, and lived for a certain time, then had the next person. Yet, there's no mention of anything they did. They didn't build anything. They multiplied, had children, and then passed the blessing, the birthright, and the faith onto their seed. This emphasizes not building and work, but life.

Two lines responding to God

We're talking about two different ways of perceiving God and responding to Him. These are religious lines at their root. One is a satanic religion rooted in the tree of the knowledge of good and evil and influenced by the serpent. The other is the line of life that is being governed by a vision of God's purpose to restore humanity to the realities represented in the Garden of Eden - God in Christ as the tree of life to be everything to man in rest. The path of this restoration is guarded by the Cherubim, acting as witnesses to the propitiation, the altar, and the sacrifice. It's important to note that the early followers of God had a promise - the promise of the seed and the blessing, which together formed the core of the gospel. These believers each had an altar and offered sacrifices to God. They recognized their need for a propitiation for their sins, and this constitutes the record of their work until we meet Noah.

Noah's testimony does involve an activity of building, which is very different in character than the building of Cain, and we will discuss it later. This building is a metaphor for the construction of the Church. So how does this apply to us? It's possible to be a believer and yet work with perishable materials such as wood, hay, and stubble. These materials will all be consumed by fire. If you don't understand that justification and Christ are everything, you could still be building in the line of Cain.

Christ is our building material, and He is constructing an ark. This ark is not meant to be a permanent fixture in this world. Instead, it will be rejected by the world. Yet, it serves as a means of deliverance for God's people. God is focused on the next age, looking forward to His salvation. The only hope for the believers in the line of life is in the salvation of God. They live on this earth as strangers and pilgrims, rejected by the world.

The lineage in Genesis 5 marks the passage of time. Each person lived for a certain number of years, then had a child, and so on. I've previously created a timeline based on this lineage, revealing some fascinating insights. For instance, I discovered that Noah was still alive during Abraham's time. Interestingly, Noah passed away on the day that Abraham received the covenant of circumcision and performed the act on Isaac.

Circumcision is typically associated with the eighth day, which symbolizes the day of the new creation. Noah, whose name means 'rest', and his eight family members, entered the ark, which was their place of rest and salvation. This ark brought them into the new creation, symbolized by the new world and the eighth day. While we live under the seven days of creation, when we are regenerated, we are brought into resurrection and start celebrating the Lord's table on the eighth day, the day of resurrection. This is the day when Jesus emerged from the tomb, the day of the new creation, and the day of the new heavens and the new earth. Circumcision signifies the cutting off of the strength of the old creation, making Abraham's act of circumcision an interesting event, especially when considered in light of its connection to the death of Noah.

The day that Noah died signified the death of the old, and God's call for something new through Abraham (Genesis 12:1-3). This new path would eventually lead to Christ. It's always supernatural, and it's always about life. God said to Sarah, 'I will visit you in the time of life, and you'll conceive.' This conception would be a miracle because Sarah was beyond childbearing years (Genesis 18:10-14). Her womb was barren, and Abraham's body was old. Yet, they believed in the word of Him who gives life to the dead and calls those things that are not as though they are (Romans 4:17). This belief is their faith. Faith is believing in God's word and His ability to bring life from the dead (Hebrews 11:1).

Isn't that how Adam responded? God gave them the gospel with the promise of the seed. The first thing Adam did was call his wife Eve because she was the mother of all living. When God speaks, it brings life. When God speaks, it's a kind of washing. God's words convey an impression of Himself that makes you realize, yes, technically, the law should condemn you. But God's intention is for you to have life. The wages of sin are death, but the gift of God is eternal life.

That's how we see the Bible, on the line of life, always looking for God's promise, His intervention. This shows us His nature. We get an impression from Him that washes and renews us. From this renewal, we minister to others, washing and renewing them.

The descendants of Seth, such as Shem, followed the times and seasons, understanding astronomy and God's prophetic program. They lived in anticipation of God's promise, in stark contrast to Cain and his descendants, who were more preoccupied with worldly achievements.

The timeline of Seth's descendants, marked by the passage of time, holds significant weight in scripture. It speaks of the importance God places on their seemingly inconsequential lives, compared to the worldly achievements of Cain's line. Cain's descendants were builders, inventors, and innovators, contrasting with the simple shepherds who offered sacrifices and lived out their faith.

This dichotomy presents two distinct ways of life: the line of works from Cain, representing an antichrist spirit that opposes Christ's testimony, and the line of faith from Seth, which waits on God's promise. In doing so, they become part of God's eternal building, their lives marked by the passage of time. Meanwhile, those who seek only the glory of man will not be remembered.

The flower fades, the grass burns and withers immediately. It seems like Cain will have bigger ministries, more fun, and be more attractive to the senses. He's got a city, he's got all kinds of stuff, but God won't remember him. But these little grace channels, all we have is Christ, and God is marking the passage of our time.

Chapter 17 Cain's line – the Identity in the Strength of the Flesh (Genesis 4)

Genesis 4:15-24 KJV And the LORD said unto him, Therefore whosoever slayeth Cain, vengeance shall be taken on him sevenfold. And the LORD set a mark upon Cain, lest any finding him should kill him. (16) And Cain went out from the presence of the LORD, and dwelt in the land of Nod, on the east of Eden. (17) And Cain knew his wife; and she conceived, and bare Enoch: and he builded a city, and called the name of the city, after the name of his son, Enoch. (18) And unto Enoch was born Irad: and Irad begat Mehujael: and Mehujael begat Methusael: and Methusael begat Lamech. (19) And Lamech took unto him two wives: the name of the one was Adah, and the name of the other Zillah. (20) And Adah bare Jabal: he was the father of such as dwell in tents, and of such as have cattle. (21) And his brother's name was Jubal: he was the father of all such as handle the harp and organ. (22) And Zillah, she also bare Tubalcain, an instructer of every artificer in brass and iron: and the sister of Tubalcain was Naamah. (23) And Lamech said unto his wives, Adah and Zillah, Hear my voice; ye wives of Lamech, hearken unto my speech: for I have slain a man to my wounding, and a young man to my hurt. (24) If Cain shall be avenged sevenfold, truly Lamech seventy and sevenfold.

Some strange things in Cain's genealogy can really lead you on esoteric hunts. I was just looking through Hebrew name dictionaries to find out the meaning of the names because the names are always significant. They tell the story.

Cain's line moves away from the presence of God, making them orphans in the world. The world system is based on an "orphan syndrome" where those without God as their provider are left to fend for themselves. Living in bondage to the fear of death and under the curse, they spend their whole life trying to mitigate its effects and soften its blow. As a result, they develop an identity around this struggle.

The world system is built on a foundation of orphanhood, godlessness, hopelessness, bondage, and fear of death. As a result, everything we do is a reaction to this condition. We strive to survive, build things that mitigate the effects of the fall, find comfort and stability, and fight against the environment. Over time, we develop an identity rooted in pride for our accomplishments.

Acknowledging that not all inventions and achievements are inherently evil is important. Even in Cain's line, there are examples of things that are not necessarily bad. For example, the inventor of air conditioning deserves recognition and appreciation. However, the root problem with the world is the identity that stems from alienation and even hostility towards God, which ultimately leads to pride. That's the root of the world system.

When John refers to "loving the world," he's actually referring to a particular identity. Despite this, the names associated with these things reveal an opposition to God and a characterization of God as a tyrant who doesn't have your best interests at heart.

He says, **"Behold, you've driven me out of this day from the face of the earth, and from Your face, I shall be hid, and I'll be a fugitive in the earth and a vagabond in the earth."** The story of Cain and his banishment is a compelling one. Cain's status as a wanderer and fugitive meant he was always on the run, fearing for his life. The Lord marked Cain and warned that anyone who killed him would face sevenfold vengeance. Despite this protection, Cain chose to leave the Lord's presence and dwell in the land of Nod, an area that represents wandering and desolation. Cain's decision to leave the Lord and dwell in desolation is reminiscent of the children of Israel's time in the wilderness. While the line of life that comes from Seth still represents rest, Cain's line represents defense and constantly being on guard.

Nod is located to the east of Eden, away from the Garden. There is speculation that Jerusalem may be the gate to Eden, as it is where God has set His name and where the Messiah is expected to enter through the east gate. Cherubim guard the gate of Eden, bearing witness to the propitiation and serving as the key to the Tree of Life. This door leads to Christ and is accessed through His blood. Sacrifices representing redemption were to be performed in Jerusalem, in the Holy of Holies. It is interesting to consider whether this is the same place as the gate.

The name Cain means "produced" and is associated with production and hard work. He is not lazy and is zealous. Cain knew his wife and conceived, which raises the question of where she came from. However, it is important to note that Adam and Eve were commanded to multiply and replenish the earth, indicating that there were other people present. Many other children would have been born, but Genesis concerns itself with the genealogies of those who built the world system versus those who are to inherit the city whose builder and maker is God. They also lived a very long time. We don't know how much time passed between the birth of Cain and his slaying of Abel. It could have been a hundred years, enough time for hundreds of thousands of people to have been multiplied on the earth. God gave humanity dominion over the earth and instructed them to replenish it, setting the stage for the eventual establishment of His kingdom on earth.

The narrative within Genesis may contain hints that suggest there is more to the story than what is explicitly told. However, it is not necessary to relentlessly pursue answers outside of scripture. In my experience, doing so can lead to a focus on Jewish mythology and endless genealogies, rather than the gospel and grace.

While some speculate that the population during Noah's flood was between six to eight billion people based on statistics, the genealogy in Genesis primarily focuses on the lines of Cain and life, which eventually lead to the end of Cain and the birthright and blessing of Christ's line.

Names of Vanity

Enoch: In Genesis, it is mentioned that Cain knew his wife, who then conceived Enoch. It is important to note that there are two Enochs mentioned in the narrative. This Enoch is significant as Cain built a city and named it after his son, which is a vainglorious act. Enoch means teacher in one sense, but disciplined in another, representing discipline and "discipleship." Cain's view is that he's a hard worker, and that was the point of his offering. By naming his child "disciplined" and building a city, he is identifying with all the tragedy of the fall and the irony of the world system. The population is growing, and the city is meant to protect them from the elements and the world. God views humanity as dwelling outside the gate in the wilderness, just moaning and crawling around as orphans. However, humans manage to devise a way to gain prestige and glory for themselves in the midst of this, which, in the light of the Kingdom we will inherit, is just ridiculous. To be the king of the universe without God is to be the king of a trash heap! The kings are going to go into the earth, and all the glory of man is like grass, and like the flowering of grass, it fades away (Isaiah 40:6-8). While they may have thought the city was glorious, to God, it's a wilderness (Isaiah 32:13)."

.

Irad: Enoch's son Irad has an interesting name that is composed of two root words. The word "Irad" is not actually in the Hebrew language, which might be confusing. While there are various forms of noun, verb, and adjective for these two root words, it appears that when combined, they can be interpreted as a "heap" of empire dedicated to the dragon. It's quite fascinating to ponder. Enoch, the city's name, is also Enoch's own name, which suggests what he valued – his own prestige and legacy. He was likely the ruler of the city. His son's name, meaning "heap of empire dedicated to the dragon" indicates a focus on the satanic lineage.

This is where the contrast between the two lines and their religions becomes immediately apparent. There is the revealed religion of God, which begins with His promise concerning the seed of the woman and His method of justifying man through propitiation, and then there is the alternative. This alternative religion views the dragon as the light-bearer who liberated humans from ignorance in Eden through knowledge of good and evil. They consider this view as beautiful, while viewing God as the evil one. This perspective may arise from their being cast out from God's presence by a rebel and their descent from this rebel who despises God's way of justifying sinners. They seek to build something of their own, and Satan continues to interact with and inspire this lineage.

Mahujael and Mathusael - The names of the next two descendants in the line provide further evidence of their view of God and their lineage's focus on destruction. One source said that the name means "God has demanded his death." Keep in mind that these are very subjective interpretations. One way to investigate is to look at the Hebrew letters, which are pictographic, and research their commonly understood meanings. Hebrew words are an assembly of pictographic individual letters and are usually a "sum" representation of the meaning of the individual symbols. I will not do this for every name but I thought it would be an interesting illustration to take these two interesting names which have very little history or documentation regarding their meaning.

Mahujael

- In Hebrew, the name Mahujael (מ_חי_א_ל) is composed of the following characters:
- Mem (מ)
- Chet (ח)
- Vav (ו)
- Yod (י)
- Aleph (א)
- Aleph (א)
- Lamed (ל)

Mem (מ): Mem originally represented water or waves and is associated with liquid or flowing concepts. In some interpretations, it can symbolize chaos or potentiality.

Tet (ת): Tet has been associated with a basket or container and can symbolize something hidden or contained within.

Vav (ו): Vav is traditionally seen as a hook or nail and can symbolize connection or attachment.

Shin (ש): Shin can symbolize teeth or flames and is often associated with sharpness, destruction, or transformation.

Aleph (א): Aleph traditionally represents an ox or bull and can symbolize strength or leadership.

Lamed (ל): Lamed can represent an ox goad or a staff and is associated with teaching or guidance.

Mathusael:

In Hebrew, the name Mathusael (ל_א_שות_מ) is composed of the following characters:

- Mem (מ)

- Tet (ת)
- Vav (ו)
- Shin (ש)
- Aleph (א)
- Aleph (א)
- Lamed (ל)

Mem (מ): Mem originally represented water or waves and is associated with liquid or flowing concepts. In some interpretations, it can symbolize chaos or potentiality.

Tet (ת): Tet has been associated with a basket or container and can symbolize something hidden or contained within.

Vav (ו): Vav is traditionally seen as a hook or nail and can symbolize connection or attachment.

Shin (ש): Shin can symbolize teeth or flames and is often associated with sharpness, destruction, or transformation.

Aleph (א): Aleph traditionally represents an ox or bull and can symbolize strength or leadership.

Lamed (ל): Lamed can represent an ox goad or a staff and is associated with teaching or guidance.

These two names are very similar and it is interesting to see the characters they have in common and the characters where they diverge. The names that were given at that time were very significant, representing the perceived purpose and plight of those who gave them.

Commonalities:

Mem (מ): In both names, Mem symbolizes the concept of chaos or potentiality. This suggests a shared theme of hidden or transformative elements.

Vav (ו): In both names, Vav represents connection or attachment, signifying a linking or binding element. This theme of connection is consistent in both interpretations.

Differences:

Chet (ח) vs. Tet (ט):

In Mahujael, Chet symbolizes a fence or an inner room, suggesting something protected or contained within. This implies a sense of guarding or preserving.

In Mathusael, Tet has associations with a basket or container, signifying something hidden or contained within. While both suggest protection, Tet's symbolism emphasizes containment.

Yod (י) vs. Shin (ש):

In Mahujael, Yod symbolizes a hand and implies power or work, suggesting a sense of action or creation.

In Mathusael, Shin can symbolize teeth or flames, emphasizing sharpness, destruction, or transformation. This contrasts with the more constructive connotations of Yod in Mahujael.

Aleph (א) and Lamed (ל):

In both names, Aleph represents strength or leadership.

In Mahujael, Lamed symbolizes teaching or guidance, emphasizing the idea of leading or directing.

In Mathusael, there's no equivalent Lamed, and Shin's symbolism takes a different path toward transformation and sharpness.

Both names have hints of occult secrets. Conveying the sense that in the midst of the chaos (which in their view is God's "fault") and that they are hiding a secret for man's protection and even teaching men to "fight back." The names are obvious parallels, one a "creative" hidden work emerging from the chaos, and the other having a destructive aspect. This is another way of expressing the occult adage, "order out of chaos."

In their view, there is nothing good for them from God. In their view, they dwell in the waste places because of God's judgment. They have to build their empire, and they have a sense of self-glory in that, and they've dedicated it to the dragon because God decreed their judgment. This a line away from God, dwelling as orphans, inspired by Satan's lies, fending for themselves, and increasingly angry. That's the sense I get from these names. Any one of them could have repented. They didn't have to stay in this line. Salvation is genuinely available to anyone who believes the gospel. And remember these are only the names of the "important" figures in the line. There were many others besides. Tracing this path does not mean that no one in that line ever was saved or believed. But this is Cain's legacy that we are looking at, passed down as a heritage through names.

Lamech, Jabal, Jubal and Tubal Cain

There are two Enochs and two Lamechs, each in their respective line. This Lamech most likely is a contemporary of Noah. Lamech had three sons, born to his two wives. The name Lamech means "to descend and to mourn." It refers to descending into a mournful state. He had two wives – Ada and Zilla. Ada gave birth to **Jabal,** who became the father of those who dwell in tents and raise cattle. Jabal's brother, **Jubal,** became the father of those who play the harp and the flute.

Jabal's name means the "course that water follows" which suggests irrigation. He developed agriculture and animal husbandry, and was the father of those who lived a nomadic life in tents - not in cities.

It's possible that some of these individuals rebelled against Cain's line and returned to a nomadic lifestyle. Abraham lived during Nimrod's time and also dwelled in tents. God's people tended to dwell in tents until they established a permanent home, such as Jerusalem. They sought a city whose builder and maker is God - a heavenly foundation. They confessed that they were strangers and pilgrims. It's noteworthy that Jabal, the father of those who dwell in tents and raise cattle, represents a nomadic lifestyle, yet he came from the line of Cain. Some people assume that the line of Cain is entirely evil, and the line of Seth is entirely good, but it's not about good and evil. It's about faith and what one believes - whether they are justified by faith or not.

View yourself as an orphan having to fend for yourself and thinking that God is against you. The names of Jabal and Jubal are not malicious like the other names. Jabal just means the course that water flows down. Jubal's name means ram's horn, which is associated with the assembly of God's people and is also a musical instrument. There's nothing malicious in these names, so they are not all bad, they are neutral. There are things in the world system that are neutral, like music and food. Loving music or good food doesn't mean that you're worldly. When John talks about not loving the world, he talks about the pride of life, the lust of the flesh, and the lust of the eyes, which all come from the tree of knowledge of good and evil (1 John 2:15-16). These desires reflect a vainglorious desire to be something, to usurp God. That's the root of the world and loving the world.Some people think that loving music or food is worldly, but those things are neutral. With Jubal and Jabel, they produce something for the world that is useful but not evil in itself. Their names do not have a malicious intent behind them, which shows the view of their parents. Lamech is interesting. I think Ada, whose name means ornament, probably had a hand in naming Jabal and Jubal and influencing them.

Tubal Cain- the World Builder

> **And Lamech took unto him two wives: the name of the one was Adah, and the name of the other Zillah. (20) And Adah bare Jabal: he was the *father* of such as dwell in tents, and of such as have cattle. (21) And his brother's name was Jubal: he was the *father* of all such as handle the harp and organ. (22) And Zillah, she also bare Tubalcain, *an instructor* of every artificer in brass and iron: and the sister of Tubalcain was Naamah**

It is interesting that they are said to be the *father* of those who handle the harp and organ and the *father* of those who dwell in tents and have cattle. I believe Jabal and Tubal may have identified themselves with God's people, meaning ram's horn and course of water, becoming nomadic and being fathers of their arts to pass on to others that they cared about.

Zilla, Lamech's other wife also bore **Tubal-Cain**, who is not a *father* but an *instructor* of every artificer in brass and iron. Tubal Cain has the name Cain in it and you could say he represents the peak of Cain's strength. Tubal-Cain is not said to be a father, but a teacher.

Being a father means caring about their person and investing in them, while being a teacher doesn't necessarily mean caring about the person, just caring about what is being taught. Paul said "you have many teachers, but not many fathers." (1 Cor. 4:15) Tubal-Cain is a teacher, not a father, of every artificer in brass and iron. Brass and iron are related to weaponry and building, so this is a negative development. Cain built a city, but this would fortify the city. He's a gatekeeper of knowledge. He trains people, but that means you have to become a disciple of his. Masonry and esoteric (occult) views of world history hold Tubal Cain in high regard and consider him the father of many of their principles. In Masonry the building crafts are closely guarded secrets requiring initiation. You're initiated into them.

This narrative contains many unanswered questions and mysteries. For example, what is the significance of these names? **Tubal-Cain**, which means "spear of the dragon" or "confederacy of the world empire. It is impossible to be too dogmatic about these things. But I stumbled upon a Masonic website that discussed Tubal-Cain's origins and the myth that he survived and preserved knowledge. They claimed that he was a mighty man who headed the first world empire and that their call to a "new world order" in unity, love, and peace was from Tubal-Cain

He was the instructor of all who use iron and brass. That means his knowledge persisted beyond the flood. Think of the Greeks and the Romans, who capitalized on knowledge of working with brass and iron to gain their military advantage. This knowledge came from priesthoods that trace their origins back to myths surrounding a preflood civilization and have Tubal Cain at the center. Iron and brass were used to create weapons, and the cultures that had iron and brass could subdue those that didn't. So, it was in their interest to preserve that knowledge and protect it, and only give it as a mystical secret to those who were initiated and proved themselves to be loyal. That's how empires survived, and the technology that fuels it was guarded. We have the same thing going on today with technology. You have to be certified, you have to be groomed in a certain way to really understand the mechanics of some of the deeper technologies.

Initiation into secret knowledge in the esoteric view ultimately points back to the tree of the knowledge of good and evil and the promise of man's deification. Even today, Masonic patterns are seen in the architecture of great buildings dedicated to some form of Tubal-Cain. There is opposition to God in this. Tubal-Cain is associated with weaponry and buildings, which fortify the city, and occult secret knowledge.

Tubal-Cain's sister, Nema, is mentioned for no apparent reason (to us). But for it to be mentioned in Genesis, means that it would have been known to the people during Moses' time as a significant name. If you lived in the time of Moses receiving his writings, you would have known who she was.

Many people believe that Nema, Tubal-Cain's sister, was Noah's wife! The significance of this, to some, is that as Ham's mother, she might have been the one to have brought occult knowledge through the flood, which was passed through Ham's line to Canaan, father of Cush, father of Nimrod, who became a "Gibborim" (same word used for the "mighty men of Genesis 6). Nimrod is the source of the present world system and its Luciferian religion, and the occultists long for the return of "pre-flood" days before God judged what they view as a "higher civilization" (Atlantis).

Lamech's Words:

Apart from Cain, Lamech, (the father of Jabal, Jubal and Tubal Cain) is the only person in the line whose words were recorded. Lamech says, "Hear my voice." Now, it says that he says to his wives, but I've read some translations that he spoke a poem. So, he actually spoke a poem of Lamech. **"Hear my voice, O wives of Lamech, hearken to my speech. For I have slain a man to my wounding, and a young man to my hurt. If Cain shall be avenged sevenfold, truly Lamech seventy and sevenfold."** That's interesting that he made that into a song. Who did he kill? My first thought was, did he kill Cain? And sure enough, there are people that believe that.

I am uncertain as to whom Lamech killed, however, his statement that his retribution would be seventy-seven times greater than Cain's reminds of Jesus' words regarding "seventy times seven" forgiveness (Matthew 18:22). There is a contrast between the blood of Abel, which cried out for vengeance (Genesis 4:10), and the blood of Jesus Christ, which speaks of forgiveness (Matthew 26:28). While Lamech boasts of his importance and ability to exact revenge, Jesus forgave those who caused his death (Luke 23:34). Lamech's speech about killing a man and a "young man" is also perplexing.

Lamech makes this declaration almost like a curse, implying that he may be hunted that and whoever kills him will be avenged "seventy and sevenfold." It is likely that Tubal-Cain, his son, will be the one to seek revenge. Tubal-Cain is known in history for his tremendous strength, and he is believed to be a mighty man, reminiscent of Nephilim lore.

Interestingly, both lines end in a building. In Cain's line, the city and empire are built up in opposition to God, with curses of God along the way. In contrast, the line of life ends with a resting place, the ark, built by Noah, whose name means rest. Its purpose is to preserve God's saved people from the judgment that is coming on all of this. All of these things are crying out for judgment, and the people in Cain's line have hard speeches against God with their evil names and sayings.

According to Jude, Enoch prophesied that God would come to judge with His saints and judge the ungodly for their hard speeches and ungodly words against Him (Jude

1:14-15). Speaking against the blood and the righteous is blaspheming God's way of justifying, which He has revealed (Hebrews 10:29). It is considered hard speech against God and their names too. It consumed them, and one cannot escape from God even if they harden themselves.

Some individuals who used to be Christian but weren't saved ended up hating God. They are now absolutely consumed with it and can't stop. It's all they think about, and they are dedicated to blaspheming and hating God. They look for Christians to stumble and will pretend to be Christians to destroy them. This is terrible because they are consumed with it. Cain's line has zeal and dedication, and it does not stop. This is why the antichrist spirit is so bad because it destroys and consumes people. They do not stop, and that's why it's advisable not to engage with those who show that their countenance is falling (Genesis 4:5-7). They are going the way of Cain, and it's better to leave them alone as they have more energy than you do (Proverbs 4:14-17). Unless God calls you to do something and stands you up in His strength, you won't be able to compete with their zeal. They can keep going and going, and it's really amazing. This is Cain's line, and it ends with proud blasphemy against God (Genesis 4:23-24).

Strength in the Flesh Contrasted with God's Power Perfected in Weakness

It's interesting that the genealogy of Adam begins to be recounted in Genesis 4 and then is recapitulated in Genesis 5. It's almost as if the vain speaking of Lamech, boasting of his strength, is in contrast to the calling upon the name of God that begins with the third generation in the line of life, Enos, which means "weakness" or "mortality."

> **Gen 4:23-26 And Lamech said unto his wives, Adah and Zillah, Hear my voice; ye wives of Lamech, hearken unto my speech: for I have slain a man to my wounding, and a young man to my hurt. (24) If Cain shall be avenged sevenfold, truly Lamech seventy and sevenfold. (25) And Adam knew his wife again; and she bare a son, and called his name Seth: For God, said she, hath appointed me another seed instead of Abel, whom Cain slew. (26) And to Seth, to him also there was born a son; and he called his name Enos: *then began men to call upon the name of the LORD.***

Now, Adam knew his wife again. Now we're resorting back to Adam and we're going back to the beginning time-wise. And she called his name Seth, for God, he said, has appointed me another seed instead of Abel, whom Cain slew. Now the line of life comes out of Seth, who is the secondborn. And there's this principle all the way through the Scriptures, we'll see it several times, that the secondborn seems to usurp the place of the firstborn, and the firstborn gets offended at that too. Cain is offended, he was the first. Ishmael was offended, he was the first. Esau was offended, he should have had the blessing. He came out first, and Jacob was holding his heel. So, God has a way of preferring the last to be first, right? Satan was first, but then God created man. He uses this to choose the things that the world despises, to humble the mighty and proud by choosing the second born. This violates the principles of honor that are ingrained in the flesh, the desire for vainglory. God is not going to satisfy that.

Abel was replaced by Seth, and to Seth was born a son whom he called Enos. The name Enos means mortal, while Seth means appointed, and Adam means man. By calling on the name of God, they acknowledged their mortality, which is a consciousness of weakness and frailty, and the realization that our existence is fleeting like a vapor. The only eternal thing is God Himself.

Cain's descendants spoke harshly against God, using religious speeches to attack His character and diminish the propitiation. They also ridiculed God's people, calling them lazy and boasting that they were the true workers who would be avenged if anyone killed them, even seventy times sevenfold. (Jude 1:11) Perhaps Lamech even believed that God would support him in his vain and boastful speeches. (Genesis 4:23-24) This behavior is similar to that of false prophets discussed by Jude and Peter in the end days who follow the way of Cain and are known for their grandiose and vain speeches. (Jude 1:16, 2 Peter 2:18) In contrast, the names in this line represent truth about their state.

We don't see the bitterness and the zeal in the line of Genesis 5, which some call, "the line of life." They're not bitter, they just confess the reality of their estate. The first three names, Adam, meaning "man," Seth, meaning "appointed" and Enos, mean mortal sorrow" state simply, "Man is appointed mortal sorrow." This is just the reality of the human condition. Mortal sorrow speaks of sorrow in a state of weakness and death. What is a man to do? They started calling on God.

The first activity recorded related to Seth's line is calling on the name of the Lord, which is significant. When the early church called on Jesus, they were referred to as "Jesus callers". (Acts 9:14) Knowing God's name is special, and calling on it means you're asking Him to embody whatever that name represents. He can be your salvation, your healer (Jehovah Rapha), your provider (Jehovah Jireh), and much more. (Exodus 15:26, Genesis 22:14) Calling on one of His names acknowledges that He is the source of whatever that name represents, and it requires you to rely on Him to fulfill that role. (Psalm 20:7-8)

This differs from the belief that one can construct a world system to provide for oneself, like an orphan trying to survive on their own. In this age, true spirituality is characterized by a sense of weakness. We've discussed this concept on this channel before. We have a treasure in our earthen vessel, and our spirituality is glorious in the New Testament because an eternal weight of glory is being developed within us, which will be revealed in the next age. However, in this age, we're surrounded by weakness, and we're in a state of weakness. God uses our weakness to encourage us to call on His name and prevent us from constructing something within ourselves. (2 Corinthians 4:7-18, Romans 8:18-25)

As Christians, we know that the power of Christ presides over us in our weakness, and His grace is perfected in our weakness. Our weakness prompts us to call on the Lord. In contrast, Cain's weakness and rejection caused him to build up his own strength. This is the difference between Cain and his son, Enoch. Cain's line is dedicated to the dragon and builds up a city, constructing a world empire in his strength. Enoch, on the other hand, calls upon the name of the Lord in his weakness.

One line represents the strength of the flesh, while the other represents weakness. Cain's line represents the strength of the flesh, while Enos, who comes from Seth's line, represents the weakness of the flesh, but the strength of the Spirit. God's power is manifested in weakness, and He is not focused on vindicating individuals in this world.

In the record of Cain's line, there is no passage of time. However, in Seth's line, time is recorded meticulously. "After so many years, this one begat that one" because God is marking their time as it is significant for the forwarding of His purpose. Even though Cain's line may seem more glorious, they will perish. This is true of the religious Cains as well. They hate you because they don't want you to know grace or how to call on the name of the Lord in the midst of your weakness. Religious Cains always tell you "You CAN do it!" and want you to rely on the flesh. Their purpose is to put a stumbling block in front of you.

They don't understand the language of weakness. When we say, "I'm weak, but I call on the name of Jesus, and He becomes my strength," they say, "You're just carnal and in unbelief. You don't believe that God said you can do it. Why would He give you the law if He didn't think you could keep it?" Maybe we're not under the law of Moses but we're under the commands of Jesus. We can keep those. They give lip service, "it's by the Holy Spirit's help." But anyone who doesn't understand this principle that Christ has to be everything is not on the way of life. They are in the way of Cain. And it'll show up in their religious service. Doesn't mean they're not saved, it just means they're not clear, and they're doing a lot of damage while they're not clear. What they're "building" is wood, hay, and stubble, and it's going to be burned.

Seth's line may build, but what they construct is unlikely to earn anything other than mockery from the world (1 Corinthians 3:12-15). The culmination of the line of life is the building of the ark, a representation of Christ and the church (Genesis 6:14-16, 1 Peter 2:4-6). Today, building the church happens in weakness by those who call upon the name of the Lord in their weakness, and He becomes their building material (2 Corinthians 4:7-18). To build with gold, silver, and precious stones means recognizing that we are weak in the flesh and calling on the name of the Lord in truth (1 Corinthians 3:12-15). We cry out to Him in desperation, and He answers the call, building something within us (2 Corinthians 4:7-18). Christ begins to make His home in our hearts, and we start to become solid, but in a different way. We do not become solid in ourselves or grow in self-confidence. Instead, we grow in confidence in Christ, with a full assurance of faith and a perfected conscience (Hebrews 10:22). We learn to abide in His presence and walk with Him, as Enoch walked with God (Genesis 5:22-24). This is the key to escaping judgment: calling on the name of the Lord, believing in the blood, trusting in His promise of the seed, and walking with God in a state of awareness of our weakness but confidence in

His strength (Hebrews 11:7). This is what ultimately builds the ark (Genesis 6:14-16, 1 Peter 2:4-6).

So, there is a building on our line, it's just not a work of hands, really. And it's definitely not from our zeal, it's from our place of weakness.

Chapter 18 Seth's Line – Rest on the line of Life (Genesis 5)

Gen 5:1-32 This is the book of the generations of Adam. In the day that God created man, in the likeness of God made he him; (2) Male and female created he them; and blessed them, and called their name Adam, in the day when they were created. (3) And Adam lived an hundred and thirty years, and begat a son in his own likeness, after his image; and called his name Seth: (4) And the days of Adam after he had begotten Seth were eight hundred years: and he begat sons and daughters: (5) And all the days that Adam lived were nine hundred and thirty years: and he died. (6) And Seth lived an hundred and five years, and begat Enos: (7) And Seth lived after he begat Enos eight hundred and seven years, and begat sons and daughters: (8) And all the days of Seth were nine hundred and twelve years: and he died. (9) And Enos lived ninety years, and begat Cainan: (10) And Enos lived after he begat Cainan eight hundred and fifteen years, and begat sons and daughters: (11) And all the days of Enos were nine hundred and five years: and he died. (12) And Cainan lived seventy years, and begat Mahalaleel: (13) And Cainan lived after he begat Mahalaleel eight hundred and forty years, and begat sons and daughters: (14) And all the days of Cainan were nine hundred and ten years: and he died. (15) And Mahalaleel lived sixty and five years, and begat Jared: (16) And Mahalaleel lived after he begat Jared eight hundred and thirty years, and begat sons and daughters: (17) And all the days of Mahalaleel were eight hundred ninety and five years: and he died. (18) And

Jared lived an hundred sixty and two years, and he begat Enoch: (19) And Jared lived after he begat Enoch eight hundred years, and begat sons and daughters: (20) And all the days of Jared were nine hundred sixty and two years: and he died. (21) And Enoch lived sixty and five years, and begat Methuselah: (22) And Enoch walked with God after he begat Methuselah three hundred years, and begat sons and daughters: (23) And all the days of Enoch were three hundred sixty and five years: (24) And Enoch walked with God: and he was not; for God took him. (25) And Methuselah lived an hundred eighty and seven years, and begat Lamech: (26) And Methuselah lived after he begat Lamech seven hundred eighty and two years, and begat sons and daughters: (27) And all the days of Methuselah were nine hundred sixty and nine years: and he died. (28) And Lamech lived an hundred eighty and two years, and begat a son: (29) And he called his name Noah, saying, This same shall comfort us concerning our work and toil of our hands, because of the ground which the LORD hath cursed. (30) And Lamech lived after he begat Noah five hundred ninety and five years, and begat sons and daughters: (31) And all the days of Lamech were seven hundred seventy and seven years: and he died. (32) And Noah was five hundred years old: and Noah begat Shem, Ham, and Japheth.

Rest vs Restlessness

I'm not convinced we possess a comprehensive understanding of what 'rest' truly signifies. When we're fond of a word but lack a full grasp of its meaning, we tend to embellish it, link it to other concepts, and before we realize it, we've morphed it into something it might not be.

There's a tendency to transform 'rest' into an achievement, something you arrive at as if it's some sort of mystical state. By the time someone finishes explaining it to you, you feel burdened once more. Rest, in truth, is Christ Himself. Remember His words, "Take my yoke upon you and learn of me. My yoke is easy, my burden is light. In me, I'm meek and lowly, and in me, you will find rest for your souls." (Matthew 11:29). Rest, in truth, is Christ Himself. (Hebrews 4:10-11). When your conscience is not at rest, which Hebrews states means it's not perfected, it indicates you're not resting in the finished work of Jesus Christ (Hebrews 10:14). The enemy accuses us night and day, and we need to learn to answer him with the blood of Jesus Christ. When we do, our conscience is cleansed, and our faith is assured.

Rest is a supernatural concept. It's something that God guides you into because, due to the weakness and opposition of your flesh, you don't enter rest automatically. Rest is always 'today.' "Today is the day if you hear His voice" (Heb 4:7). It's constantly presented as something to enter into, yet in ourselves, we can't. So, what does this imply? It means that each day, I need to learn to depend solely on Christ. Only He can bring me to rest. If it's entirely up to me, I'll be in a state of agitation, of restlessness.

Restlessness takes on different forms, but the ones that Hebrews focuses on are linked to unbelief and issues of the conscience. When your conscience is not at rest, it indicates you're not resting in the finished work of Jesus Christ for your sins. Your agitation over your condition, your past, your history, and your sins tempt you to resort to something other than Christ to deal with your conscience.

We all experience this restlessness to some extent. Our conscience produces our restlessness from our past. The enemy accuses us night and day, and we need to learn to answer him with the blood of Jesus Christ. When we do, our conscience is cleansed, and our faith is assured.

This restlessness can only be truly appeased through faith in the blood. We are only accepted, and can only find genuine rest when the blood of Jesus Christ purges our conscience. This purification, coupled with exercising faith, brings us closer to Him. With this closeness comes a feeling of thankfulness, and a sense of peace that everything is okay.

I aim to demystify the concept of "rest". Rest is not a supernatural state of existence where you're entirely immersed in the spirit. Rather, rest means not trying to satisfy my restlessness, my unbelief, or my plagued conscience with anything other than faith in the blood of Jesus Christ. By having faith in His blood, I draw near to God as an empty, needy vessel, declaring, "Lord, apart from you, I can do nothing. I need you and I believe that you're there."

I'm not expecting spectacular outward results to verify that God is present. Instead, I understand that my faith is the assurance of things that I do not see. This sentiment echoes the book of Hebrews, which states that "the just shall live by faith", defining faith as the vision that everyone has of Christ in chapter 11. We walk by faith in that vision, to the point where it governs our lives, leading us away from the world's clamor and striving, which are rooted in restlessness.

We end up being strangers and pilgrims, much like the examples of Abraham, Isaac, and Jacob who dwelt in tents rather than in Babel, the empire of their day. Living in tents demonstrated that they had no lasting home there. Their sights were set on a city built by God. Their faith was grounded in unseen things. They were not seeking immediate results but were resting in the knowledge that God had a destiny for them related to Christ. Even though they didn't visibly see it, they found rest in this faith.

As we saw in the last chapter, Cain dwelt in the land of Nod, which can be likened to wilderness wandering. This wandering is the embodiment of restlessness, the antithesis of Eden in Genesis, or the contrast to the Good land which was the rest for the people of God in Numbers. Cain moved away from the gate where the propitiation was accepted and the cherubim were placed as witnesses.

I believe that Abel and the patriarchs in his line remained near that altar. They maintained a relationship with God through that altar, and I believe they stayed near Eden. In doing so, they experienced a semblance of restfulness. In contrast, Cain's lineage was characterized by a lack of rest, leading to all the evil, wickedness, and mystery that we examined in our previous discussion.

Rest comes from living in the presence of God, while restlessness is a result of being separated from Him. In the Bible, Eden is described as the place where God rested on the seventh day after sanctifying, having rested from all His works. Then He put Adam and Eve in this garden and gave them everything that was pleasant. That garden was really their covering, their life, and their supply. It was all pictures of Christ for their enjoyment. They had a miniature prototype of the New Jerusalem, at least in type, and that was a rest. It was God's rest and their rest on the seventh day.

But then, they got kicked out of the garden after the Tree of Knowledge of Good and Evil. Yet, God immediately intervened with the Gospel and then the covering of the lambskin. He gave them an altar and a way to sacrifice, and Abel picked up on that, we know. That was a prefigure of the Sabbath system, which is the seventh-day system, the Sabbath feasts. All of this commemorates rest.

But rest also acknowledges a position of weakness. As the line progresses, we witness a growing restlessness that culminates in Lamech, the only one in the line to speak, apart from Cain. In a poem, he confesses to killing a man and declares his intention to seek even greater revenge than Cain (Genesis 4:23-24). In Nod, Cain's line wanders in the wilderness, building things that glorify themselves and make a name for themselves. They even communicate their views on God. They must fend for themselves and protect themselves because they are orphans. When naming their children, they speak harshly about God and identify with the serpent. All their work stems from a place of restlessness that comes from being outside the presence of God. This all comes from Cain's statement, that he is a fugitive, a vagabond, and cursed from the earth (Genesis 4:16-18, Genesis 4:20-22). When you are in "Nod," when you are not enjoying the presence of God, everything you do is in vain. It doesn't matter if it's religious or not.

"Remember the root of the difference between Cain and Abel and the two lines is the offering. Abel's offering declared him righteous because it represented faith in the propitiation blood (Genesis 4:4). It showed he agreed with God's way of justifying sinners, and so he confessed. He confessed in his offering that he was a sinner, that he needed redemption, and that only God could provide it (Hebrews 11:4). Only God could bring him into fellowship, and only God could give man hope of restoration and eternal life.

Remember that the altar was at the gate of Eden, guarded by the cherubim who guarded the way to the Tree of Life (Genesis 3:24). God has given us hope in this seed, Christ. We look to Him to bring us back in, and we make this offering as a picture, knowing that only He can deal with our sins. Only He can deal with the fall. We're not trying to deal with it; we are resorting to Him. In contrast, Cain said he was going out of the presence of God and he would have to deal with his situation. He was an orphan, and everything that came out of his line came from that place of alienation.

The Line of Life

Gen 4:23-26 And Lamech said unto his wives, Adah and Zillah, Hear my voice; ye wives of Lamech, hearken unto my speech: for I have slain a man to my wounding, and a young man to my hurt. (24) If Cain shall be avenged sevenfold, truly Lamech seventy and sevenfold. (25) And Adam knew his wife again; and she bare a son, and called his name Seth: For God, said she, hath appointed me

another seed instead of Abel, whom Cain slew. (26) And to Seth, to him also there was born a son; and he called his name Enos: then began men to call upon the name of the LORD.

We have previously seen that there was no time recorded on Cain's line, which represents vanity and restlessness. Now we come to the "Line of Life". We see Adam know his wife again, and she bore Seth. Then Seth called his name Enos, and people began to call upon the name of the Lord. Interestingly, this is mentioned again in Genesis 5 when Seth lived for 105 years and begot Enos, who then lived for 90 years and begat Kenan.

Enos' name is mentioned again in the previous chapter, where it says that's when men were calling on the name of the Lord. It's a special "marker" when the Lord brings up something out of place, as with the mention of Tubal-Cain's sister Naamah. There are no sisters mentioned in this bloodline, so it's significant when Naamah is suddenly mentioned. If something is out of place, the Holy Spirit is trying to highlight it.

Right after the record of Lamech's horrible poetry, there's an out-of-place mention of Adam, Seth, and Enos. It's out of place because the genealogy officially starts in the next chapter. It's like resetting the lines back at the beginning, but it mentions Enos, and in his days, men began to call upon the name of the Lord. Enos means weakness, and they knew they were weak, so they called upon the name of the Lord. Calling on His name invokes the presence of God.

We call on Him to be whatever we need Him to be. We're not looking to be "spiritual," we recognize we're frail. Rest is not an ultra-spiritual state of mystical existence. That is too burdensome. It is a place of weakness where you are looking for rest.

> "Come to me, all you who are weary and burdened, and I will give you rest. Take my yoke upon you and learn from me, for I am gentle and humble in heart, and you will find rest for your souls. For my yoke is easy and my burden is light." - Matthew 11:28-30 (KJV)

Jesus wants to provide you with rest. However, it seems the only people who discover this rest are those who realize they can't find it themselves. There's a certain weakness in this realization. So there is an aspect of this line which seems characterized by weakness.

Another Lamech

> And Lamech lived an hundred eighty and two years, and begat a son: (29) And he called his name Noah, saying, This same shall comfort us concerning our work and toil of our hands, because of the ground which the LORD hath cursed. (30) And Lamech lived after he begat Noah five hundred ninety and five years, and begat sons and daughters: (31) And all the days of Lamech were seven hundred seventy and seven years: and he died. (32)

In the Genesis 5 line, we encounter all these names we'll look at in a bit.. It's noteworthy and clearly by design that the only one who's speaking is recorded in the line of life another Lamech, who would have probably been contemporary to the original Lamech. Lamech lived for 182 years and begat a son whom he named Noah. Noah means rest! This Lamech said, **'This shall comfort us concerning our work and the toil of our hands, because of the ground which the Lord has cursed.'**

Both lines end with a Lamech and with the record of the speaking of their Lamech. Both Lamech's represent the "fruit of the lips" and the "abundance of the heart" (out of the abundance of the heart the mouth speaks) and represent the way of each line. The name Lamech means to mourn. Both Lamechs are mourners. But the Lamech on the line of life mourns while anticipating redemption. He names his son Noah, saying 'This is the way God is going to comfort us.' We acknowledge that our situation is due to the fact that God cursed the earth. We need to be comforted concerning our toil. They don't take pleasure in their toil; they know that it's a result of the fall.

In contrast, Cain's line boasts in their toil. From the beginning with Cain, he did not understand that the toil was something negative. God was not interested in man toiling for him, and he did not respect that offering. So there's a fundamental difference between Cain's line and Seth's line. Seth's line stays by the altar, calls on the name of the Lord out of weakness, recognizes hope in their redemption, and they really do have a kind of rest.

Now, in the line of Cain, we saw that there's no recorded passage of time because God doesn't remember; he doesn't consider it significant. I believe that's what it means. On the other hand, you have a record of all these works. City building agriculture, musical instruments, secret knowledge, weaponry, murder, and polygamy.

Yet all we see in the Genesis 5 line is 'someone lived this long and begat so and so, then lived a little more or a lot more, and begat sons and daughters.' All they did was live and beget. That's why we call it the line of life, and this is why it seems to convey an impression of rest. The focus of God is life. Even in creation, the focus was life. It was to recover the earth on the third day. In order to separate the land from the sea, and then make it a productive place for life to grow, there is a certain order to life and complexity; from plants to animals, birds, and then finally, man. The tree of life symbolizes this emphasis on living things. Even after the fall, the first thing Adam does after God's pronouncement of the gospel and covering them with skins is to name his wife "Eve, the mother of all living." There's a focus on life because life means the seed. This is a big deal for God's people.

One of the reasons why being barren was considered a curse in the Old Testament was because everyone hoped to be the one to bring forth the Messiah. The biggest blessing would be to bring forth the Messiah. From the very beginning, when Eve had Cain, she said, "We've gotten one from the Lord." Even when Abel was killed and she had Seth, which means appointed, she said, "He's been appointed in place of Abel." We see this at the end of Chapter Four when she said, "God has appointed me another seed instead of Abel, whom Cain slew."

For them, the seed and the life didn't mean anything unless it pointed to Christ, who was the "Seed of the woman" who would bruise the serpent's head and restore everything. (Genesis 3:15) It's not about life for life's sake. That's just vanity. (Ecclesiastes 1:2) Yes, they lived a long time, but it's all just futility and vanity. (Ecclesiastes 1:2) Everything under the sun is vain until they're brought back to what God originally created. So, there's a recognition that this is not our home. They are strangers and pilgrims and they're not building anything. (Hebrews 11:13-16)

That's not to say that these people didn't have their own lives. However, God's record focuses on the line of life that leads to Christ, who is the resurrection and the life (John 11:25). The genealogy of Jesus Christ is being recorded with these names, including the names from Genesis 11 that lead to Abraham from Shem. These names can also be found in Luke's genealogy, which traces the bloodline that finally brings forth the seed of the woman who is their hope. That's what they were living for - they didn't care about anything else.

The Restful Walk with God of a Believer

Prior to Noah, the only activity we have recorded on the line is that of Enoch, who walked with God and "was not." This is a restful sort of thing. He was walking with God for a long time, which just means abiding with him, abiding in him, and having fellowship. How did he have that fellowship? Well, he believed in the seed. He believed in the gospel and he had the offering at the altar and called upon the name of the Lord in weakness.

These are the people who called upon (Genesis 4:26) the name of the Lord in weakness. They are invoking the presence of God. They each also followed the pattern of Abel, offering the firstling of the flock with the fat portion. We know that because after the flood, Noah's first act was to offer a burnt offering (Genesis 8:20). These are the activities on the line of life. To believe in the blood, to look for redemption, to call upon the name of the Lord in weakness, and in this, walk with God.

We have the same. We have the blood of Jesus Christ, which is our propitiation, our altar. We also have the name of God, which is Jesus Christ. We come to the Father in His name (John 14:6), and we believe in Him. This belief brings us into fellowship and into the spirit. The difference is that our inheritance is so much more because the work has been finished. God is really able to perfect our conscience. He has given us the Holy Spirit, which is Christ Himself as life. We're members of the Body of Christ. We've been baptized into His death and made alive together with Him.

However, the principle of our life, of how we live it, is still the same. We call on the name of Jesus and remember His offering, and believe in it. This is our altar. We walk with Him, we abide in Him, and we just remain with Him. It's a position of rest. But ever since the fall, rest has always been available for the people of God. Today, that's the point Hebrews makes, and it's made in the Psalms as well. It's always today. The seventh day is a day that's always available today. God's seventh day is a day to enter into by faith, and that faith is an acknowledgment of the finished works of God.

God has decreed it, He's going to bring it to pass because in His eyes, it's already done. He is the God who calls those things that are not as though they are (Romans 4:17), and gives life to the dead. That's how Abraham walked. He had an altar in the name of God and walked with God. Romans 4 tells us how he walked. He walked by believing in Him who justifies the ungodly, who calls those things that are not as though they are, and gives life to the dead. Abraham believed that God would give him a seed. He lived on a line of life.

Now we do as well. But what they called the seed, we name Jesus Christ. Christ has come. For us to walk in the line of life, we believe God's going to bring forth fruit. Furthermore, as they believed the seed would come through their line, we believe that Christ will be manifest in us. This means the fruit of the Spirit will manifest in our life, there will be a transformation. But again, that is God's work, not ours. None of the patriarchs, none of the fathers, none of these people in this line could make Messiah come or force him to be born. Only God could do that, and He finally did it in His own time, "in the fullness of times" (Gal 4:15). But they all lived in anticipation nonetheless.

We're the same way when it comes to fruit. According to Galatians, by the Spirit, we eagerly hope for the righteousness in which we hope. We're not trying to generate the fruit of the Spirit or activate it or produce it. No, we're believing in Jesus, walking with Him, and calling on His name. We're believing and we're standing at the altar. In fact, we've presented ourselves on the altar according to Romans 12. We've taken a step further and said we put ourselves on the altar as a living sacrifice, acknowledging that we're dead with Christ, that we're holy and accepted, and that we're alive together with Him. Now we're a living sacrifice and we're expecting Him to manifest Himself in our life.

We don't have control over how fruit is produced. When you try to control it, you fall back into dead works, wandering instead of resting. The rest of faith is exactly that, a state of waiting. I am not going to do anything to try to generate this on my own. Instead, I am waiting for God to produce it, living in faith that He will.

Abraham provides an example of what it means to wander versus to be in faith. When he was wandering in unbelief, he was trying to help God produce the seed (Genesis 16:1-6). He went into Hagar and had Ishmael, which led to all kinds of strife in his house. God didn't communicate with him for 13 years (Genesis 16:15-16).

When God returned, He gave Abraham the circumcision covenant and said, 'I'm going to visit you at the time of life, and Sarah's going to conceive. There's going to be a seed.' At that point, Abraham knew it would have to be supernatural because Sarah was barren and he was past childbearing. He didn't consider the deadness of his own body or the barrenness of Sarah's womb, but gave glory to God, believing that God was able to give life to the dead and call those things that are not as though they are (Genesis 17:1-22, Romans 4:17-21). He trusted that God would fulfill His promise.

The way they looked to the seed to be produced is the same way we look for fruit to be produced. This is directly related to the Christian life. Just because you look back at the Old Testament and see it as pre-Christ does not mean it doesn't have to do with your Christian life. Justification has always been the same; it's always been by faith. Walking with God in principle has also been the same. It's about calling on His name in your weakness, knowing that He has to be everything that you cannot. That's Enos calling on the name of the Lord and offering the blood, not your own toil from the ground.

Serving by Resting

You need to understand that God didn't decree toil because that's what He wants, but because of an adverse condition that He wants to fix. You're looking forward to redemption and groaning for that day. You are now a stranger, a pilgrim, because you're governed by a vision that this is not how things are supposed to be. Your hope is tied up in Christ. Their hope was tied up in the seed, the promise of the seed, to deliver them.

We operate the same way. Our faith is exactly the same. The only difference is the seed has already come and now we're looking for the fruit. But the way we look for the fruit is the same kind of walk. The walk we walk is the same walk Enoch walked, and I know that from Hebrews 11. If you look at Hebrews 11, you'll see it's not a list of "superheroes of faith." Instead, Hebrews 11 is a description of the vision that guided the fathers and what they believed. What you find out is that what they believed is the same thing we believe, and the faith that they had is the same faith we have. That is the rest. Resting is faith. We have believed to enter into that rest, and it's something that needs to be remembered.

Every day, I find myself needing to halt my relentless restlessness that would otherwise lead me to wander and produce unfruitful works. I need to approach the altar and offer up Christ by faith. You see, He has already offered Himself. As Paul stated in Philippians 2:17, "I'm being poured out as a drink offering on the sacrifice and service of your faith, I rejoice…"

Our faith is our service and our sacrifice. Christ is our offering. We believe in Him and call upon His name in our weakness, trusting that He is the one who must be everything to us. We yearn for Him to produce His fruit and ultimately, to deliver us from our toil. This is the comforter we believe in, the manifestation of the Spirit, which we long for. However, it's God who must fulfill this.

This is the difference between wandering and resting. Resting is when God fulfills His promises and we believe in Him. Wandering occurs when we believe His promises aren't enough. We feel the need to help Him out, to offer up some toil. Wandering stems from a restless conscience, unsatisfied and feeling distant from God's presence.

It's the feeling of being an orphan, of needing to fix your own situation. On the other hand, abiding in God, walking with Him, staying in the line of lif,e and resting are all about acknowledging our weakness and fragility as mortals. It's about calling on God to be our everything, trusting Him to produce what we cannot. This is the message presented in Hebrews, Genesis, and throughout the scriptures.

We see a contrast, two manners of life. One is from restlessness, trying to generate something for yourself, whether it's religious or otherwise. The other is a form of resting that does involve a struggle due to our flesh, but we're conscious of our weakness. We call on the Lord. We're not trying to enter rest on our own. Instead, we're asking the Lord, who is our rest, to guide us. This is a daily struggle.

Enoch walked with God for 360 years before he was raptured. What does that walk look like? To walk with God means, every day, I stay in the line of life. I acknowledge my inability to do anything without Him. I am weak, He is strong. I live by faith in His love for me, in His sacrifice for me.

Every day, I strive to refrain from doing my own thing. I aim to abide in Him, to wait on Him. Eventually, yes, fruit does come forth. There are those who say we don't engage in good works. However, this is my good work: I testify of Christ and glorify Him. I'm on the line of life, bearing fruit. We are producing fruit, praise from our hearts to Him, and fruit in that others are entering the line of faith.

The progression of faith and glorification of Christ is exemplified in the line of life. Cain's line, however, views the line of life with skepticism. They question its productivity, contrasting it with their own tangible achievements. Yet, the line of life remains steadfast, nurturing their offspring and maintaining their faith.

Many out of One Man

The Book of Generations of Adam provides a profound insight into this concept. It harks back to the creation of mankind in the likeness of God. The creation of male and female, blessed and named Adam, forms the basis of our belief that we are all in Adam. We are many, yet we originate from one man. All of Adam's seed, our DNA, was fashioned in him. This is why his fall led to our fall. We inherited his nature.

Interestingly, God's dealings with one person, Adam, resulted in the transgression of one leading to death for all. However, the same principle applies to Christ. He is one man, yet a corporate man, embodying the new man and the new humanity. We, as many members, have been transferred out of Adam and into Christ through death and resurrection. This shift has allowed us to become part of Christ.

Adam's expulsion and disqualification due to sin made us heirs of wrath, death, and sin. Conversely, Christ, as the new head of the new humanity, offers us acceptance and reconciliation to God when we believe in Him. His righteousness is credited to us, just as Adam's sin was imputed to us. Despite not sinning in the same way as Adam, death and sin came to all of us.

Christ's one act of obedience, giving His life for us, made the many righteous. We all became righteous through Him. Now, instead of a "river of death" flowing out of Adam, there is a "river of life" flowing out of Christ into the new humanity (John 7:36-39). This is the new creation.

This concept is where Paul gets his idea in Romans 5. In God's dealings, there are just two men - Adam and Christ. God dealt with Adam in Christ, the last Adam. He put Adam to death in Christ, and all those from Adam died with Him. However, those who believed were also raised together with Christ in His resurrection.

The line of life promises a new humanity, an exit from Adam and into Christ. This is a repair of the situation caused by the fall of the original man. He created them male and female, blessed them, and called them Adam. As we saw previously, He reckons them as Adam even though he created "them" male and female. The day they were created marked the beginning of a new era.

Names

Now let's look at the names on this line. We've seen that the name 'Adam' translates to 'man', and following him, we have Seth, whose name means 'appointed'. Seth then begat Enos, a name symbolizing 'mortal' or 'mortality'.

Moving forward, Enos begat Kenan, a name that signifies 'sorrow'. So, in effect, we have 'Man appointed mortal sorrow'. Enos then begat Mahal, which means 'the blessed God'. This is where we begin to see the divine intervention in the lineage. Mahal begat Jared, a name that means 'to descend'. Some suggest that this period symbolizes when the fallen angels descended and started creating Nephilim.

Following Jared was Enoch, whose name means 'to teach' or 'discipline'. Enoch begat Methuselah, a name that translates to 'his death shall bring'. Methuselah lived 300 years, while Enoch lived for 365 years, walking with God until God took him. This is an example of pre-judgment deliverance.

The authenticity of the current circulating Book of Enoch is questionable, but we know (Jude 1:14-15) was able to quote from Enoch. Enoch prophesied judgment when the Lord would come with all his saints to judge the ungodly sinners speaking against God.

Methuselah, whose name means 'his death shall bring', begat Lamech. Lamech, I believe, is the contemporary of the other Lamech in the lineage. Both of them spoke something to sum up their line. One spoke about vengeance, and the other about comfort. Which line would you like to be on?

Lamech then begat a son, Noah, whose name means 'rest'. Noah was the symbol of comfort concerning our toil and the work of our hands because of the ground which the Lord had cursed. Noah lived for 500 years and begat Shem, Ham, and Japheth. Their genealogy continues in Genesis 11 with the table of nations, marking the end of that line until the time of the flood.

The two Lamechs were contemporaries of each other. One believed he was going to be avenged, but the other knew God was going to comfort them. Enoch knew that judgment was coming, as did Lamech's son. Lamech knew about the impending judgment and named his son Methuselah, which means 'his death shall bring'.

When you chart it out, you find out that Methuselah died the year the flood started. His life was a prophecy of the countdown of God's judgment. His death signaled the end and he died when the flood started. We've reviewed the names and their meanings, but I'll leave you with this thought: every name carries a message, a prophecy, a divine decree. The popular view, championed by Chuck Missler, emphasizes that these names spell the message "man was appointed mortal sorrow. However, the blessed God shall descend teaching that His death shall bring an end to our lament." This can also be interpreted as "bringing rest from our lament." This is essentially the gospel.

Did the authors know they were spelling out sentences? I don't believe so. I believe God orchestrates history. One of the ways He shows His genius and sovereignty over human history is through these names. This is not unique to Genesis 5.

We're discussing the line of life, a way of life not characterized by anything but the hope of life, which yields fruit and rewards (Genesis 5:1-32). It's what builds. This line of life resulted in a building. Didn't Paul say that we're building on a foundation with gold, silver, and precious stones? (1 Corinthians 3:12) Cain's line, however, was building with corruptible materials that couldn't withstand the flood (Genesis 6:11-13).

Just like those in the flesh today, they are building with corruptible materials that won't withstand the fire. But gold, silver, and precious stone will pass through the fire because they're born out of the hope of life that comes from walking with God from a place of weakness. This is achieved by acknowledging your need, calling on Him, relying on the blood, and believing God to bring forth the fruit.

This is the same faith as those who were weak, called on His name, believed in the blood, and believed God to bring forth the seed. We have a different object - Christ - but for us, it's Christ in us, and there will be fruit that we will see in eternity. We may not recognize it now, but there's more fruit than we know, born out of the fragrance produced from living this way.

Outwardly, it may not look like we're doing much, but God reckons it by the passage of time. It looked like Cain's line was doing a lot, but he didn't acknowledge any passage of time with them. Yet, He recorded the years of all these fathers who seemingly did nothing. We know how they lived and so we have the accusation, but we don't need to believe it. We're justified by what we believe, which is the blood. Our Advocate's blood silences the mouth of our accuser.

Chapter 19 Flood, Judgment and salvation (Genesis 6)

Introduction: A sober minded approach

Gen 6:1-8 And it came to pass, when men began to multiply on the face of the earth, and daughters were born unto them, (2) That the sons of God saw the daughters of men that they were fair; and they took them wives of all which they chose. (3) And the LORD said, My spirit shall not always strive with man, for that he also is flesh: yet his days shall be an hundred and twenty years. (4) There were giants in the earth in those days; and also after that, when the sons of God came in unto the daughters of men, and they bare children to them, the same became mighty men which were of old, men of renown. (5) And GOD saw that the wickedness of man was great in the earth, and that every imagination of the thoughts of his heart was only evil continually. (6) And it repented the LORD that he had made man on the earth, and it grieved him at his heart. (7) And the LORD said, I will destroy man whom I have created from the face of the earth; both man, and beast, and the creeping thing, and the fowls of the air; for it repenteth me that I have made them. (8) But Noah found grace in the eyes of the LORD.

We have come to one of the more intriguing Chapters in Genesis. The section is replete with types, dates, and the typological significance of the Ark as it points towards Christ, (landing on the day Christ resurrected).

This part of Genesis delves into the Nephilim, a topic of great interest for many. It was this aspect that the Lord used to pique my interest in the Gospel. I grew up in an atheist home but, loving science fiction, always felt there was "more" out there. In my early twenties in the 1990s, I found myself extensively reading about whether aliens had visited Earth and influenced world religions. Then someone directed me to Genesis 6. It speaks of similar beings, referring to them as fallen angels. I was told these entities had formed the religions, that they were the "gods of old" - fallen ones who intermingled with humanity, corrupting our gene pool. Thankfully the Lord led me from chasing them down that rabbit hole and instead captivated me with the story of His prophetic plan for history. This opened my eyes to see the Lord's narrative behind world events.

Today I have very little appetite for these things. They have unfortunately become a subculture and a genre among Christians and are being used to send new believers on endless quests into darker and darker themes. I call it "giving Satan a colonoscopy." I have grown weary of it. Nowadays, people have become like Indiana Jones, hunting for the Nephilim all over the world. It's become a Christian sci-fi genre, a money maker. More importantly, it's a back for works and all kinds of heresies and works doctrines (Titus 1:14). For example, today many in the prophetic community have linked the genetic tampering in Genesis 6 with the pharmaceutical industry and vaccines to establish "do not taste, do not touch, do not handle" ordinances

(Colossians 2:21-22), and to establish criteria around whether they can accuse someone of not being saved. Even so-called grace teaching, gospel-believing teachers who have gotten into this stuff had people fearing they had lost their salvation or had their DNA tampered with so that they were no longer human and possibly had taken the "Mark of the Beast:" They claimed to have inside information that the vaccine would be sprayed into the air as an aerosol and change our "God gene," making it impossible to be saved. This contradicted the gospel they had previously defended. At this time many people were "failing" simple gospel tests.

I do not wish to undermine the significance of this aspect of Genesis. This does not mean that I no longer believe what I initially did. I still hold that the fallen angels, the sons of God, did what Genesis says they did. The judgment referred to in 2 Peter 2:4 and Jude 1 regarding the angels who left their first estate and pursued unnatural desires, remains valid. Noah's purity in his genealogy, all these matters are still significant.

However, in his letters to Titus (1:14) and Timothy (1 Tim. 1:4), Paul warns us to avoid these myths and endless genealogies. These lead to speculation rather than God's economy which is in faith. Paul also says that the end of the "charge," is love out of a pure heart, unfeigned faith, and a good conscience. Some have turned aside from this, desiring to be teachers of the law, and have turned to vain jingling. Their words poison churches and overthrow households.

1Ti 1:3-7 As I besought thee to abide still at Ephesus, when I went into Macedonia, that thou mightest charge some that they teach no other doctrine, (4) Neither give heed to fables and endless genealogies, which minister questions, rather than godly edifying which is in faith: so do. (5) Now the end of the commandment is charity out of a pure heart, and of a good conscience, and of faith unfeigned: (6) From which some having swerved have turned aside unto vain jangling; (7) Desiring to be teachers of the law; understanding neither what they say, nor whereof they affirm.

When you look through the New Testament, you will see Paul's warnings. He often connects heresy and legalism with myth, genealogies, mythology, "Jewish myths," and wives' tales and fables. He refers to them as "fable," "wives' tales," and "endless genealogies.". We often get caught up in trying to figure out who the Nephilim families are, and the thirteen Illuminati bloodlines. All that stuff, man, what comes out of it are ordinances: 'do not handle', 'do not taste', 'do not touch'. (1 Timothy 1:4, Titus 1:14; Col 2:21-22)

An example of this is the "vaccine scenario." Some individuals who seek to cause fear love to promote the idea that vaccines will turn people into Nephilim hybrids and alter their DNA, rendering them ineligible for salvation. The grace community, who were effective at spreading the gospel of grace, began preaching this idea.

We fail to understand that considering these notions and leaving the possibility open for them to be true can bring harmful things into the body of Christ. It can impact our perception of God and what is required of us. I made a comedy video by "Pastor So-and-So" about Halloween handing out King James Bibles and saltine crackers to children. He mentioned that half of the kids that came to his door were wearing zombie makeup and because they were wearing makeup he called them transvestites. He believed that half of them were Nephilim vampires, and said he was wasting his Bibles because these kids could not be saved, as Nephilim cannot be saved. This was satire, but not far off from the kinds of comments, I saw on walls of people in the so-called "grace community" who should have the Gospel as the plumbline.

These things can contribute to a culture of irrationality and dehumanization. During a time when there was much speculation about whether Kanye West had his conversion, some were more inclined to believe he was an MK Ultra clone or Nephilim hybrid, rather than hoping he had truly found faith. Some argued that he was a completely different person, an MK Ultra clone with a dissociative personality that had been fractured due to CIA Monarch mind control. While that's not totally impossible, I found very few "Gospel-believing" Christians who were even willing to hope that he might have been saved at that time.

This kind of thinking completely pollutes your mind and conscience and defiles you. On one hand, I praise God that I know about the Nephilim and that God used that to lead me to the Lord. God used it to lead a lot of people to the Lord. But remember, what actually leads us to the Lord? Is it the stories about the Nephilim? No, it's the gospel. God was able to inject the truth in spite of the fact that I was fascinated with the tales.

The gospel was intertwined with all the "garbage". Years ago, if you were to listen to my testimony, I would try to tell you everything I had learned about the world empires. I learned that certain priesthoods had cultivated secret knowledge and passed it on. They were behind all the ideologies of the world empire, shaping people's views. These people believed they were in contact with gods who, according to the Bible, are fallen angels.

'Okay, but how did you get saved?'

I would answer that God has a plan. There's a cosmic war for our soul and Israel's presence in the land proves that there is really warfare, and that the Bible is true.

'Okay, but how did you get saved?'

Eventually, I had to grapple with the fact that Christ died for my sins according to the scripture. He rose for my justification according to the scripture. This is how I can have peace with God, as a sinner like me. That somehow found its way into my belief system, but as long as I was entertaining all of this stuff, it was difficult for me to even tell someone how to be saved. I felt like I had to lead people through all of this complicated information to get them to the gospel and I rarely arrived at the point! I still believe these things and will share them in the right context. We'll touch on them several times in these chapters. However, this is not the testimony of Christ; it's a sideline.

One thing that exhausts me is the overwhelming amount of misinformation. It is possible to be exposed to dehumanizing and depersonalizing concepts. When one strictly bases their relationship with God on ancient stories without considering the Person and work of Christ and interpreting everything in that light, it just leads to "vain jangling". I have found that most people who become heavily involved in this are against grace and view their Christian life as one bound by ordinances. These people are not enjoying the Christian life, but instead are exhausting themselves with ordinances as a way to shield themselves from the Nephilim.

When you think like that, the love of God becomes alien. I remember scoffing at people who didn't understand the depth of the mysteries I knew regarding all this stuff. They just wanted to focus on the love of God. I thought I was the mature one. I had it backward!

If a kid comes for Halloween candy, he's a human being as far as I can tell. He's got two feet, two hands, and eyes. He's saying 'trick-or-treat.' He's a human being and a candidate for the grace of God. That's how I'm to view him. There are literally people who dehumanize others and say, 'Well, you're probably a Nephilim.' There are people who dream that I'm a Nephilim. It's ridiculous. It doesn't take a whole lot of wisdom to see the damage that entertaining these things to an extreme has done. But at the same time, God wanted us to know the background.

God didn't give us the Book of Enoch or include it in the canon. But he wants us to understand that this stuff is real. There's stuff going on behind the scenes. There's a reason why Joshua had to kill all the women and children, even the cattle, in some of these cities populated with Nephilim descendants (Num 13:33; Deut 2;20). That's real. However, I don't believe they're as present as you might think. I think they were mostly in Canaan, and I believe Israel dealt with them as they conquered the land.

God's economy produces love from a pure heart, sincere faith, and a good conscience. A good conscience means that I know that the blood of Jesus gives me access to God as a sinner, and there's nothing in my way. I can come to Him freely and boldly on the basis of the blood. I don't have to be subject to any rules or ordinances to do that. I am not in debt to anything. But the speculation from the wives' tales and the myths brings in things to undermine the Gospel. As I said, we've got people who are super solid in teaching grace when they teach the Gospel.

It's truly amazing how gifted they are. For the Gospel's sake they are brothers and sisters, and I love it when it's so clear, when there's an authority with the gospel. Yet, because of their entertaining of speculative stuff, they've been derailed.

What does that do? It undermines your ability to believe in your security. It's a wives' tale that comes in alongside the gospel and damages people's faith and can overturn households. Then there are people who, on the tails of the vaccine thing, are saying, "Even if it's not the mark of the beast, you better not take it because you're sinning against your own body and it's connected to the abortion industry." They make a moral thing out of it.

This is "do not handle, do not taste, do not touch" ordinances (Colossians 2:21-22). Paul said we're not to be subjected to them. They're of no value against the indulgence of the flesh (Colossians 2:23). Jesus said, "It's not what enters the body that defiles it, but what comes out of the heart" (Matthew 15:11). Sin is not about what comes into me, sin is what comes out of my heart and my motives. That's what God's looking at (1 Samuel 16:7). He knows we are swimming in a toxic stew (Romans 3:23).

We currently live in a generation where we are often unaware of the contents of our food. The presence of preservatives affects the behavior of our children, and there are concerns regarding this issue. While it is true that these concerns are valid, some people go to extreme lengths to protect themselves and base their reality solely hysterical misinformation and end up resisting the implications of the Gospel even though they've been saved by it.

This really produces a schizophrenic split. People who love grace end up acting like a legalist, living in a mix of fear and boldness. Somedays, you're going towards God; other days, you think your "God gene" is going to be turned off, and it's "game over!" Where does all that come from? That's the impact of wives' tales and fables that overthrow faith.

Not the Time for Nephilim, Time for the Ark!

So for this Chatpter, that's pretty much what I have to say about the Nephilim. This is not the time for Nephilim, this is the time for the Ark! When you realize the time that we're living in, where Noah is getting ready to go on the ark. He's got seven days; he's supposed to get the animals on. That is not the time for him to start wondering about the real motives of Cain naming the city after his son Enoch! If he were to get bogged down tracing the underpinnings of the world that was about to pass away, it would have hindered his building work!

I believe we are at a time of the end, and we need to be laser-focused on the Gospel and what saves us. We need to maintain a good conscience so that we can be bold when He appears. We need to abide in the Lord so that we can have confidence when He comes and not shrink back in shame.

I believe that there's a lot of grace to be found in Noah's flood, but we're not going to focus on that here. Even this has been turned into a sensational distraction. Nowadays, you can visit a full-size replica of Noah's Ark, complete with a zip line, snacks and a gift shop. It's become a sort of entertainment, like a musical. But imagine if someone were to build a model of Auschwitz and install a zip line through the area where the ovens once stood. To me, this would be very distasteful.

This shows that the story of the flood has become so ingrained in our culture that we've forgotten how offensive God's judgment and wrath can be to mankind. The flood should be regarded with solemnity. The main point of Genesis 6 is that "God repented that He made man," but Noah found grace in His eyes and was chosen to start anew. This was all done to preserve the seed so that Christ could come. The only reason we exist is because God saved Noah through the flood.

Noah had three sons with him: Ham, Shem, and Japheth, and their descendants are our ancestors. The reason God did this was so that Christ could be born (Genesis 9:18-19). In a way, the fact that we exist at all after the flood is due to

God's mercy and plan of redemption. Although we are naturally "heirs of wrath" and "alienated from God through wicked works in our mind," and destined for judgment because of our own sins and as descendants of Adam, the fact that there is a human race on earth today that has been able to populate it demonstrates God's mercy and patience (Ephesians 2:3, Colossians 1:21). It shows that His purposes are greater than anything else, and His purpose is to bring forth Christ and the Church (Ephesians 1:9-10).

Since the resurrection, the Church is commissioned with the building up of the "real ark" through edification. It's crucial that we maintain a sober view, particularly when it comes to the Nephilim and other such fables. We may miss the point with the flood often reduced to mere entertainment in children's stories and the like. We've used it to argue against an old earth, but we've overlooked its spiritual significance.

Peter showed us that the flood and our baptism are intertwined (1 Peter 3:20-21). Our baptism signifies our death to the world and its elements, all of which are passing away and under judgment. This includes the fables and wives' tales (Titus 1:14). From our perspective, these should be under the sea. We need to be in the ark, high above it all (Genesis 7:17-20). As these elements wash away, our perspective should also change.

We cannot continue to be fascinated with worldly things and maintain our joy. We cannot enjoy grace and find rest in the ark while simultaneously 'dining from the cup of demons' (1 Corinthians 10:21). As Paul stated, we cannot drink from the cup of demons and from the Lord's table. Eventually, the mixture has to be purged out.

There is a time and a place for everything, as scripture tells us (Ecclesiastes 3:1-8). I'm not advocating for complete ignorance, but we've had years to familiarize ourselves with these tales. Now, there's an urgency to focus on the gospel, which produces love from a pure heart, genuine faith, and a good conscience (1 Timothy 1:5). A good conscience allows us to be bold unto the Lord at his coming (1 John 2:28). We need to be free, without spot or offense (Ephesians 5:27).

"Let your love abound more and more in wisdom and discernment. Test what is excellent and aim to be sincere, without offense, on the day of Christ. Be filled with the fruits of righteousness, which are by Jesus Christ, for the glory of God. Discernment is not about figuring out if Kanye West might be a Nephilim. It's about approving of God's work so you can be without offense (Phil 1:9-11)

Offenses in the New Testament are not about causing anger, but about causing stumbling in people's walk with the Lord (Matthew 18:7). Offenses damage their conscience and their view of the gospel, leading them to submit to legalistic ordinances that bring them into bondage, rather than to the gospel which brings freedom (Galatians 5:1). Stumbling, offenses, and false teachings are related to myths that overturn the faith (1 Timothy 1:3-4). This is what offense truly means.

Some people may say, "You offended everyone with your Pastor So-and-So videos." However, the truth is that my Pastor So-and-So videos did not make anyone question their salvation. On the other hand, these vaccine scenarios are toxic for the faith. They cause people to stumble and produce offenses that are contrary to the Gospel.

> **Gen 6:1-8** And it came to pass, when men began to multiply on the face of the earth, and daughters were born unto them, (2) That the sons of God saw the daughters of men that they were fair; and they took them wives of all which they chose. (3) And the LORD said, My spirit shall not always strive with man, for that he also is flesh: yet his days shall be an hundred and twenty years. (4) There were giants in the earth in those days; and also after that, when the sons of God came in unto the daughters of men, and they bare children to them, the same became mighty men which were of old, men of renown. (5) And GOD saw that the wickedness of man was great in the earth, and that every imagination of the thoughts of his heart was only evil continually. (6) And it repented the LORD that he had made man on the earth, and it grieved him at his heart. (7) And the LORD said, I will destroy man whom I have created from the face of the earth; both man, and beast, and the creeping thing, and the fowls of the air; for it repenteth me that I have made them. (8) But Noah found grace in the eyes of the LORD.

Corrupting the Imagination of Men

The passage begins, "*It came to pass when man began to multiply on the face of the earth and daughters were born unto them, that the sons of God saw the daughters of men that they were fair; and they took wives of all that they chose.*" The Lord then declares, "*My spirit shall not always strive with man, for he is flesh: yet his days shall be 120 years.*" We see there were giants in the earth in those days, and also after that when the sons of God came into the daughters of men, they bore children unto them. These offspring became the mighty men of old, men of renown.

The lore that was passed down concerning the sons of God, the human wives, and the Nephilim shows up in all of the world empires after the flood and is the basis of most of the state religions up until the time of Rome. The tales of the Greco-Roman pantheon are highly descriptive. In addition to Hercules, some other examples of the offspring of fallen beings and human wives in the Greek and Roman pantheon include Perseus, Theseus, and Helen of Troy. These figures were believed to possess extraordinary abilities and played significant roles in various myths and legends. Now, the stories are likely exaggerations and a mix of truth and legend, but what stands out is the morality, or lack thereof, of these fallen creatures. Their stories are filled with the most abhorrent acts, including matricide, patricide, and even more gruesome deeds.

Whether these stories are factual or not, and I believe there is a basic kernel of truth that Genesis and Jude and Peter allude to, the stories reflect what captivated the imaginations. And it was the imagination of the hearts of the pre-flood men that God said was "only evil, continually." The saying goes, 'You become what you worship.' Arguably, the most violent culture we know of is the Roman Empire, with crosses lining the streets and gladiator fights serving as public entertainment. Their plays and dramas revolved around these gods and their horrific tales. This is what they celebrated, and, consequently, this is what they became.

Man was really wicked. Some argue that this wickedness was because the angels mated with humans, creating these offspring. This is true to a certain extent, but remember, sin and death reigned from the moment Adam fell. Our judgment was sealed due to Adam's disobedience. We are all sinners because of Adam, not because of the Nephilim. I believe that the Nephilim's biggest impact is on the imagination of men though. Are they real? It almost doesn't matter. Yes, they are real, but the main point I want to emphasize is that man's fascination with certain things can corrupt him. We've already discussed this from the perspective of how it affects Christians. Christians who delve into such matters become increasingly offended and consumed with everything but Christ, resulting in a loss of their purity.

Paul warns:

> Tit 1:14-15 **Not giving heed to Jewish fables, and commandments of men, that turn from the truth. (15) Unto the pure all things are pure: but unto them that are defiled and unbelieving is nothing pure; but even their mind and conscience is defiled.**

Notice how Paul connected Jewish fables with man-made commandments, resulting in a departure from the truth and subsequent corruption of the mind and conscience. These "Jewish Fables" are essentially rooted in Nephilim Lore, the book of Enoch, and various speculations about gene pools and genealogies. They lead to disbelief, corruption, and legalism, where nothing is considered pure. Regardless of what you may think of

Kanye West's conversion now, at the time I originally shared these messages, I was astonished by how some Christians preferred to perceive him as an MK ultra clone or a Nephilim, rather than as a human being who might have a hunger for God.

In the time of the flood, man was occupied with increasingly vile things. Eventually, the imagination of his heart was only evil continually. The Nephilim, whether there were only a few or many of them, captured the imaginations of the people, diverting their eyes from God and resulting in a loss of the fear of God. Consider the superhero movies of today. They're overwhelming, with buildings toppling and trains and plains being thrown around like playthings. The kind of catastrophic, cataclysmic power as these beings fight each other fills you with a sense of powerlessness and frailty and mortality. What is man in the face of all that? Weak and powerless! When the superhero throws a building at a plane, thousands of people could die. But that's not the focus. In other words, man's life becomes inconsequential. Can you see how this is a kind of propaganda orchestrated by Satan and full of his hatred for man?

This kind of power skews your perception of yourself and of God. You lose sight of God and worship power. Power becomes your fascination. Either you're afraid of it or you glory in it. But the more that happens, the more corrupt man becomes. There's less and less light in man.

Calvinists, those who are really fascinated with predestination, especially their perverse doctrine of "double reprobation" (God's fashioning of "vessels of wrath" to do the evil He planned for them and forcing them to do so), are fascinated with power. They believe that might makes right, and when you question this and point out that it is evil, they'll say, 'Who are you to question God.' They will appeal to His power. This is because Jesus Christ is not in their mind. They despise the lowliness and meekness of the one who said "come to me, all you who are weary and burdened, and I will give you rest." They argue that if God wanted everyone to be saved, and some were not saved, then He is a "failure". Everything is about winning and losing. This is the way the world thinks about "heavenly things," and it shows that their imagination is defiled. They cannot approve of Christ, who came not to be served but to serve.

What our culture celebrates reflects its condition. We have gangster rap, pop culture which is so bad. Sexual perversion, murder, and violence fill not only the number of acts committed but also the number of imaginations. Everybody's watching the movies, everybody's listening to music.

God's looking at the heart, and what we imagine definitely has real-world consequences. I've been watching some of these true crime documentaries lately. It's just amazing what people are capable of, and the things that actually happen, because of the kinds of things they can imagine. But it all comes from the heart. God was grieved about the condition of man's heart.

When man is given over to be just flesh and God says "my spirit won't strive with him anymore," it means "there's nothing I can do. There's no room for me." Yes, it's because of the Nephilim, but the emphasis in Genesis is *the reputation* of the Nephilim. They were "men of renown". This speaks of what they were *known for* and what made an impression on the imagination of men. Man became corrupt through it.

God Grieved

So God reached a point where he said it repented that the Lord that he made man and the earth, and it grieved him at his heart. Consider verse five: *"God saw that the wickedness of man was great in the earth, and that every imagination of the thoughts of his heart was only evil continually."* This is perhaps the strongest statement of judgment about man in the entire scripture. The wickedness of man is great, and the imagination of his heart is only evil...continually!

This is the opposite of *"You shall love the lord with all your heart, soul, mind, and strength."* Christ is the one who is the reality of this command. Every thought of his heart is to glorify the Father, and every imagination of his heart is pure and glorifies God continually.

> *John 6:38* **"For I came down from heaven, not to do mine own will, but the will of him that sent me."**
> *John 8:29* **"And he that sent me is with me: the Father hath not left me alone; for I do always those things that please him."**
> *John 12:49-50* **"For I have not spoken of myself; but the Father which sent me, he gave me a commandment, what I should say, and what I should speak. And I know that his commandment is life everlasting: whatsoever I speak therefore, even as the Father said unto me, so I speak."**

The Bible says God was Grieved. In the New Testament, there are only two instances where God is said to be grieved. The first is found in Ephesians 4:30 (Eph 4:30), where believers are admonished not to grieve the Holy Spirit of God. This grieving occurs when believers walk in the futility of their minds, being insensitive to the new creation realities and ignorant of spiritual truth (Eph 4:17-19). It is a result of not living with an acknowledgment of the high vision of God's heart and failing to appreciate what God has provided in Christ. The second mention is in Hebrews 3:10-12 (Heb 3:10-12), where God is said to be grieved with the children of Israel in the wilderness who refused to enter His rest due to their unbelief.

This grieving is related to their rejection of God's promises and their inclination to shrink back in fear rather than boldly take the land (Heb 3:18-19). Incidentally, the fear that kept the Israelites from taking the land was the fear of the Nephilim! (Num 13:33). Both instances highlight the importance of living in alignment with God's truth, having faith in His promises, and not allowing unbelief or insensitivity to hinder our fellowship with Him (Eph 4:20-24; Heb 4:1-3). The only times God is grieved in scripture is when men are occupied in such a persistent way with lies and unbelief that they have no heart for truth. This is what grieved God in the wilderness (Heb 3:16-17), and this is what grieves the Spirit in Ephesians 4.

Everyone's Speaking Revealing Their Hearts

There are a few *firsts* in this chapter. Genesis 6 is the first time we see the word grieved, the first time we see the word **grace,** the first time we see the word **righteous** and the first time we see a **covenant.** The word covenant is in this chapter too.

Remember, the last time we saw God was making the promise of the gospel in Genesis 3. But before that, everything was good. Then we had Cain's line. So we had God creating things by decree. It was through speaking and declaring things "good" and blessing them. We saw holiness, the seventh day rest, the garden, the charge "be fruitful and multiply," and God's speaking, "let man have dominion." Everything was wonderful. Then we had the fall.

Then we saw God saying, "Man has become like us, knowing good and evil." He then issued his decree against the serpent, set up the cherubim to guard the way to the Tree of Life, and promised the gospel. He slew an animal, symbolizing the propitiation and showing the way of redemption. This was followed by a period dominated by Cain's line, with God remaining silent and man speaking.

During Genesis 5, we encountered the descendants of Seth. We heard Adam and Eve speaking about Abel and Seth, naming their descendants. Lamech said, "God's going to comfort us concerning all of our toil because of the curse." God remained relatively silent during this time, communicating only through man.

Here, in Genesis 6 we see God speaking again, and the focus shifts to the *heart:* God's heart and man's heart. Man's heart was filled with every evil imagination continually, while God's heart was grieved. When God was grieved, it was because man was unreachable due to his mind being filled with things that opposed God.

We've discussed grieving a few times, particularly in regard to grieving the Holy Spirit. Ephesians 4 speaks about this, warning us not to be like the Gentiles, walking in the futility of their minds and being insensitive to the life of God (Ephesians 4:17-19). Their understanding was darkened, their hearts were numb through hardness, and they lacked feeling. They pursued all manner of lasciviousness with greed. (Ephesians 4:20-24).

Grieving the Spirit is presented as a state of being so absorbed in everything else to the point where you've lost all your feeling towards God. He can't touch you; He can't reach you. This state can befall a Christian who becomes fascinated with worldly problems and various cultural causes.

Being a 'culture' warrior, prioritizing America first, or striving to preserve our 'God-given' country - all of these can distract from Christ. There's a zeal that doesn't necessarily involve direct involvement in evil things, but you're still saturated and captivated by these issues in your imagination. This preoccupation can affect your spiritual life and grieve the Spirit to the point where He can't reach you.

At some point, it does all come back to Satan and his angels, the principalities against which we wrestle. In the times before the flood the renown of these beings impacted the imagination, not only of the general populace but of God's people as well.

But again, this is the first emphasis we see on God's *heart* in the scriptures. God went from declaring everything as good in Genesis 1 and 2 to being grieved and repenting. Incidentally, when we see God repenting, it proves that repentance isn't solely related to sin. It wasn't a sin for God to create man. Repenting, in this context, means to change your mind, and this change leads to a decision to go in another direction.

God declared, **'I will destroy man whom I have created from the face of the earth, both man and beast, and the creeping thing and the birds of the air. '** It repented Him that He had made them. While man continued in his wicked imaginations, oblivious to God's decree, this decree was in God's heart, in His council.

God did have Enoch and the prophets, however. Abel was a prophet, and everyone who came after him in the line of life was a prophet. Noah was a preacher of righteousness, and Enoch testified to the impending judgement.

Enoch knew God was coming to judge all this wickedness. Jude quoted him in his epistle. Jude and Peter also both spoke of the angels who did not keep their first estate but left their own habitation. He reserved them in everlasting chains of darkness for the judgment of the last day. (Jude 1:14-15)

Enoch, the seventh from Adam, prophesied of these events, saying 'Behold, the Lord comes with ten thousands of his saints to execute judgement upon all and convince those that are ungodly among them of all their ungodly deeds which they've ungodly committed

and of all the hard speeches which ungodly sinners have spoken against Him' (Jude 1:14-15). Remember what we saw about Cain's line. We saw speeches against God. Even their names were speeches against God, and the whole culture was full of such speeches (Genesis 4:17-24).

However, in Seth's line, they were calling on the name of the Lord, even in weakness. I believe they were doing so in a good way and walking with Him. There was this relatively narrow group of people that were walking with God. As a whole, the culture was given over to evil. The imaginations of their heart were only evil continually, they were making hard speeches about God, and they were captivated with the Nephilim and with the evil works of fallen angels. God said, 'I'm going to destroy them." Everyone's speaking reflected their hearts. The cursed spoke hard speeches against God from their darkened imaginations. Seth's line called upon the name of the Lord because of their faith. God was grieved in His heart and spoke the judgment of man, and His prophets confirmed His   word.

Chapter 20 God's Positive Focus (Genesis 6)

Gen 6:8-22 But Noah found grace in the eyes of the LORD. (9) These are the generations of Noah: Noah was a just man and perfect in his generations, and Noah walked with God. (10) And Noah begat three sons, Shem, Ham, and Japheth. (11) The earth also was corrupt before God, and the earth was filled with violence. (12) And God looked upon the earth, and, behold, it was corrupt; for all flesh had corrupted his way upon the earth. (13) And God said unto Noah, The end of all flesh is come before me; for the earth is filled with violence through them; and, behold, I will destroy them with the earth. (14) Make thee an ark of gopher wood; rooms shalt thou make in the ark, and shalt pitch it within and without with pitch. (15) And this is the fashion which thou shalt make it of: The length of the ark shall be three hundred cubits, the breadth of it fifty cubits, and the height of it thirty cubits. (16) A window shalt thou make to the ark, and in a cubit shalt thou finish it above; and the door of the ark shalt thou set in the side thereof; with lower, second, and third stories shalt thou make it. (17) And, behold, I, even I, do bring a flood of waters upon the earth, to destroy all flesh, wherein is the breath of life, from under heaven; and every thing that is in the earth shall die. (18) But with thee will I establish my covenant; and thou shalt come into the ark, thou, and thy sons, and thy wife, and thy sons' wives with thee. (19) And of every living thing of all flesh, two of every sort shalt thou bring

into the ark, to keep them alive with thee; they shall be male and female. (20) Of fowls after their kind, and of cattle after their kind, of every creeping thing of the earth after his kind, two of every sort shall come unto thee, to keep them alive. (21) And take thou unto thee of all food that is eaten, and thou shalt gather it to thee; and it shall be for food for thee, and for them. (22) Thus did Noah; according to all that God commanded him, so did he.

Yes, God pronounced His judgment, but even in His grieved heart, His eyes are on His purpose. "But Noah found grace in the eyes of the Lord." God does have a decree of judgment, but He always continues moving forward in life. His focus is positive. We can learn from this because our focus needs to be positive as well. We are like Noah, living in a time when wickedness and transgressions have reached their peak, and people are once again fascinated by the powers of the old world.

"Their imaginations are evil, and the whole earth is filled with wickedness." What is our focus? Is it on the wickedness or on God's move? Remember, Noah found grace in the eyes of the Lord. Do you have grace? You do if you're justified through faith. However, you can grieve the Spirit and become numb to the realities of grace while still walking according to the course of this world. Are you tracking the powers of this world and consumed by them? Noah was not!

'These are the generations of Noah.' Now, this is the third time we see 'the generations of.' The first was 'the generations of the heavens and the earth when God created them.' The second was 'the book of generations of Adam,' man that God created male and female who created them. And we see the genealogy coming out of Adam, we saw that in Genesis 5. Interestingly, in Cain's line there are no generations. Things happen, but there's no book of generations because God does not count them.

This is the book of life. Remember, the Lamb has a book of life (Revelation 21:27) and really, the book of life is based on what God has wrought. It's everything God did. He created, He formed Adam and Eve and then in them, the life came forward. Seth, Abel, Seth, that line that walked with God and knew God and believed in God were all responding to Him. Through them, there was the knowledge of God's promise, His judgments, His purposes. So, they represent God's move (Genesis 6:8-22).

The statement, "These are the generations of Noah" represents the next creative act of God, in a sense. Again, God just, decreed judgment on the whole of the human race and said He's going to destroy all of it. What's God's next move? Is He focused on the judgment? No, now He's working with generations, which speaks of Life, and speaks of the Seed, speaks of Redemption and everything Christ represents including the blessing, the inheritance and the Kingdom God wants to give to man. God is undeterred. Now He recorded Noah and their names.

This is the generations of Noah. Then it says, 'He begat three sons, Shem, Ham, and Japheth.' This is the record of the people that are going to populate the earth after the judgment. Looking forward, we must recognize that God deals with us in a particular way. He sees us in advance and knows us according to the future Good works, and blessings and works of God in our lives as a result of His visitation.

When He was working with Noah, Ham, Japheth, and Shem, He was looking past the flood, and already building the "table of nations" that would be documented in Genesis 10. He was considering the life that would come forth. He was looking into the future. That's how He deals with us. He's always looking toward the future. Noah is all about future thinking. He was going to build an ark to preserve life for the future. Yes, there's a judgment, but God's focus is on life. To walk with God is not to focus on the judgment but to focus on the life. That's where the grace is.

Remember, Noah walked with God. These are the generations of Noah. Noah was a just and perfect man in his genealogy. The only other person we see that it says walked with God was Enoch, and then Adam walked with God in the cool of the day. To walk with God is to have your conversation in this world with God. The only way you can do that is by faith. Faith is a vision of what God has provided and what He is doing.

God had already provided them with quite a bit. They knew about the Fall. They knew how man was created, what he was created for - to express God in His image and likeness and to have dominion. They knew about the Tree of Life, about Eden, the Fall, and God's judgment. Yet, they also knew that God had promised a seed, and that seed is Christ. They believed in Him, and that's how they were justified. They knew that the way God was going to ultimately deal with sin was through blood, and they had an altar. This is the line that walks with God. To walk with

God is to walk by faith, and faith is supplied by a vision that comes from God. That's why we become the representative of God's future, even in a time of judgment where it seems like all God has said is "I'm going to destroy the earth." That's not the case. That's not what He's focused on.

The earth was corrupt before God. The earth was filled with violence. There's one more thing I need to mention. Noah was a just man. He was justified by faith, perfect in his generations. We know that this is, on one hand, a mention of the tampering of the gene pool because the Nephilim are the product of fallen angels who desired to corrupt the gene pool in an attempt to thwart God's plan to bring forth the seed. It's very important that Jesus' genealogy is spotless. His lineage can be traced all the way back to Adam. He is the "Last Adam" (1 Cor 15:45). I'm not referring to moral corruption, but corruption from this Nephilim activity, and also corruption of the line as it relates to the passing of the birthright, which represents God's promise to give man dominion over the works of His hands. Adam was a king, and the line of Seth is a kingly line.

Noah was perfect in his generations. This means that he's directly connected to Adam, free from the blemishes of the genetic alterations happening around him, but also he is the heir of the promise that has been passed down. We even see the re-establishment of the dominion with him in the preparation, as God re-established his dominion over the animals. The gathering of animals by Noah echoes back to the task of Adam, who was to name all the animals as they were presented to him (Genesis 2:19). Noah's role in preserving the animals during the flood is a continuation of the responsibility given to Adam in the garden. (Genesis 6:19-20). But he is also part of the generations of God's work. When God records the generations, it signifies his divine intervention.

The Vision of God's Purpose and the Purification of the Imagination

Noah walks with God. I believe all these elements are interconnected. The generations mentioned in the Book of Life, the generations of the heavens and the earth, which God created, then the generations of Adam and Eve, and finally the generations of Noah - they all represent God's ongoing action to preserve life, even in the face of judgment.

God said unto Noah, 'The end of all flesh has come before me, for the earth is filled with violence through them. Behold, I will destroy them with the earth.' This primarily refers to the Gibborim, the giants, the tyrants, the fallen ones. The earth is filled with violence through them, both directly and indirectly, because they have seized control. They've become men of renown, which means their reputation has spread, captivating the imagination of the people.

Imagination is what we worship. It is okay to use our imagination. However, we need to have a pure imagination filled with thoughts about God's plan. The more we understand about God's heart and His work in redemption, in the New Jerusalem and in the kingdom, the more our imagination is purified. When you read the Bible, please use your imagination.

Cain had no imagination when he considered what God wanted. His offering from the toiled ground showed that his vision was limited to just ordinances and commands. His imagination was polluted. Abel, on the other hand, had a fertile imagination that took into account not only what God said but what God did. The coats of skin that God made by killing an animal left such an impression on Abel that he became a shepherd. That's the power of imagination at work. Your imagination reflects who you want to be and what you aspire to become. It's a form of worship, so it's crucial to be mindful of what fills our imagination. Our imagination should be filled with the things of God, which is quite possible since He has given us so much in His word to ponder.

God decided to destroy everything due to the wickedness that came through the reputation of the men of renown, the Nephilim. Otherwise, He wouldn't have mentioned them. He instructed Noah to make an ark of gopher wood, with rooms inside, and to cover it inside and out with pitch. Interestingly, "pitch" comes from the same Hebrew word for atonement, and it is a type of Christ in the Church. We could get bogged down into the details, like its size and the number of levels, and there's all kinds of symbolism in there that you could pull out. But the main thing is that God set Noah to a positive work in a time of judgment. His imagination was full of details about God's plan, which is a redemptive plan, a saving plan, and a building plan.

God is building something. God has decreed judgment on everything, and yet here's someone building something. There was no rain and there was no such thing as a flood. Noah is working based on a vision no one else can see because he has a pure imagination informed by God's speaking, and yet everything he is doing is deemed useless before men. He was scoffed at while he's building this thing, but he's building for a future because he's walking with God by faith.

We are Noah really, in this age at the end of the age. Noah represents us, and Peter shows us that by saying that the flood of Noah was a type of baptism, which is our answer of a good conscience from God (1 Peter 3:21). It signifies we recognize we are dead to this world and that the world is judged (Genesis 6:13). That's the decree that went out from God, that the flesh is judged. Baptism recognizes that the flesh is judged and there must be a new creation (2 Corinthians 5:17). My life has to be for something other than this world and what's in it.

Yet I can't make anything happen because I'm judged too. It's not that Noah wasn't wicked. We know after the flood he was drunk in his tent. He had that vineyard, he got drunk, he was naked. He was not called righteous because he was good. Justified men are righteous because they believe on him who justifies the ungodly, even though they work not, and their faith is counted to them as righteousness (Rom 4:5). That's what Paul says justification is. They are judged with the human race, but they found grace. The wages of sin is death, but the gift of God is eternal life through Jesus Christ our Lord (Romans 6:23).

We are judged. We kind of get this idea that we've been forgiven and not judged. No, that's not the right view. We've been forgiven and judged. We were crucified with Christ, we were buried with him in baptism into his death, and his death was the death of everybody. That was the ultimate culmination of God's judgment on flesh. "I'm done with it. My spirit is not going to strive with it" (Genesis 6:3), there has to be a new creation, which He created in Christ.

It is a building work that God is doing from the material of Christ himself, in the people who have found grace to walk with God and be justified by faith. We now receive His life, and God begins to do a building work, which is the building up of the Church, which is the vessel that preserves us into the next stage and into the incorruptible Kingdom (Eph 2:21-22; 1 Cor 3:6-10).

So, Noah built, he's told to build all this stuff. I'm going to skip all the details about the floors and the wood. It's worth study but beyond the focus here.

Life and Nourishment

> "Behold, I, even I, do bring a flood of waters to the earth to destroy all flesh where is the breath of life from under heaven and everything in the earth that shall die. But with thee, I will establish my covenant and you will come into the ark, you and your sons and your wife and your sons' wives with thee."

Here's the first use of the word 'covenant' in the Bible. We've already seen the first use of the word 'righteous' or 'just'. He was a just man, which means righteous, which means he was justified by faith. We also see the first word use of the word 'grace' and I think even 'wickedness' is the first time used in Genesis 6.

The Significance of the Covenant

So, it's really pivotal. "I'm going to establish my covenant with you." This covenant, I believe, is the everlasting covenant between the Father and the Son to make Him the shepherd of the sheep. He doesn't really make that covenant with us because we are not parties of the covenant. Christ and the Father are the parties of that covenant.

But he establishes it with us. Who is going to benefit from this covenant? Well, those who are justified by faith, who walk with God, and who have found grace. Now at this time, Enoch, Methuselah, and Lamech are all getting old. We know Methuselah died the year that Noah went into the ark and the flood came.

So really, at this point, Noah is the last left who's walking in grace. It's amazing that how very few, eight people, eight people understood God and were not defiled in their imaginations and overtaken by this world. Remember, Peter said, "If few of the judgment begins in the house of God and a few of the righteous or the right, if the righteous are scarcely saved, what shall happen to the ungodly in the sinner?" (1 Peter 4:17)

The Scarcity of True Believers

I have found as a Christian, a very disappointing realization that there are actually very few who are actually saved. There are so many counterfeits and so many that look like they're saved, and yet when you start really getting into what do they believe about the gospel, you find that they don't believe it. And that's what God's long-suffering is all about. This whole time of Noah building the ark and being a preacher of righteousness is called the time of God's long-suffering. Peter refers to it. In God's long-suffering in the days when he waited, what's he waiting for? Well, he's waiting number one for the ark to be built, but he's waiting for anyone who might repent and get on the ark.

But he already knows what man is. So, judgment is coming far as man is concerned, the end of all things is coming. That's how Noah saw the world. That's how Enoch saw the world. That's how Lamech saw the world. It's how Methuselah saw the world. They named their kids accordingly. But Lamech knew. Lamech named his son Noah, a name which means 'rest'. He hoped Noah would be a comfort, a solace for mankind, easing the toil brought about by the curse. While Enoch had prophesied judgment the people's imaginations were not consumed by this. Instead, they looked forward to the next age, to the comfort that God would bring. Each person hoped that their offspring would be the prophesied 'seed of the woman'.

Lamech likely hoped that Noah would be this seed, the one to destroy the serpent. It is for the purpose of bringing forth Christ that Noah was allowed to live. He found grace and was justified. Justification, especially in the times before Christ, meant being qualified to walk before God, even after judgement had been passed. This grace, this justification, was for the purpose of being part of Christ's kingdom. It was all related to Christ, all Christ-centric.

The only reason Noah, along with the eight souls with him, was allowed to live was because God had made a promise. God was to establish a covenant with Noah. This promise was to make Christ the shepherd of the sheep. Christ would lay down his life for the sheep and bring many sons to glory. This purpose, to bring forth Christ, was the secret in God's heart from eternity past. God was intent on fulfilling this covenant.

When people were justified, when they walked with God and found grace in His sight, it was for this purpose. God said, "I'll establish my covenant with you. You will benefit from this covenant, but my eyes are on the covenant and my eyes are on bringing forth Christ, the seed." Noah found grace in God's eyes and was allowed to build the ark and survive, so that his descendants could populate the earth, ensuring the coming of the seed. God was establishing His covenant with this seed. It was all for Christ.

God commanded Noah to bring into the ark two of every sort of living creature, male and female, to keep them alive. Noah was also to gather all the food that was eaten to sustain both him and the animals. Noah did as God commanded. Noah's obedience was a vision, not the following of an ordinance. There's a difference between blindly following an ordinance because God said so, and having a vision. Noah was a friend of Go; he walked with God, and he understood what God was doing. His heart and his imagination were in sync with this divine vision.

The text appears to be saturated with God's purposes, in contrast to the imagination of the people's hearts, which were only evil continually and the Nephilim. However, Noah's eyes and heart were focused on God, and he walked with God. It was deeper than merely adhering to commandments; it was about following a divine vision.

Of course, Noah obeyed all that God commanded him. Yet, in this context, God's commandment is seen as the forwarding of His vision. It's not about rules and regulations, but about saturating your imagination with a view of God's heart, His desires, and His actions. The things you do in response, naturally align with this vision of God. In essence, you become what you behold.

God's focus here is on life. His instructions to Noah were geared towards preserving life: building an ark for safety, and gathering food to keep the occupants nourished. You might wonder, what did Noah do during the flood? The flood lasted for ten months. Yes, it rained for forty days, but Noah was in that ark for ten months. A large part of his time would have been spent feeding animals and ensuring there were enough food supplies. This act of providing nourishment to all these animals demonstrates a form of stewardship, aimed at keeping them alive and sustaining them.

Nourishment During Judgment

This reminds me of how God often focuses on nourishment during time of judgmentnt. In Revelation 12, during the tribulation, God takes the Jews to the wilderness to nourish them. During the time when God judged Egypt and brought Israel out with a mighty hand, His focus was on the nourishment of the children of Israel. He provided them with a diet of manna. Nourishment, in this context, is synonymous with knowing Christ.

We see that during times of judgement, there is usually a famine. This is a time when people's imaginations are polluted because they lack spiritual food. The Word of God is restricted, which can sometimes be a form of judgement. However, during these times, God provides those who know His grace with a feast and nourishes them.

There is a stark contrast between Noah and those perishing. Noah, his household, and all who were with him, symbolized by the animals, were being nourished while everyone else was perishing. Death and destruction were upon the people due to God's judgements, but life was granted to Noah and his family through nourishment.

So, what do we do when we know that we're at the end? We know that the Lord is coming, His judgements are starting to manifest on the earth, and we are aware of the impending conclusion. Do we focus on that? No. Our focus should be on the edification of the body of Christ, which is achieved through nourishment. We feast on the Word, especially in these end times.

The stuff happening outside, I'm less and less aware. Somebody asked me, as I am a wedding musician, what my stance was on the Equality Act. To be honest, I hadn't been paying much attention to it. It's been like this in the wedding market for years. All my advertisers have rules about discrimination. What I do is I trust myself to the Lord and take it on a case-by-case scenario. I just trust Him to save me, preserve me, and guide me.

I'm not here to take a stand against anything. I really am not. I'm not trying to change anything. We know the writing is on the wall. What are we focused on? We're focused on nourishing and preserving life. If you want to discuss commandments, this is it. The commandment is eternal life (John 12:50). This is the commandment Jesus received from His father, that He may give life to the sheep (John 10:17-18). He lays His life down for the sheep (John 10:11). That's the commandment Jesus said He received from the Father, and it's called the new commandment, which is true in Him and also in you (John 13:34).

The darkness is passing; the true light now shines for us. The light is already shining. We're already in the eighth day, already in the next day. We're already past the flood and the judgments. We're already preserved from it. We are nourishing ourselves in Christ and being kept alive while everyone else is being delivered over.

The main thing that marks and separates out God's people at this time is the building of the ark and the food. There has to be building and nourishment, and they go together. The body of Christ is built up by speaking the truth to one another in love (Ephesians 4:15). It's being filled with the Word of Christ, with wisdom. Let His word dwell in you richly in wisdom, teaching and admonishing one another (Colossians 3:16), and even speaking to one another in hymns, psalms, and spiritual songs (Ephesians 5:19).

There's a fellowship that grows richer and richer. If you want to say what was going on in the ark, you know, the last seven days, Noah was putting the animals in the ark. It took him seven days to get everyone in there. What were they doing in there, waiting for the judgment? They were being nourished. You might think that must have been miserable, but in type, it represents the Church and our feast.

We are sitting at the table in the presence of God's enemies, and He has set a feast in front of us. That feast is Christ, and He is our nourishment, our supply. The more we focus on Him and enjoy Him together, the more we are preserved and made alive at a time when there's judgment everywhere. We have joy on our faces.

Gen 7:1-24 And the LORD said unto Noah, Come thou and all thy house into the ark; for thee have I seen righteous before me in this generation. (2) Of every clean beast thou shalt take to thee by sevens, the male and his female: and of beasts that are not clean by two, the male and his female. (3) Of fowls also of the air by sevens, the male and the female; to keep seed alive upon the face of all the earth. (4) For yet seven days, and I will cause it to rain upon the earth forty days and forty nights; and every living substance that I have made will I destroy from off the face of the earth. (5) And Noah did according unto all that the LORD commanded him. (6) And Noah was six hundred years old when the flood of waters was upon the earth. (7) And Noah went in, and his sons, and his wife, and his sons' wives with him, into the ark, because of the waters of the flood. (8) Of clean beasts, and of beasts that are not clean, and of fowls, and of every thing that creepeth upon the earth, (9) There went in two and two unto Noah into the ark, the male and the female, as God had commanded Noah. (10) And it came to pass after seven days, that the waters of the flood were upon the earth. (11) In the six hundredth year of Noah's life, in the second month, the seventeenth day of the month, the same day were all the fountains of the great deep broken up, and the windows of heaven were opened. (12) And the rain was upon the earth forty days and forty nights. (13) In

the selfsame day entered Noah, and Shem, and Ham, and Japheth, the sons of Noah, and Noah's wife, and the three wives of his sons with them, into the ark; (14) They, and every beast after his kind, and all the cattle after their kind, and every creeping thing that creepeth upon the earth after his kind, and every fowl after his kind, every bird of every sort. (15) And they went in unto Noah into the ark, two and two of all flesh, wherein is the breath of life. (16) And they that went in, went in male and female of all flesh, as God had commanded him: and the LORD shut him in. (17) And the flood was forty days upon the earth; and the waters increased, and bare up the ark, and it was lift up above the earth. (18) And the waters prevailed, and were increased greatly upon the earth; and the ark went upon the face of the waters. (19) And the waters prevailed exceedingly upon the earth; and all the high hills, that were under the whole heaven, were covered. (20) Fifteen cubits upward did the waters prevail; and the mountains were covered. (21) And all flesh died that moved upon the earth, both of fowl, and of cattle, and of beast, and of every creeping thing that creepeth upon the earth, and every man: (22) All in whose nostrils was the breath of life, of all that was in the dry land, died. (23) And every living substance was destroyed which was upon the face of the ground, both man, and cattle, and the creeping things, and the fowl of the heaven; and they were destroyed from the earth: and Noah only remained alive, and they that were with him in the ark. (24) And the waters prevailed upon the earth an hundred and fifty days.

We are still in the flood account. We already know that the Lord commanded the flood as a judgment. In Genesis 6, we saw that the hearts of men, and their imaginations were "only evil continually." Noah was chosen to build an ark and was separated because he found grace in God's eyes and was justified by faith. He walked with God, just like Abel, Enoch, Methuselah, and everyone in the line of life in Genesis 5. They all had these characteristics. They were justified by faith, found grace in God's eyes, and walked with God.

Noah is the first one in that line who seems to have been given a specific task (at least according to what we have in the account). The emphasis in Genesis 5 was on life and multiplication, and now Noah, the culmination of that line, is told to build an ark and he's given a lot of specifics.

A Focus on Life

In Genesis 7, we will see references to the passage of time. It is important to remember that God does not give us a lot of documentation regarding the works on the line of life, because the only works He is concerned with are those that multiply forward and preserve *life*. Noah was told to build an ark to keep creatures *alive* during the time of judgment. Everything is going to be judged, including all of Cain's works and the cities he built. The entire world system created by the line of Cain in Genesis 4 will be washed away in judgment. Noah's work of building the ark is about salvation and life, which is what is on God's heart. Yes, Noah did a work for God, but it was the culmination of the line of life. His work was to preserve the seed.

Remember, Noah was chosen because of his genealogy and his faith (Gen 6:8-9). Regarding his genealogy, he is in the line of the heir, which is Christ, representing the promise God made to the woman in Genesis 3:15. Noah's genealogy also represents God's move to intervene with grace when judgment has been decreed.

In Genesis 3, there was a judgment because man had taken from the tree of knowledge of good and evil. But God's response was to promise the woman a seed who would crush the head of the serpent. He covered Adam and Eve with skins so that they remained alive. The animal that was slain was a substitute for their life. God intervened with a promise and an action related to life. Adam responded to God's work and promise by calling the woman Eve, the "mother of all *living*."

Cain and Abel's story follows, with Cain choosing the opposite of life by murdering Abel. However, Abel's blood "speaks" even though he is dead (Heb 11:4, 12:24, 4:10). Seth comes to replace Abel in Genesis 5, and in this genealogy there is also a focus on life, with many children and naming them in the line of life. There is little evidence of what they did, but we know they had an altar. Abel had an altar, and Noah, as we will see in Genesis 8, also built an altar and presented burnt offerings.

Burnt offerings are a special offering in the Old Testament, related in a sense to sin, but there is a focus on the "fat portion" and the sweet savor (which means the smell of the burning fat). There were different types of offerings, and as Christians we are familiar with the trespass offering and the sin offering. These are related to dealing with sins so that one can live and not die. But the burnt offering signifies one's *life* before God, and we need a substitute for this as well.

Leviticus mentions various offerings, each representing different aspects of the accomplishment of Christ's death (Leviticus 1-7). Some argue that the victory of Christ was only His resurrection, but the Bible presents the cross as a victory (1 Corinthians 15:54-57). The cross is where Christ spoiled the principalities and made an open show of them, triumphing over them (Colossians 2:15). It is where He made peace, created the new man, and defeated Satan (Ephesians 2:15-16). The cross is His accomplishment. The burnt offering represents Christ's work, not just for forgiveness but to become one's whole *life*. Because of this aspect of Christ's offering, we are, in our living, a fragrance of Christ unto God (2 Corinthians 2:15). It is a sweet smelling savor that was entirely for God and not related to sin (Ephesians 5:2). It is a picture of Christ's satisfying life lived for the glory of the Father (John 17:4), and the aroma goes up continually to God as a fragrance on all those in whom Christ *lives*.

Note that there is an accumulative record of "practices" of the people in Genesis. For example, Enos, Seth's son, was born in the time when people began to "call upon the name" of the Lord. Enos means weakness, and their calling upon the Lord was a recognition of their weakness, mortality and need before God and a sign that their hope was in God and His move in life and His seed. This becomes a walk with God. Enoch walked with God. We walk with God, which means we walk by calling upon the name of the Lord, acknowledging our need for Him, and relying on His strength in our weakness. This is the walk on the line of life, and that is what it means to walk with God.

They also had an altar. Abel's offering was of the firstling of the flock and the "fat portion." This is a "burnt offering." The altar with the fat portion signifies that our life must be Christ, and we exchange ourselves for Him, and it is his aroma that ascends to the Father and is pleasing to Him, not our own. Living in hope concerning the seed of the woman and recognizing our weakness while placing our hope in God, living by faith in Christ as a way to be pleasing to God, calling upon His name. This is how we live.

We live by calling on the name of the Lord, and when you call in the name of the Lord, that represents that God is everything that you're not. What is He? He's whatever name He presents Himself as. God revealed names for Himself in the Old Testament to show what He was to the people. For example Abraham called on Jehovah Jireh, that means the Lord is my provider. Some called Him Jehovah Rapha, the Lord is my healer. He is the thing you're calling on, you're calling on him to be in you what you need. That's how they lived in their weakness, in the midst of the judgment all around them. Enoch knew the judgment that was coming and he prophesied about it. They knew that the wicked generation around them was headed for judgment. They knew their own weakness and inability to do anything and they looked to the Lord to deliver them. Today the name of God is represented as Jesus which means Jehovah Saves. He is our salvation and we call upon Him.

The wicked came out of Cain's line, seeking to be justified by works first and foremost. And then Cain is known by all these outward works and the things he built.

The works that the line of life produced did not seem useful to man. They didn't have any value to man, but they were valuable to God. Calling on the name of the Lord in weakness, walking with God, and living by faith in Christ - this doesn't look very useful. We are on the line of life as Christians. We need to stay on it. We do have works, but they're not the kind of works that really are for the benefit of the world. They're first and foremost works seen by God, but obscured in the eyes of the world. The world doesn't value anything we do.

Religious people don't value our works. They say we don't work, and in a way, we don't. We are recognizing our weakness. We are calling on the name of the Lord. We are living by faith in Him. We're covered with the righteousness of Christ, and we are living by faith in Him and presenting ourselves in Him to God and trusting that He makes us a fragrance of God, a fragrance of Christ unto God. This is our "offering" and our "altar." He is a fragrance in us to God, and that's why God satisfied us. It's all based on Christ.

To the world, that looks like not working, but to God, those are the works that He accepts. They're hidden, um, but then eventually they are manifest. There is a manifested work, and that's what Noah represents. Noah's building work was the *manifestation* of the line of life. It was like the culmination of all their hopes and expectations that God would preserve life and that He is to keep life alive in spite of judgment and in the day of judgment.

This line from Adam and Eve to Abel, to Seth to Noah is about keeping life alive and preserving life because of judgment. That was all that was on their mind. They should have been judged, but God covered them with the skins. He substituted the animal in their place, and then they lived in hope of the seed of the woman. Adam called the woman Eve, the mother of all "living." It's all focused on life, keeping alive.

Against this, there is a backdrop of judgment. You have to have an offering to deal with God because you need to be justified. That's related to judgment. You need to present the offering on the altar with the fat portion to live before God, and to have your life. It's not just about preserving your life, but for your life to be enjoyable to God and satisfying to Him. That's an offering too, and that is also a picture of Christ. Christ is your justification, and He's your sanctification. He's the beginning and the end of the Christian life.

Preserving Life

> **Gen 7:1-3 And the LORD said unto Noah, Come thou and all thy house into the ark; for thee have I seen righteous before me in this generation. (2) Of every clean beast thou shalt take to thee by sevens, the male and his female: and of beasts that are not clean by two, the male and his female. (3) Of fowls also of the air by sevens, the male and the female; to keep seed alive upon the face of all the earth.**

So from the beginning with the sacrifice of a lamb to cover Adam and Eve, it was about preserving life, and now at the end of this line before the flood, it's about preserving life. Noah is told to take animals after their kind. Noah is told to bring them into the boat, why? To keep them alive, and then food for nourishment. The ark was a place of life. Everything outside the ark is death and not mentioned, but washed away by the flood. When we stand before Christ, the works of the world will be burned up in the fire.

The ark was a benefit only to those that were justified by faith at that time, you know, because they were on the ark. The only benefits of the Ark are for those who are on the ark and are participating in God's salvation. So we have to have a view of works related to life. Cain thought that God would reward him for the toil of his hands, digging in the ground from the cursed earth and bringing forth food from the sweat of his faith. So he offered that, thinking God would reward his hard work. And yet, all of those things he toiled in were a result of the the fall and not God's focus at all. God's focus was on bringing forth the seed and making a way for man to be brought back to God and brought back into the rest where he wouldn't have to toil.

There's nothing virtuous in toiling away under the curse in the sweat of your brow. That's just what you got to do to survive. So many people believe that God should reward them for this kind of toil. No, the ones that are remembered, the book of generations, are the works of those who had the offering and the altar, who cried out to the Lord in the midst of their weakness and hoped in the seed that would come, knew that the world was under judgment and looked to a deliverance. That's it. And yet their generations are counted, and the passage of time is counted with them, whereas in Cain's line, with all its record of their works, the passage of time is not marked.

Brought to Rest

This is what Noah, whose name means *rest*, really represents, bringing man back to God. Lamech named him and said, "Because this one will comfort us from all over our toil because of the curse." See, we don't recognize our suffering as particularly virtuous. We recognize it as a byproduct of the fall, and our focus is on how is God going to comfort us. So we call in the name of the Lord in our weakness, and we look to Him, and we expect, we desire Him to bring us into rest. And that's what He wants. That's actually what He wants. He wants to bring us into rest.

That's what shepherding (1 Peter 5:2) is like. Consider the reward mentioned by Peter. Peter says, 'Shepherd the flock of God which is amongst you, serving as overseers, not by compulsion but willingly, yet not aggressively, but gently; nor for dishonest gain, but eagerly; nor as being lords over those entrusted to you, but exemplary; and when the Lord appears, you will receive the crown of glory not readily fading away.' (1 Peter 5:2-4) Now, I happen to believe that's for everybody who has any part in building up the body and edifying the saints, not 'pastors' who lord themselves over the flock. Shepherding and bringing people into rest is the opposite of being lords over their faith and lording it over the flock and putting them under the law and making demands on them (Matthew 20:25-26, 1 Peter 5:3). What does a shepherd do? He leads me beside still waters and he makes me lie down his rod and staff comfort me. Even when I go through the valley of the shadow of death (Psalm 23:4) he feeds and nourishes me (John 21:15-17). He restores my soul (Psalm 23:3), I go astray, but he bore all my iniquities (Isaiah 53:4-6). He's shepherding me into glory (John 10:27-29), he's shepherding me into rest (Hebrews 4:1-11), he's making me lie down. Surely goodness and mercy shall follow me (Psalm 23:6), he makes the table for me in the presence of my enemies (Psalm 23:5). I don't have to worry about anything (Philippians 4:6-7). The Lord is my shepherd, I shall not want. A shepherd shepherds (John 10:11), a shepherd points to the chief shepherd (1 Peter 5:4), and the chief shepherd's job is to bring you into rest (Hebrews 13:20)

This is what the ark represents. Noah represents rest. And if you go with Noah, you're going to be brought to rest. And he's been given to comfort the people because of all the toil on the earth. That's what Lamech said. Noah is doing a work, but it's a work related to Christ, to the preserving of life, to the forwarding of the redemptive plan, to salvation. Not putting burdens on people, and lording it over their faith and all that, but witnessing to Christ's righteousness and showing the way to salvation and preserving people alive. It's not Noah's fault that no one got on the ark other than the eight, you know, but he did get all the animals, and the animals, in a sense, are a picture of us.

That's what I'd like to emphasize with the flood. Man is wicked, he's judged. God repented that he made him. There's no hope. All of the works that are done are in vain. They're all going to be destroyed, washed away in the flood and not remembered. The only work that counts is to believe in the promise and to be justified by faith in the blood and to present Christ on the altar to God as a burnt offering, knowing that He is satisfying to Him and He is my life. I may be weak but I am calling on the name of the Lord in that weakness and walking with God by faith, knowing that the world is judged and everything under it is vain, everything on it is vain, and knowing that God is going to preserve us alive and responding to that.

Noah's Response is Obedience to a Vision

Noah's obedience, was his response to his vision that he saw God's heart. Just like Abel becoming a shepherd. He became a shepherd to offer the lamb, the firstling of the flock with the fat portion. It shows us that he had a vision of God's heart. He looked past the literal of what God said externally, related to the sorrow and the suffering and the toil, which Cain only saw, and looked to God's heart and considered the fact that God had spared Adam and Eve and covered them with the skins. And that caused him, that so affected him, that he became a shepherd. We know he's a prophet. Prophets become shepherds. If you have a vision of Christ and you understand His heart, then you're going to have a shepherding heart. You understand that God's intention is to bring people into rest.

This is the culmination of the line of life. Lamech knew, God is going to comfort us concerning all this toil. That's why he named Noah "rest." Noah's work is related to bringing life, preserving life, and bringing salvation, and bringing them into rest. When we get to Genesis 8 and he's on dry land, we will see that God actually lifted the curse off the earth. There's a specific mention. So, in type, the new ground that Noah lands on represents the rest of God.

Rest is freedom from the curse and the toil. What does it mean to rest? It means I am not living as a slave anymore, in debt to God because of my transgressions, toiling away to preserve myself and thinking that's virtuous. Rest means I'm trusting Christ to provide everything and even bless me, even though I'm one of the sinners,. Even though I was of the world that was judged, I found grace in His eyes, and I was saved, and preserved and nourished and fed and brought into rest. That's really what it means to be in rest. I'm not responding to my sin by toiling away, I'm calling on the name of the Lord, walking with God, and being shepherded and shepherding others into rest.

When Cain went out from the presence of God, his response to his alienation was to build. He built a city and named it after his son Enoch, and then his descendants built the world system. They built and built and built, and those are dead works because they come from a sense of alienation from God, a sense of debt, a sense of needing to justify themselves and make a name for themselves and have their own glory because they don't get glory from God. That's what dead works are, really.

Seth's line has no record of any of that kind of stuff. They just call on the name of the Lord in weakness and believe in His promise. And then out of that line does come a building work, the ark, but it's really to salvation and life. And out of our line as the church comes a building, which is the church. The church is a building, and it is produced by vision, by people who simply are being built up in the faith. Faith is a vision. The way the church is built up is in the faith. We're rooted and grounded in faith, and we're built up in faith and in love. That is not the work of our hands. That is us being regulated by seeing God's heart and knowing His love. And then that nourishes and supplies us, and it makes us participants in His shepherding work to bring people into rest. And that's what Noah was doing. He was shepherding people into rest. He shepherded the eight into rest, as well as all the animals. That was a shepherding work.

If you've been tracking with all these messages, you definitely get the point. So then, Genesis 7, we see God repeating Himself. He's already decreed that Noah is going to get on the ark in Genesis 6, but then He says it again in Chapter 7, but there are some distinctions. In Genesis 6, there were two of every kind, animals of every kind. In Genesis 7, there is a distinction between clean and unclean animals. And the clean animals get seven. There are seven of each clean animal on the ark, and two of the unclean.

Genesis 7:2-3 - "Of every clean beast thou shalt take to thee by sevens, the male and his female: and of beasts that are not clean two, the male and his female. Seven days shall there be no rain; and yet will I require a account of thee in respect of every beast, and of every fowl after their kind; and of every thing that creepeth upon the earth after his kind." 2. Genesis 7:4 - "For yet seven days, and I will cause it to rain upon the earth forty days and forty nights; and every living substance that I have made will I destroy from off the face of the earth." 3. Genesis 7:10 - "And it came to pass after seven days, that the waters of the flood were upon the earth." 7. Genesis 8:4 - "And the ark rested in the seventh month, on the seventeenth day of the month, upon the mountains of Ararat." 9. Genesis 8:10 - "And he

stayed yet other seven days; and again he sent forth the dove out of the ark." 10. Genesis 8:12 - "And he stayed yet other seven days; and sent forth the dove; and she returned not again unto him any more."

When you see a chapter full of sevens, like the book of Revelation is full of sevens, there's a specific emphasis on the fullness of God's work. For example, in Revelation 15, there are seven angels with seven plagues, which are the last of the judgments of God before the end of the age. These seven plagues are poured out from seven golden bowls, and they correspond to the seven seals and seven trumpets that have already been opened and sounded in earlier chapters. You could spend a life time just collecting the sevens in the Bible and you'll see that its one of God's favorite numbers!

The Work of God

The ark is a work of God and has His signature all over it. Also there are all kinds of specific references to time in Genesis 7 and 8. There's 40 days, seven days, and then it'll rain, and then 40 days the water was on the earth, but then 150 days the water was covered the face of the earth, and then another 40 days, and it goes on and on. They were on the ark for a long time. Yes, it rained for 40 days and 40 nights, but actually they were in that ark for months and months.

In other words, all of a sudden in this Genesis narrative that has had not much specific detail related to works, there really has not been much for the line of life. Suddenly we have a highly detailed account, with many markers of time and structure, starting in Genesis 6 with all the detail about the ark. It's got one window and three floors, and it's covered with pitch, and there's all these details. We don't see this level of detail in Genesis 5. Genesis 5 is like a sketch but here we have a painting with tons of detail. You're dealing with the work of God, there's all kinds of detail, and God provides the plan, the blueprint, when He talks about His salvation in life. When you're talking about the good works which we were prepared for, which are related to the building of the body of Christ, which is actually a shepherding work, there is a lot of detail!

In Ephesians, there's a high vision full of detail provided by God. It's not up to you to figure it out; it's all furnished. So we need a spirit of wisdom and revelation. In Ephesians 1:10, it says that God desires to make known to us the mystery of His will with a view unto an administration of the fullest times to head up all things in Christ. The way He heads up everything in Christ is to make Him head over all things to the church. So the church, we do have a work. We do participate in the building and the administration of the fullest times to head up all things in Christ by the building up of the church over which He is head over all things. The church being built up is our work, as the ark was Noah's work. Both of these works speak to the same thing - the building up of the rest of God and man, and both of them are the culmination of the line of life - walking with God, calling on Him in weakness, relying fully on Him and living because of Christ.

People want to talk about works and rewards, but works that God rewards are related to building. Those are the only works that are not vain, those are the only works that won't be burned up, and they are related to a shepherding work to bring people into rest. That's what we're doing. We're taking the burdens off of people. We're here to comfort people because of the toil.

Noah didn't have the capability of taking the toil away from people. The judgment did that. People think judgment is a negative thing, but as Christians we should see it as the removal of the toil and all the works and all the death and all of the sin, and our being brought into rest. Noah didn't have the capability of doing any of that but he did have the capability of pointing them to the ark and saying, "Get in, there's food in there." The main focus was that he was to bring food in there to keep everybody alive.

In the ark, there's no toiling away to dig in the ground and from the sweat of your face to bring forth food. It's already there. You enjoy the provision that's already been supplied by God's commandment. That's our life in the spirit, and shepherding points people to food. Christ is the food. I hope you're getting the point that this is all a picture of Christ and His salvation, and we need to see Noah in the light of grace, and we need to see his work as a picture of our work in the church, which is related to preserving life, bringing people into rest, and supplying them with food.

If you're not supplying food, if you're not bringing people into rest, but you're sending them out to toil you're doing an evil work of scattering. Remember Jesus said "He who does not gather with Me scatters" (Mt 12:30). If Noah had been building on the ark, standing by the ark, telling people, "Hey, you need to get to work out in the field, you better be toiling, because judgment is coming!" They definitely wouldn't have known to get on the ark. No, he told them, "Get on the ark." In fact, the very thing he was telling them to do was to stop their work and come rest. That was his gospel. "Come, get on the ark. Everything you need is in there. It's been provided for you." Anybody who would have gotten on the ark would have benefited from somebody else's work, work that had been finished.

That's why in this chapter, in Genesis 7 there is such a prevalence of the number seven because the emphasis is that this is God's work. Yes, He had a man to do it because Noah is also a picture of Christ in that regard. But Christis really the man through whom God has accomplished His work, and that work is to shepherd us into rest and provide for us, to keep us alive, to save us, to make us pleasing to Him, and to feed and build us up to become a vessel to express Him and contain Him, to be full of life. Noah's ark was a vessel full of life in a world of death, and the only works that mattered are related to that vessel, either getting on it, building it in the first place, or getting on it and helping to feed the animals, which is a shepherding work.

Works on the Ark

I guess if you were on there, there were probably tasks related to feeding. What else are you gonna do? They were on that ark for a year. You think, "What did they do?" Well, it's a lot of work to feed the animals and keep them alive. Noah was in charge of their life, just like Christ is in charge of our life. But the work is related to feeding the animals with the provision that's already been put there in advance. The provision was all on the ark before God shut the door. It was based on the enjoyment of the provision and the food and the feeding and the distribution of the food, the stewardship in the ark was based on what had already been supplied.

We are not developing anything of our own. We're not coming up with our own food. It's already all in the ark. It's the riches of Christ. And yes, in the ark, we have a stewardship to keep the animals alive and keep them in a state of comfort and rest while God carries the ark. Meanwhile, God is preserving the whole thing, just like God is building the church. God is the one who delivered Noah. God is the one who saved everybody in the ark, saved them from the judgment, and used the ark as a means to transport them into the new world. And He's the one who governed when the water would abate and making sure that the ark didn't get destroyed. Noah had no power over that.

All Noah had power to do in the ark, was to keep animals alive and keep them nourished. That's our work. God's work is to save, and our work is to make sure everybody is feeding on His salvation. And we can't force anybody to eat, but we can distribute food. So that's our work.

There are good works in the New Testament, but you have to see it in the light of what God's doing. It's not random. Noah didn't tell people, "Okay, you toiled really good in the field. I watched you, so you get a stateroom in the ark." None of the works that are related to the curse are mentioned or profitable when it comes to the ark. Once you're on the ark, none of that stuff is referenced anymore.

It's a whole new day. And that's where we are. We see we're already in the ark. We know that's a picture of the time of the end. But getting in the ark and getting the ark ready and being in the ark really is our whole Christian life.

We got in when we were justified. We are in God's salvation. We are in His building. And now our work is really this nourishing and preserving of life.

Distinguishing Clean and Unclean

The Lord says, "Come, and all thy house into the ark, for thee have I seen righteous before me in this generation. Of every clean beast, you shall take to thee by sevens, male and female, and of beasts that are not clean by two." (Genesis 7:1-2) In the last chapter, we saw two of every kind. Now, we're seeing a distinction between clean and unclean. First of all, that is a distinction that we don't know how Noah made. Later, God has given us information regarding what is considered clean and unclean. In Leviticus, it is defined for us that animals that chew the cud are considered clean, while those that do not chew the cud are considered unclean. (Leviticus 11:3) This distinction is related to how they eat. The focus here is on nourishment and supply, which is what we are doing in the church. Even in God's salvation and within the church, there are vessels of honor and dishonor, clean and unclean, based on how they eat.

Christ is our nourishment, and the word is our nourishment. A clean animal, such as a cow, has multiple stomachs and chews its food multiple times to fully digest it. This may sound gross, but it allows all the nutrients in the food to become a washing and a real nourishment to the animal. They are washed inwardly and assimilate the new nourishment from the food they eat. On the other hand, unclean animals like dogs barely digest their food and will eat anything without distinguishing what they are eating or how they are eating it. They just eat it and it goes right through their system. This is why they are considered unclean.

Jesus warned us not to give that which is holy to the dogs and not to give our treasures to swine, which are two examples of unclean animals. They cannot take it or digest it. (Matthew 7:6) The difference between those who are on milk and those who are on meat is how they handle the word. Do they make distinctions in the word between what is truly their food and what is not?

Cain did not distinguish what God had said. He barely paid attention and offered his toil without understanding the significance. Abel, on the other hand, meditated on what God said and did, and his response to the word showed that he thoroughly digested everything. He became a shepherd, understanding the nature of God and his intentions. We are not just taking commandments and obeying them. We are sitting at the feet of Jesus, assimilating his word and being washed by it until it transforms us into something else.

Noah, as the culmination of the line of life, had a vision and responded to it. He knew the significance of finding grace in God's eyes and understood the judgment on the world. He knew that an offering was required and how man was justified. His response to the word was the obedience of faith. It was a work of faith because it was based on a vision laid out by God. Our response to this vision is God's work in us, which comes to us as food. The food cleanses us, and how we eat makes us clean.

Even on the ark, God preserved clean animals and saved them. He preferred to have more clean animals than unclean animals. Clean animals could be offered on the altar, which is why Noah offered seven clean animals after the flood. They were presentable, holy, and acceptable. Similarly, when we present ourselves to God, we are clean. Our reasonable service of worship is to present ourselves as living sacrifices, holy and acceptable. This is based entirely on the vision we have received and "digested."

The unclean animals on the ark, however, indiscriminately ate whatever they found without meditating on it. They are like members of the body of Christ without vision, and the word is not nourishment to them. They cannot handle spiritual things. Clean animals, on the other hand, are related to spiritual things. They can be offered on the altar.

The unclean animals, like the raven could live in the time of judgment by eating the flesh of carcasses. It did not have to come back to the ark. The dove, a clean animal, found no rest for the soles of its feet and returned to the ark. This is a picture of a double-minded person who can listen to grace messages and then go listen to law messages, thinking there must be a balance between the two. They are not digesting anything and have no rest. They are always under condemnation because they eat everything without distinguishing what kind of food they are consuming. They are not digesting Christ as their food.

A "clean animal" understands that presenting oneself to God as a living sacrifice means knowing that we are dead with Christ and risen with Him. We know we are holy and acceptable. A clean person gets free from condemnation by digesting what they eat, digesting Christ as their food. We are clean animals on the altar presenting ourselves as a "living sacrifice" to God, holy and acceptable (Rom 12:1-3).

The first thing we see on the ark is there's this distinction between the clean and the unclean. Remember that both were on the ark, so we are not saying that unclean means "unsaved". Only Noah would have understood a distinction between clean and unclean. The world perishing outside certainly wouldn't know. They just knew there were people getting on the ark, but God does make a distinction in the house.

We need to understand if someone's clean or not because it affects how we deal with them and what kind of food we give. Jesus said, "Don't give your treasure to the swine and the dog because they're going to turn around on you." That means I need to be able to discern who's a swine and a dog and not give them the choice portions. A dog really shouldn't get steak from the table if he'll eat the cardboard box instead. It doesn't mean they're not in the house, but when it comes to shepherding, this has to do with knowing someone's state, knowing whether they're in rest, knowing if they can enter rest, and knowing if they can take it and giving them accordingly.

Noah is a shepherd, and I guess those family members would have been shepherds with him in the ark. To shepherd just means to feed and keep everybody alive. There's a distinction between clean and unclean, but that's not for us to make a judgment and say, "Well, you're gonna be punished." No, because everybody on the ark, clean and unclean, gets saved and brought through. When it comes to how do I feed you and what are you going to respond to, there is a distinction for shepherds to make between clean and unclean. Again, who would have known what clean and unclean means? In those days, the book of Leviticus had not been written. Noah knew, and he's the one that mattered because he's in charge of keeping everybody alive. A shepherd makes a distinction between clean and unclean for the purpose of his shepherding, not for making judgments.

How do Ravens Respond?

We are going to quickly "zip" through chapters seven and eight while maintaining the emphasis that this is a picture of the building of God, and in the building, the work is about shepherding and nourishing. In the building, the saved people are either clean or unclean depending on how they respond to the nourishment. And that's really related to the vision of Christ as our life, Christ as our food, Chris as our drink. He's not only my justification, he's also my sanctification. He's my whole life. He becomes the clean animals that are able to be offered on the altar and become a pleasing aroma to God. Meaning that they are a burnt offering.

It says in chapter 8 that he offers them as a burnt offering. A burnt offering means that Christ is the aroma.

Right? We are the fragrance of Christ unto God. We are accepted based on Him and we're satisfying to God based on Him, meaning we're saturated with Him. And it's because we're clean animals. We've been digesting Him, we've been washed with Him. He is our element, and we're filled with Him. Practically, that means when I'm in the Word, I'm making a distinction, I'm rightly dividing, and I'm looking for Christ, and I'm feeding on Him. I'm being satisfied and refreshed in Him. I'm being shepherded by Him. I'm being brought into rest by Him, and I'm really enjoying it. And that makes me an aroma pleasing to God, not because of me, but because of Christ in me.

So, there is a distinction. There are vessels of honor and vessels of dishonor in the house, and it's all about being a clean animal. We need to be careful what we eat and how we eat. That's the work on the ark. Either you're shepherding and feeding others, or you're making sure that you're eating right. And that's there's nothing else to do on the ark. I don't want to keep going ahead, but later we learn there's only one window in the ark, and it faced heaven. While the ark was floating, everything on the earth was death, and there were dead bodies floating all over the place. That's what the ravens ate when Noah was trying to determine if there was dry land.

Noah opened that window and sent out a raven, and the raven didn't come back because it found food. It went circling the earth. But then he sent out a dove, and the dove did come back because it didn't find food. Why? Because it was a clean animal. It's not going to eat death. But Noah, being a picture of us, doesn't know the condition of the earth. He doesn't know if the water has abated or not because he's only got one window, and it's facing heaven. In the ark, our eyes are single in Christ Matthew 6:22-23 (KJV).

> "The light of the body is the eye: if therefore thine eye be single, thy whole body shall be full of light. But if thine eye be evil, thy whole body shall be full of darkness. If therefore the light that is in thee be darkness, how great is that darkness!"

We're really not supposed to be so consumed with the world. The only thing we are recognizing is the difference between life and death. We are focused on our shepherding and on the animals. We're focused on the nourishing supply of Christ and clean animals in their response. We can measure how the world is doing by *how the ravens respond.* We do have some unclean ones among us, and they go out from us and they don't come back because they find death to feed on.

There are plenty of people that have disappeared from our YouTube channels, and you know that they're over there on those death channels, listening to the slanderers and the accusers, not distinguishing between clean and unclean, not distinguishing the kind of food they're eating, and they're back on the commandment works channels because they couldn't figure it out. They didn't have a vision. Well, that tells me something about the temperature out there. I don't know how everything's going out there. I try not to look. I've learned don't go to the other channels and listen to what they're saying and read their comments on their walls. But you can tell if someone's unclean on your channel. You can see, "That guy cannot seem to arrive at a spiritual conclusion." You know that he's a raven. You know that when he goes out, he's probably not gonna come back. You can see it. Whereas the ones that are really getting it and are feeding on Christ, you can see that they're clean. You know that they may go out, but they'll always come back because they're not gonna find rest out there.

It's interesting that the raven went to and fro. It didn't find rest, but it found food out there. What did it find? Dead carcasses. Whereas the dove found neither food or rest and had to come back. The dove came back because it can't live on carcasses. Someone who is clean knows what rest is, knows what nourishment is, and knows where it is.

So, I don't worry too much about "ravens" when you're dealing with a bunch of people. We go through seasons, sometimes of dryness spiritually speaking, and when we're dry, the flesh comes out, and you can see some people start to act out in their flesh. Sometimes people are really worried about it, "Oh my gosh, what are we gonna do about this person?" But I know that they're clean animals, and that the food in them and the vision that's in them and the way they eat, I know they're not gonna find any rest out there, and I know they're not gonna find any food.

So, even if they kind of depart for a little bit because they're in a season of dryness, I know they'll be back. And I don't have to go get them. I don't have to go beg them, "Hey, how are you doing? Do you need me to pray for you?" You know, the Lord's got them because they're clean animals. The only way to become a clean animal is by being shepherded by the Lord and nourished by Him. This proves that we have a high priest who takes care of us. In our shepherding work we are also clean animals in the sense that we recognize God's work. To be able to recognize a clean animal as someone who truly digests Christ and knows how to rest in Him means that I have to be a clean animal. Only someone who is clean can discern between clean and unclean.

The clean animals ultimately won't depart, even though they may have to fly out for a little bit. We all get restless, you know. So, that's just a word if you've got people you're taking care of. If you know that there's a good solid basis in the truth and they know that Christ is their life, you don't have to worry too much because everybody wanders, but they'll come back and you can rest. Look at Noah. He let the raven out and he let the dove out of the boat, but he stayed at rest. He didn't know what was going on out there. He would just kind of know by whether he saw the raven again or whether he saw the dove again. But he knew that the dove was a clean animal. He knew that the dove would come back. You don't have to worry about it. The Lord takes care of His own.

So, on the one hand, yes, we are shepherds and we're feeding and there's work, but it's all God's work. That's why there are so many sevens in chapter seven. Seven is the number of God's work in rest. God is the one working. He's the one preserving everybody alive. We have a part to play, something to do, so we're not bored out of our minds. There is an enjoyment in it. Our satisfaction comes from enjoying this work of God, and this is our service. Just like

Adam and Eve in the garden, they were given work to tend the garden, but it was all a matter of cultivating what God was already producing. That's all Noah was doing in the ark with the animals!

Chapter 22 Recognizing Our Place in God's Work. Shepherding Nourishing and Building(Genesis 7)

The Ark: A Type of Christ and the Church

The point that we saw so far is that the ark is a place of life and nourishment. It's a type of Christ and the church, and we are on the ark today. We're on the real ark, and the building work is the culmination of the line of life.

The service to God results in a building work, which is a work of preservation. Noah built the ark according to the vision related to God's judgment but also related to the preservation of life. The reason life is going to be preserved is strictly because of the mercy of God, due to the everlasting covenant between the Father and the Son. The Son, who is the heir of all things, will be born into humanity and will defeat Satan, crush the head of the serpent, and restore the way to the Tree of Life for those who believe.

As we have seen, those who believed walked with God and believed in the promise of the woman's seed. They believed in the message behind the altar where they offered the offerings, understanding that death, resurrection, and bloodshed were necessary for them to stand before God and be reconciled to Him. This was the way to approach God and, ultimately, the way back into Eden. They called on the name of the Lord out of their weakness. The line of life in Genesis 5 culminates with Noah, the last of the line whose name means rest. He is given a task to build, the only one in that line given a work to accomplish, related to shepherding the animals and those who would come into the ark to preserve them.

The Line of Life: Acknowledging Weakness and God's Judgment

Initially, Adam fell, and as a result, sin and death entered the world. The earth was cursed for their sake, and they were cast out of the Garden of Eden, destined to return to the dust of the ground. However, God showed mercy and comfort to the descendants of Adam by sending Noah, whose name means "comfort and rest." Through Noah, God would give them respite from the toil caused by the cursed ground. The line of life accepted the judgment they were living under, while the line of Cain rejected it. The latter believed that their toil on the ground, a result of the curse, was an acceptable offering to God. Cain tried to offer up the fruit of the ground to God, showing that he did not understand the nature of the situation and rejected the basic premise that things are not the way they're supposed to be. When he went out from the presence of God, everything he did was to build and develop things to mitigate the effects of the curse. However, the line of life acknowledged that we suffer in this world because of sin. This acknowledgment is also crucial for us, as it involves recognizing our weakness and God's judgment on the flesh.

Then there's another judgment, which is that "man has just become flesh, and I even repented that I made him." Every imagination of his heart is evil continually. That's true of everyone. The only way to be found and find grace in God's eyes, which Noah did and so did all those in the line of life, is to be justified by faith, to believe God's promise. And then from that kind of walk of faith, issues a work, and it's a building work for the preservation of life. Everything on Noah's ark passed through the judgment and remained, right? Well, that's what we are doing in the church. We are producing the building of God as we walk in faith, which is the church. And in the church, the building work is preservation. In fact, everything wrought in the church that's of faith, of gold, silver, and precious stones, is something that will survive the fire. See, then the world was judged with water, but now the world's going to be judged with fire. And everything that passes through the fire and remains with us will be the result of this building work, with incorruptible materials. Noah built with his hands. He built a wooden ark, which was a picture. But we have the reality, which is Christ in the church. There is a building work, and that building work can only be produced by those who walk in the line of life. God didn't go to Cain's line and say, "Build an ark." No, He went to Noah, who walked with God, found grace in His eyes, and was a just man who was justified by faith. He had the altar; he called on the name of the Lord in weakness. He had an acknowledgment that they lived in the conditions that they did. His name meant God's going to comfort us concerning the cursed ground.

It was cursed for our sake because of our sin. There's an ownership there. We own the fact that we suffer in this life due to sin. We don't have an idealistic view that we can fix it and make it all better. And see, religion does that. Religion tells you that if you walk right with God, you're not going to suffer. You know, you can mitigate the curse, especially if you build up our systems, you can mitigate the suffering. You'll be blessed. But with the line of life, there comes basic acceptance. I'm weak, I'm in a fallen world. There's sin, there's consequences, and I live with them. And yet, I have a rest and comfort because I'm looking forward past the flood, past the judgment, into what remains. And my life is built of things that will remain. Like Jesus said, you know, put your treasures where your heart is. Your treasure will be where your treasure is. So put...don't build your treasures on the earth where moth and rust will corrupt, but put them in heaven. That's the next age. Noah, in his building work, was preparing for the next age. And everything he did was about preserving things into the next stage and remain, which in a sense were a reward to him when the flood was passed and he came out on dry ground. The animals coming out, the food coming out, and then the blessed situation he was in was a reward of rest. God even rolled back the curse, as we'll see, and blessed and restored the dominion over the animals like in Eden. It's a type. They landed on the day of resurrection. They're brought into this new era as the result of a building work.

Building Work: Preserving Life for the Next Age

Similarly, church is being built up to preserve us in life into our next stage. And the fire is going to test all the works, and everything that is not of that building work is going to perish and just be burned off.

Noah probably had all kinds of stuff in his house that didn't make it into the ark. He was 600 years old when he entered the ark. 600 years is a lot of time to do stuff. How much of it do you think made it into the ark? Space was a factor, right? And he's a builder, so who knows? Maybe he had built things before. Maybe he left a wooden rocking horse that he had made for Tubal-Kane as a favor. The point is, there's all kinds of stuff we do that's not going to make it through. That's just part of life. Our Christian life is a full spectrum picture of what it means to walk by faith. We call on the name of the Lord in weakness, having an altar in Christ Himself. He is our offering and our justification. As we walk with God, He reveals to us the judgment on this world and the blessed state of the saints in the future. Out of this revelation comes a building work, where we become a blessing to others and bring them into the ark. It is both a shepherding work and a building work.

Everything that is in the ark passes through the flood, remaining incorruptible and untouched by the fire that tests all works. Our service in God's building is preserved, and what remains after the fire is our reward. It is a reward that belongs to Christ, but He shares it with us. We each have our reward because we have planted and watered.

Noah, however, does not have a right to do anything or inherit anything. He is included with those who have been judged in the time of the flood. He is under the curse of sin and part of the generation that is described as "all flesh" with every imagination of the heart being evil continually. Those who came out of the boat are also under the same condition.

Noah found grace in God's eyes. He was justified by faith, preserved from the judgment, not for his sake, but for the sake of the seed. The ark was built to keep the seed alive, including the seed of all the animals and, ultimately, the seed of Christ. The covenant between the Father and the Son is established, and we are beneficiaries of that covenant.

Noah's building of the ark was a proclamation of righteousness. He preached while he built, and his building itself was a form of preaching. In the same way, we build by speaking. The gifts given to the church are for the perfecting of the saints and the building of the body of Christ. All members participate in the ministry by speaking the truth to one another in love (Eph 4:11-16.

In the line of life, as seen in Genesis 5, the naming of the children was prophetic. The names described the generation they lived in and what was happening on the earth. It also reflected God's promise and the fact that He is the one saving them. When the names are put together, they spell out a sentence that speaks of the appointed man's mortal sorrow and the blessed God descending to bring an end to our lament and bring us into rest.

And that's the only work we see in the line of life versus all Cain's works. All Cain's works are perish, right? Cain's line in Genesis 4 was full of works, but Noah's line or

Seth's line was full of life and speaking and believing and walking with God.

Eventually, that produces a kind of building work. But even that work is a speaking work because we're told that Noah is a preacher of righteousness, yet we don't see him say anything about what his building work was. His speaking and his speaking was his building, and that is also a type of what we do. And that building work is shepherding. It shepherds people onto the ark as we speak of Christ and we speak of the seed that was promised and what he accomplished. And we speak of his blood and the way for sin to be dealt with. Men are brought to God and are made a part of this building. They are regenerated, and they're even washed and transformed. And that is all God's work, and yet it's attributed to us as our remaining fruit. He gives us a part in it as a privilege. Jesus is the one who gave his life. All we're doing is speaking about what he did. We do suffer for it. There's a fellow partaking of his suffering. Paul said, "I fill up in my body that which is lacking of the afflictions of Christ for his body's sake, which is the church, which I became a minister according to the dispensation of God, which is given to me to preach this mystery, which is Christ in you, the hope of glory" (Col 1:24-27).

There is suffering because we're persecuted, and so was Noah. We suffer because of what we are in the world, and we've judged ourselves, and we agree with God's judgment. We've been living with a sense of futility as Noah did for the last hundred years while he was building that ark. His life meant nothing. You know, he knows everything's gonna perish, so why build it? Why do anything in a sense? And yet he's singularly focused on the building work of God to bring people, and nobody would come except the eight. Those eight had to all be involved in the building, even if they weren't directly using the hammer and nails when the ark was being built. When they were on the boat, they would have had a responsibility to nourish the animals, everything.

Once you're on the ark, everything is about keeping alive and giving life-giving food and nourishment. And Jesus said to us, you know, who is that faithful steward to whom the Father will or the Master will appoint head of his household to give meat in season? And he said, "Blessed is he who he finds doing that when he comes. He'll sit down and gird himself and serve them" (Lk 12:42-44). My prayer has always been in this last couple years, "Lord, grant me the mercy to be found giving meat in season."

Noah's Generation

There are two groups of people. There are people who are offended and not giving out any food, and people who are really giving out the food and doing the building work to preserve life. And they're doing an incorruptible work of building to build the ark, the church, you know? But you first have to accept the judgment. Judging ourselves is represented by baptism. If you don't accept God's judgment, you will not build an ark, you'll continue building something out in the world.

And I said, there's this, you know, in the so-called grace community, there are people that do not accept the judgment. They're enemies of the cross. They don't believe that the flood is for them. They believe it's for "those people out there." They believe there's something good in them that qualified them to be on the ark. No, God condemned all flesh, including Noah's.

Noah's Flood is about preserving life for the next age, which will be rewarded. But it's also a picture of baptism (1 Peter 3:20-21). Peter told us that it's a sign of baptism where we are separate, we are reckoned as dead and buried in the tomb. The Noah that came out on the other side is, in type, a new Noah. He lived 600 years before the flood, and Genesis 6 says, **"These are the generations of Noah. And he had Ham, Shem, and Japheth... "**

"Whenever God says, "These are the generations of something," it is as if He is saying, 'Now I'm going to show you who this person is' (Genesis 2:4). There are several statements of Generations in the first chapters of Genesis. 'These are the generations of Adam' (Genesis 5:1). Then the next one is, 'These are the generations of Noah' (Genesis 6:9). But it's interesting because after the flood, it shows up again in Genesis 10:1, 'These are the generations of Noah' (Genesis 10:1).

> **Genesis 10:1: "Now this is the genealogy of the sons of Noah: Shem, Ham, and Japheth. And sons were born to them after the flood."**

Baptism and New Creation

Why does Noah get two mentions of his generation? In a figure, he died and was risen. The flood was his baptism into a new sphere with a new start. The Noah and his life was left under the water, and the new Noah and his life lands on dry ground on the seventh day of the second month, which, incidentally turns out to be is the day Jesus Christ resurrected. The day of resurrection is the new creation.

So Noah acknowledged that this was his death. He didn't bring his rocking horse and all the different things he made in his life, his 600 years of walking with God, or his 600 years, of living in the old creation. All came to an end in the ark, and whatever came out of the ark is something new, on a new day, with a new situation, a new group of people. 8 people came out, and 8 is the number of resurrections, the beginning of a new day or week after the 7th. The church celebrates the lord's table on the day of resurrection, the 8th day, not the 7th day (sabbath).

What was preserved in the ark is the "remaining fruit" of Noah. We recognize that God has judged everything we do, good and bad. It's all under the water, buried. And the only thing worthy of being rewarded is that which is preserved through the building and shepherding work that we do to nourish those on the ark, to shepherd people onto the ark, and to build the ark, which is all our preaching of righteousness. Noah was a preacher of righteousness. What is righteousness? Christ is the righteousness, the seed, and the blood, the one who is the heir with whom the covenant was cut. Remember, the surviving world is for Christ. Noah was righteous – because he believed the testimony concerning the Seed, which is Christ. And Noah was perfect in his genealogy, which means he was the proper vessel for furthering the propagation of the seed, which is Christ. It is Christ who will inherit everything on this side of the flood!

The reason why the human race is even preserved is because Christ, the seed of Noah, is the heir of all things, and God is going to bring him forth. He is also the Savior and his blood reconciles us to God. And it is faith in him that justifies it. And that's what Noah would have preached. Same gospel. The gospel has not changed. It's just that in each generation, God has moved forward with his plan so that where we stand today is different than when Noah stood.

Now we're members of the body of Christ. Now we've received the Spirit, the life-giving Spirit of Christ. The Spirit of Jesus Christ has regenerated us. We are members of the real ark, the real building of God, and we're being built together as a habitation of God in spirit (Eph 2:21-22). And this is our vessel to carry us into the next age. And those that we build with today and nourish with life will be with us on the other side, and they are our fruit and our reward. And yet we didn't do anything. All we did was point to Christ and his work, and he is the reality. It's his life that supplies him. He's the food. Yes, Noah became a steward in the ark, and so did the other of the eight to feed the animals. But the food is Christ. He's the one who supplies them with the nourishment. He is the nourishment.

And he's their righteousness. He's their qualification to be on the ark. He's the only reason they exist. Otherwise, they would have all been destroyed in the flood. Again, God repented that he made man, and the only reason he made an ark was to preserve the seed alive so that Christ could come. And everything going forward is for Christ's sake.

And after Noah's account, there's again two chapters, Genesis chapter 10, chapter 11 .This will be the account of Noah's descendants, and only one line is the just line Shem's line, that God remembers. And first, they show the works of Ham, the descendants of Ham and Japheth. It's very much again

like Genesis four and five and we'll see their works and we'll see Nimrod come out of that and Canaan and all the enemies of God will come out of Ham. Japheth is ambiguous, he's somewhat on Ham's line but he also dwells in the tents of Shem. He has some salvific inheritance aspect to his inheritance, but Shem's line is the focus and Christ comes out of Shem's line. Shem's line will produce Abraham, with whom God again promised and established his covenant, the everlasting covenant that he refers to all through Genesis 7, 8, the everlasting covenant

The Everlasting Covenant: Christ as the Heir of All Things Preface

The Everlasting Covenant makes Christ the heir, and it's for the sake of that covenant that we're alive today. Even the people who aren't being saved, the only reason they live is because of the covenant that God made not to flood the earth again, and that's for the sake of the seed and to bring forth Christ. It's the only reason we exist. Everything is Christ, and Christ is everything. It's fundamental that we would understand the judgment. The flood judged everything good and bad, wiping it all away, and God's decree on us is the imagination of our hearts from youth is evil. We have no trust in our own righteousness. We're still walking on this line of life; we call in the name of the Lord in weakness, aware of our mortality, aware that the only way that we can be justified and stand before Him is through the blood and by faith in the seed.

And that issues in a walk that produces the building. This walk has its works and its reward, but what kind of works? Building, nourishing, and shepherding work. That's not our work, but Christ Himself the Great Shepherd of the Sheep (according to the Everlasting Covenant – Heb 13:21). What is our part in it is the preaching of righteousness. We speak the truth to one another in love. And what truth is that? It's the truth of who Christ is. That's what Noah would have preached; that's what everybody on the line of life preached. They preached Christ, not themselves.

Chapter 23 – remembered for Christ's sake (Genesis 8)

Genesis 8:1-22 KJV And God remembered Noah, and every living thing, and all the cattle that was with him in the ark: and God made a wind to pass over the earth, and the waters asswaged; (2) The fountains also of the deep and the windows of heaven were stopped, and the rain from heaven was restrained; (3) And the waters returned from off the earth continually: and after the end of the hundred and fifty days the waters were abated. (4) And the ark rested in the seventh month, on the seventeenth day of the month, upon the mountains of Ararat. (5) And the waters decreased continually until the tenth month: in the tenth month, on the first day of the month, were the tops of the mountains seen. (6) And it came to pass at the end of forty days, that Noah opened the window of the ark which he had made: (7) And he sent forth a raven, which went forth to and fro, until the waters were dried up from off the earth. (8) Also he sent forth a dove from him, to see if the waters were abated from off the face of the ground; (9) But the dove found no rest for the sole of her foot, and she returned unto him into the ark, for the waters were on the face of the whole earth: then he put forth his hand, and took her, and pulled her in unto him into the ark. (10) And he stayed yet other seven days; and again he sent forth the dove out of the ark; (11) And the dove came in to him in the evening; and, lo, in her mouth

was an olive leaf pluckt off: so Noah knew that the waters were abated from off the earth. (12) And he stayed yet other seven days; and sent forth the dove; which returned not again unto him any more. (13) And it came to pass in the six hundredth and first year, in the first month, the first day of the month, the waters were dried up from off the earth: and Noah removed the covering of the ark, and looked, and, behold, the face of the ground was dry. (14) And in the second month, on the seven and twentieth day of the month, was the earth dried. (15) And God spake unto Noah, saying, (16) Go forth of the ark, thou, and thy wife, and thy sons, and thy sons' wives with thee. (17) Bring forth with thee every living thing that is with thee, of all flesh, both of fowl, and of cattle, and of every creeping thing that creepeth upon the earth; that they may breed abundantly in the earth, and be fruitful, and multiply upon the earth. (18) And Noah went forth, and his sons, and his wife, and his sons' wives with him: (19) Every beast, every creeping thing, and every fowl, and whatsoever creepeth upon the earth, after their kinds, went forth out of the ark. (20) And Noah builded an altar unto the LORD; and took of every clean beast, and of every clean fowl, and offered burnt offerings on the altar. (21) And the LORD smelled a sweet savour; and the LORD said in his heart, I will not again curse the ground any more for man's sake; for the imagination of man's heart is evil from his youth; neither will I again smite any more every thing living, as I have done. (22) While the earth remaineth, seedtime and harvest, and cold and heat, and summer and winter, and day and night shall not cease.

As a picture, we see that everything living is in the ark. The focus is on life - on keeping alive, preserving, and nourishing. The animals are in there, and the food is in there. And it's just interesting that God has this emphasis on food gathering in times of judgment. In the Bible, when there is judgment, there are often famines in the land. And we know that God said He's going to send a famine, not for food, but for the word (Amos 8:11). And yet, in the midst of the famine, God always provides for His people.

And I've always believed that before we go home, there will be a time of refreshing for those who are abiding in Christ. And that refreshing is really their eyes being on the prophetic word which they have. They do well to heed it as a light that shines in the darkness until the day breaks and the morning star rises in their heart (2 Peter 1:19). So the word is the lamp, and the word is the food, and the word is the nourishment until Christ appears. And we know from Ephesians that He washes the church. He said He washes us with the washing of the water of the word (Ephesians 5:25-27). He sanctifies us through the washing of the water of the word to present the bride to Himself. And yet, we know that in the world and in religion, there's a famine for the word.

It's sad that people say they never heard the gospel, 1 Corinthians 15:1-4, until they came to YouTube, even after 40 years in Christianity. You can't hear the undiluted gospel in churches because there's a famine for the word. There's plenty of Bible, but there's a difference between Bible and the word. The word focuses on Christ. Christ is the word. You can come to the Bible and not come away with Christ. It really depends on what you're looking for. The Bible is not food for you if you're not seeing Christ in it.

Jesus said, "You search the Scriptures daily and think that in them you have life" (John 5:39). If the word was spirit and life apart from Christ, then why would He say, "But you won't come to me that you may have life" (John 5:40)? They're searching the Scriptures. Christ is the word, right? Yes, Christ is the word. So we come to Christ, and then the word becomes spirit and life to the degree that it ministers Christ to us. And that's got to do with where our heart is turned. If our heart is not turned to the Lord, but we are just focused on ourselves, then we don't see Christ. But if our heart is turned to the Lord, it says, "We all, with unveiled face, beholding as in a mirror the glory of the Lord, are being transformed into the same image from glory to glory, even as by the Lord's Spirit" (2 Corinthians 3:18). The Spirit does the work of ministering Christ to us through the word, and that's our food. And in this time of judgment, we are in a time of judgment, just like Noah was, even though the judgment hadn't occurred yet. He was preparing for it by putting animals in the ark and bringing food in to sustain them. Now he's in the ark during the flood.

The Significance of Being Remembered by God

It says, "God remembered Noah and every living thing and all the cattle that was with him on the ark" (Genesis 8:1). This is the first time the word "remembered" appears in the Bible. God remembered. And if you look through the Scriptures, you'll see that whenever God remembers somebody, it's preparing for a significant move. For example, well, here, if we do cross-references, He remembered Abraham and sent Lot out of Sodom and Gomorrah (Genesis 19:29). He did that for Abraham's sake, right? He remembered Rachel and hearkened to open her womb (Genesis 30:22).

he idea is that time is passing and judgments are coming, and yet something adverse to the promise is happening. And so God remembers. And when God remembers, it's not like He forgot. It means He's specifically focusing on His purpose with that person. The Israelites were in Egypt for 400 years. That was all part of God's plan, but it was a place of affliction for them. He heard their groaning, and God remembered His covenant with Abraham, Isaac, and Jacob (Exodus 2:24). It's significant to be remembered by God. In Malachi, it says that there will come a time when everybody is speaking hard speeches against God and saying, "Who will show us any good?" And these sinners get away with anything, you know? And then it says, "Those who knew the Lord spoke often to each other about Him, and a book of remembrance was written about them. Their names were put in a book of remembrance, and God said, 'They will make up my jewels. They will be jewels of my crown when I put this all on display,' meaning the redemption of His people" (Malachi 3:16-17).

Being remembered by God means that you're part of His purpose. And we've seen that God has a book of generations of His works and His people. There's the book of generations of the heavens and the earth, which God made, and the book of the generations of Adam, in the line of life. And we'll see the book of generations of Noah's descendants. It's significant what God remembers. It means that He's acting on our behalf based on a memorial of some kind, something that He's pointing to. And it's always for the sake of His covenant. It's for the sake of His Son. It's the sake of Christ.

God remembered Noah because of the covenant He's going to establish with him, which is the everlasting covenant, between God and the Son, between the Father and the Son that makes Him theHeir of all things. Everything God is doing anytime He moves forward in His program and does something for people, it's because of the covenant and it's because of Christ. That's what He's focused on. When it comes to baptism,you know, the flood washed away everything that wasn't for the purpose of bringing forth Christ. That's why Noah found grace in God's eyes. He was perfect in his genealogy and he lived by faith and walked with God. The faith was, of course, Christ. Christ is the content of the faith. And remember again, Cain and Abel, the difference between the way they looked at the Word. Abel saw Christ, Cain did not. Cain represents the famine of the Word and Abel represents our feast. Praise God if you looked at Christ and you say, "Look, I don't want anything but Him," you are in that moment remembered of God. You are in the list of people remembered by God. And when God moves, it's in your favor.

That's why all things are working together for our good. It's because of Christ. We're co-heirs with Christ. It's for Christ's sake. And so we need to have our focus on Him. And again, the point of baptism is that everything but Christ is done away with. Christ is the one raised from the dead. We are raised together with Him as part of a new creation created in Him. He created it on the cross and brought it forth in resurrection.

Noah's ark lands on the seventh month, on the 17th day of the month. And that is the day when Jesus was resurrected (Genesis 8:4). God remembered Noah and every living thing (Genesis 8:1). And see, we live before God, even though we're dead. We're dead to this world, we're dead to sin, we're dead to the law, we're dead to the principalities, we're dead to Satan, dead to our reputation, and dead to everything that's under the flood, under everything that got buried is gone. Our past is under the waters. And how does God remember us? He remembers us as the living in the ark. To live before God, to be alive before Him means that He remembers you and that you're accounted among the living, and your name is remembered.

To be dead before God means that He doesn't remember you at all. And that's how those who don't have Christ, ultimately they will be forgotten. They are not remembered. The scripture pretty much bears it out. And that's why the scripture says, "You come to know God, or rather, be known by God" (Galatians 4:9). We are known by Him. And all over, think about it, the whole earth was covered in judgment. Nothing is alive. And yet, there's this, in the scheme of things, a very tiny little wooden boat on the water. I mean, it was big, it's the size of an aircraft carrier. But if you look at the whole earth, it's covered by water. It would have been a speck. And yet, God's focus is on that speck. You know, God is interested in what He and the people He remembers. And He does remember you.

And He does it for Christ's sake. Just like He remembers Noah for Christ's sake.

With baptism, the point is that your whole purpose is Christ. You have no right to exist apart from Christ. At this point, nobody had a right to exist. God had repented that He made man. The judgment was that every imagination of man's heart is evil continually. But because God has a covenant, which He said He was going to establish with Noah (for the sake of Christ), and because God still has the purpose of bringing forth the seed, and when God promises something, He will surely bring it to pass. Noah lives.

You have to see that you are for Christ. Otherwise, you would just stay in the tomb or not even be in the tomb - you'd be under the water. Noah is for Christ. We're for Christ, whether we want it or not. It's not about whether you feel spiritual. When you are in the ark, you are remembered by God. And what God does is for you. This is how it is in Christ, regardless of our condition, mood, or spirituality. God is still working all things together for our good. Nothing can separate us from the love of God, which is in Christ. There is nothing that can work adversely to His purpose - it all works for His purpose. God's love and remembrance of us is unswerving and immutable.

Noah's name is "rest." This means we can realize that nothing can stop God's good intention for us. If we are in those names that He remembers and we're in the book of life, then God is for us, no matter what our condition and what our mood. God remembered Noah and every living thing, and made a wind to pass over the earth, and the waters assuaged. This wind reminds me of Genesis 1, where God's Spirit hovered over the waters. Why does He do it? Because He responds to judgment with life. Whenever Satan does something and everything has to be destroyed, God's intention is to side with life. He is forwarding the purpose of His kingdom and subjects His creation to Christ and those who stand with Him in the end. Regardless of the fact that the earth fell and we became evil, we are remembered.

He mentions here the seventh month on the 17th day of the month. Now, that's according to this earthly calendar, but in Exodus, God established a new calendar when Israel was brought out of Egypt and into the wilderness (Exodus 12:2). The seventh month became the first month of this new Levitical calendar. We know that according to the feasts, Christ rose on the 17th day of the seventh month, which is the 17th day of the first month of the new calendar. This is how we arrive at the significance of this date.

God's timetable is not according to the old creation, but rather the new creation in Christ. When the ark comes to rest on Ararat, which means "the curse is reversed," it is on the day of Christ's resurrection. This is a picture of how we come to rest in the blessing, remembered by God, with all that He does for our good and for Christ's sake.

Rest is not just about us not doing, but about God manifesting the works He ordained, despite our human fallenness and condition. He deals with us according to His covenant with Christ and His remembrance of us as those alive in the ark, even when we feel spiritually dead. God looks at us as being with Noah, who represents Christ. He remembers Noah, and therefore remembers us, working for our sake because of Christ.

When all is deemed dead and no one can do anything of value, God still deals with us from His perspective - not because of our sins and history, but because we are with Christ and remembered by Him. These are the days when God is operating, bringing His rest and redemption. Even when we intervene, like Noah building the ark, God is reckoning us as being on that ark, where His care and provision are focused.

This is the part of the story where Noah sends out the raven, and we know that the raven found food out there, so it wasn't time. The raven didn't come back. But then he sends out the dove three times, and the dove finally comes back with an olive branch, meaning now we know that there's life out there and it's sustainable. So God spoke to Noah in verse 15 and said, **"Go forth from the ark, you and your wife and your sons and your sons' wives with thee. Bring forth with thee every living thing that is with thee, of all flesh, both fowl and cattle and every creeping thing that creepeth upon the earth, that they may breed abundantly in the earth and be fruitful and multiply upon the earth."**

That sounds very similar to what God said to Adam, right? Noah is standing in Adam's place, a sort of "second Adam" in a new Eden, and He is a figure of Christ, the Last Adam, and the Second Man.

(18) And Noah went forth, and his sons, and his wife, and his sons' wives with him: (19) Every beast, every creeping thing, and every fowl, and whatsoever creepeth upon the earth, after

their kinds, went forth out of the ark. (20) And Noah builded an altar unto the LORD; and took of every clean beast, and of every clean fowl, and offered burnt offerings on the altar. (21) And the LORD smelled a sweet savour; and the LORD said in his heart, I will not again curse the ground any more for man's sake; for the imagination of man's heart is evil from his youth; neither will I again smite any more every thing living, as I have done. (22) While the earth remaineth, seedtime and harvest, and cold and heat, and summer and winter, and day and night shall not cease.

The Burnt Offering: Christ's Life for the Father's Delight

As we've seen, the burnt offering is a picture of Christ, representing His living fully for the Father's delight. This reflects the union and love within the Triune God, which is the basis for God's preservation of life. It is God's satisfaction with His Son that allows Him to continue working among men.

This is why Adam and Eve were not killed immediately - God covered their sin with an animal's life. It is also why Noah was preserved alive during the flood, for Christ's sake. Noah acknowledged this by offering a burnt offering, recognizing that his relationship with Christ qualified him for God's blessings, not his own condition.

After the flood, God blessed Noah and his sons, telling them to "be fruitful and multiply and replenish the earth." This "replenishing" suggests there may have been a previous judgment and destruction, before God started moving for Christ's sake to re-establish mankind.

Just as with Adam and Eve, Noah was given authority and dominion over the earth and its creatures. This represents a new creation, a restoration of what was lost due to the fall. God swore He would never again curse the ground, and established a covenant with the sign of the rainbow. The reason the tribulation ends is because of this covenant and God's purpose in Christ.

Throughout, we see God's work centered on Christ - preserving life, rolling back the curse, and blessing mankind, not because of their own merit, but because of their relationship to the One God remembers. This points to the ultimate fulfillment in Christ, for whom and through whom all things are made and sustained.

In Matthew 24 we are told there will be great tribulation on the earth, never such as never has been or ever shall be. And all flesh would not perish or all flesh would be saved except for the elect's sake because of God's remembrance. He's going to cut the tribulation short. This is the same kind of reasoning. God preserves life. His focus is to bring forth good and blessing for his people because of Christ. That has not changed. So, we just need to flip the script and remember that yes, God judged, but his focus is life for Christ's sake.

Chapter 24 – Dry Ground and the Everlasting Covenant (Chapter 9)

Genesis 9:1-17 KJV And God blessed Noah and his sons, and said unto them, Be fruitful, and multiply, and replenish the earth. (2) And the fear of you and the dread of you shall be upon every beast of the earth, and upon every fowl of the air, upon all that moveth upon the earth, and upon all the fishes of the sea; into your hand are they delivered. (3) Every moving thing that liveth shall be meat for you; even as the green herb have I given you all things. (4) But flesh with the life thereof, which is the blood thereof, shall ye not eat. (5) And surely your blood of your lives will I require; at the hand of every beast will I require it, and at the hand of man; at the hand of every man's brother will I require the life of man. (6) Whoso sheddeth man's blood, by man shall his blood be shed: for in the image of God made he man. (7) And you, be ye fruitful, and multiply; bring forth abundantly in the earth, and multiply therein. (8) And God spake unto Noah, and to his sons with him, saying, (9) And I, behold, I establish my covenant with you, and with your seed after you; (10) And with every living creature that is with you, of the fowl, of the cattle, and of every beast of the earth with you; from all that go out of the ark, to every beast of the earth. (11) And I will establish my covenant with you; neither shall all flesh be cut off any more by the waters of a flood; neither shall there any more be a flood to destroy the earth. (12)

And God said, This is the token of the covenant which I make between me and you and every living creature that is with you, for perpetual generations: (13) I do set my bow in the cloud, and it shall be for a token of a covenant between me and the earth. (14) And it shall come to pass, when I bring a cloud over the earth, that the bow shall be seen in the cloud: (15) And I will remember my covenant, which is between me and you and every living creature of all flesh; and the waters shall no more become a flood to destroy all flesh. (16) And the bow shall be in the cloud; and I will look upon it, that I may remember the everlasting covenant between God and every living creature of all flesh that is upon the earth. (17) And God said unto Noah, This is the token of the covenant, which I have established between me and all flesh that is upon the earth.

The flood is over. Noah's on dry ground. And again, it's like baptism. Peter's the one who tells us to look at it like baptism and that it's a demand of a good conscience before God (1 Peter 3:21). Baptism is not something that cleanses the filthiness of the flesh, but it's a demand of a good conscience before God. I used to think that that meant the demand is on us to provide God with satisfying our conscience by obeying Him to be baptized. But when I studied Peter this time around, I saw that actually the demand is from us to God.

When we get baptized, we are demanding - we are identifying with the Lord's death, and the termination of our past, and our sinful state, and our condition, and any consideration of it. We are demanding that our conscience line up. "Lord, I agree with you That I've been crucified with Christ, buried with him in baptism, raised together to walk in newness of life (Romans 6:4), and that Christ is my life now. And Christ is my righteousness. And if you've been baptized into Christ, you've also put him on (Galatians 3:27)."

Christ is the one that God now deals with to deal with us. Christ is the son of his love. There is no reason for Christ to have a guilty conscience of any kind, and he has actually credited that to us. So when we recognize our identification with Christ in baptism, we are actually demanding from God a good conscience. We're saying "I demand that my conscience line up. I'm not going to stand on the ground of trying to merit something, that's based on a reality that's been buried in the flood."

God's Indirect Dealings through Christ, the Ark

Remember, God repented that he made man there at the flood and destroyed them all. The only reason Noah comes forth is as a type of Christ and as the incubator for Christ to carry on the seed, to keep the seed alive. Everything going forward is Christ. God's purpose and his story in the Old Testament going forward will all be about God bringing forth the seed and securing the realm that he'll rule, the kingdom, and giving him the covenants and the promise. There are some major covenants: one in this chapter having to do with the fact that God's never going to judge the earth again because Christ's kingdom needs a footstool. Then, there's the covenant of Abraham that gives them specific blessing of multiplication in land, and then there's a covenant of David that gives him resurrection as the sonship as a man to be, that the seed of David would be uplifted, to be Glorified as God's son. Out of that comes the high priesthood of Christ, his identification with the body, and his kingship. So everything in the stories is about Christ going forward if that's what God is focused on.

It's always in spite of human failures, human condition and human failing. That's what grace is. God's grace is God dealing with Christ instead of dealing with us. That started at the flood when Noah got on the ark, which is a type of Christ. God didn't deal with Noah directly in the flood. He dealt with the boat. If the boat was safe, Noah was safe. The boat was what was above the waters. The boat was what was not submerged. The boat was what landed.

Noah didn't land. The boat did. Noah was in the boat. God preserved that boat, and that boat is a type of Christ, and we've been baptized into him. He's landed on dry ground, which is the resurrection and the new creation and the kingdom and righteousness, peace, and joy in the Holy Spirit (Romans 14:17). All of that is ours because we're in Christ. His condition is our condition.

The way God deals with us it's as if we are Christ because he deals with Christ. He deals with us indirectly. Some people don't like that. They don't understand it. They want God to deal with them directly as if it's your personal relationship with God. But no, we do have a personal growth in the personal growth in the knowledge of God, and yet that's a knowledge that's available to all the saints. There's one faith, one baptism, one Christ, one Lord, one faith (Ephesians 4:5). One spirit, one body, one God and Father who is over all and in all. It's one relationship. One fellowship. A unity in the body of Christ, because it's one person. God deals with us, if we can get a hold of this, in Christ, for his sake, and as if we are Christ on because of his merits and his blessing and his inheritance. In fact, we are co-heirs with Christ (Romans 8:17). We are not - we don't have our own inheritance. We've got something even higher. We've got Christ's inheritance that he's sharing with his body. We're inheriting it together.

So, that's what the reality of baptism is all about. Eventually, seeing what was accomplished in baptism should satisfy your conscience. That your performance is not the issue. Christ's righteousness is the issue. His being satisfying to God is the issue. His being the beloved son in whom the father is well pleased is the issue (Matthew 3:17). His obedience to lay down his life for the sheep is why the father loves him. He said in John 10, "Father loves me because I gave my life for the sheep (John 10:17)."

Blessings and Grace on Dry Land

God is interested in Christ's life being multiplied and given, and He deals with us based on the fact that we have that life. This is why Noah is blessed, as we see for the first time since the fall in Genesis (9:1). God blessed Noah and his sons, saying, "Be fruitful and multiply, and fill the earth." "Replenish" is not the same as "subdue." Upon revisiting Genesis, I found that God told Adam and Eve to "replenish and subdue the earth" (1:28), but here, it is simply "replenish." This is not a warfare word, but a positive command for repopulation.

God also reinstates the dominion He gave to man, saying, "The fear of you and the dread of you shall be upon every beast of the earth, and upon every fowl of the air, upon all that moveth upon the earth, and upon all the fishes of the sea; into your hand they are delivered" (9:2). I don't know what things were like before the flood, but it seems that they got out of control. The whole earth was filled with violence, and all flesh had corrupted its way (6:11-12). This was not a peaceful time, but a violent one. I have a feeling that the end of the time before the flood was as violent as anything we've seen on earth. People's imaginations were only evil continually, and they were full of violence (6:5; 8:21).

Every moving thing shall be food for you, just as the green herb I have given you all things (9:3). Eating meat is not necessarily something new, as we know that God initially decreed vegetarianism. However, Tubal Cain's son was the father of those who herd cattle, which was a food thing (4:22). They were not supposed to be eating meat, but they were. Here, God acknowledges that man is still man and will do what he will do. Sometimes, it feels like God is picking his battles, as my son gets away with things he shouldn't. But as a parent, you can only fight so many battles.

God is blessing man, but He is also acknowledging that man is still man. He says, "Only you shall not eat flesh with its life, that is, its blood" (9:4). This is important to God because the blood is the life, and it is precious. The blood of His Son is precious because it is the life. God will require the blood of man at the hand of every beast and at the hand of every man (9:5). This is a little different from before, when Cain killed Abel, and Lamech killed someone, but God did not decree their deaths directly. Now, God is saying that by man, He will require the blood. If a beast kills you, the beast will be slain. If a man kills you, the man will be slain. God is holding people accountable through human government, which is the institution of capital punishment.

Re-Emphasizing the Image of God in Man

Whoever sheds man's blood, by man his blood shall be shed, for God made man in His own image (9:6). In the old days, God did not seem to decree the death of Cain or Lamech directly. But now, He is saying that man's blood will be avenged by man. This is why capital punishment is now a thing. God requires it, but man executes it. This is not a big deal, but it is more significant than what I am seeing. I don't think it is just about capital punishment because God is reiterating that He created man in His own image. He is decreeing blessing here and restoring the concept that man has dominion. He is reminding man that his blood is precious and that he was made in the image of God.

After the whole thing with the Nephilim in Genesis 6, man had become degraded. The men of renown, those who had reputation and filled everybody's imagination, were these Nephilim. They were the offspring of the sons of God and the daughters of men, who were these gibbereen, tyrants, giants (6:4). Their reputation skewed mankind's vision of mankind and made man smaller than he was in his own estimation. This is the same thing that happens when we watch superheroes like Superman and Batman. It makes you feel weak and powerless, and human life becomes worth nothing when there is that scale of violence. When man is worshiping these people who have power, he has a weaker estimation of himself. Eventually, it says that the earth was filled with violence through them (6:11-13).

On this side of the flood, God is reiterating the blessing, which is the first time we see the word "blessing" again since the fall (9:1). He is restoring the concept that man has dominion, saying his blood is precious, and reminding man that he was made in the image of God. I think this is important because in spite of the fall, in spite of the fact that man's imaginations are evil from youth, God is still dealing with His original purpose and has not diverted from it. He is still going to give His dominion to man, have him in His image with His likeness, and give him the blessing, which we know eventually is our blessed state in Christ (Romans 8:29; Ephesians 1:3-14). But that's what grace is. Grace is God moving for Christ's sake and dealing with you according to His covenant, regardless of your condition and regardless of your background and track record. Baptism seals that in our conscience (Romans 6:3-4; Colossians 2:11-12).

Whether you go into the water or not, or whether you just learn about your death with Christ, the point is to get your mind renewed so that you can see that God deals with you on the basis of Christ, and you are blessed. Your life is sacred before Him, and He is redeeming it with blood. The blood of Christ shows you your value. You have not ceased to be valuable. Yes, you were corrupted. Yes, you were destroyed, in a sense. But if you believe in Christ, you are not part of that destruction. You are put in the boat, and then from that point forward, God deals with you according to His covenant (1 Peter 3:20-21).

Covenant

Genesis 6 was the first time we saw the word "covenant." God said, "I will establish my covenant with you" (6:18). Noah walked with God, had faith, was justified by faith, and found grace in God's eyes (6:8-9; Hebrews 11:7). Grace is related to the covenant. What is grace again? Grace is God dealing with you and establishing His covenant with you, not based on you, but on Christ. And this covenant that He is dealing with, this everlasting covenant, is really the covenant for Christ. Christ is the ultimate heir of the covenant. This is not a covenant that God made with man where there are terms on man. These are unilateral things that God has set out to do and are secured by the obedience of Christ. There are two parties in a covenant, each with obligations. But in chapter 9 here, God is establishing a covenant with Noah, and yet there are no obligations on Noah. The same thing happens in Abraham's day when God secures the covenant with him, and there are no obligations on Abraham. Abraham is put to sleep during the time when God cuts the covenant. Who does He cut it with? Christ, the oven, and the torch go through the pieces as we will see (Genesis 15:7-21).

Galatians 3 tells us that God confirmed the covenant that we are heirs to with Christ in Abraham's time. This covenant is with Christ, and He is the heir of it. The only reason we have any relationship to it is because we are baptized into Christ, and it puts Him on (Galatians 3:16-29). This is the glorious good news of Galatians 3, that there are no obligations on us to be heirs. We just had to be baptized into Christ, who is the heir. He is Abraham's seed, an heir according to the promise (Galatians 3:16, 29). And He is the seed That God preserved Noah to keep alive (Genesis 6:18; 1 Peter 3:20-21).

In this chapter, God is establishing a covenant with Noah and his seed, but the seed is Christ (Genesis 9:8-17). We must see that there are no terms and obligations on us. There is only one covenant that had terms and obligations on the people, and that was the law. That was a covenant that Moses mediated between God and man (Exodus 20:1-17; 24:1-8). But the everlasting covenant that really secures our salvation is of grace, and it is a covenant that goes all the way through the scriptures (Jeremiah 31:31-34; Hebrews 13:20-21). It has different aspects to it, but Christ is the other party in the covenant. It is between Christ and the Father (Hebrews 8:6; 13:20-21). And it makes Him the shepherd of the sheep (John 10:14-16; Hebrews 13:20). His blood is the blood of that covenant (Matthew 26:26-28; Hebrews 13:20).

The covenant that we are a part of has nothing to do with us. God is keeping us, and our condition is based on our position in the ark (Genesis 7:1-5; 1 Peter 3:20-21). God preserved the ark, therefore everybody in the ark lived (Genesis 7:1-24). God preserves Christ, and it is His salvation, His inheritance, and everybody in Christ safely and securely can know that they have a part in it (Hebrews 7:25; 9:11-15). And they have full qualification for the blessing (Ephesians 1:3-14).

There is absolutely nothing keeping you from being able to come and fellowship with God right now, if you are a believer or if you are a non-believer (Romans 5:1-2; 8:1; Ephesians 2:8-9). If you are a non-believer, believe (John 3:16; Romans 10:9-10). If you are a believer, believe (Romans 12:1-2; 2 Corinthians 13:5). Demand a good conscience (1 Timothy 1:5; Hebrews 13:18). You have no business hanging around in condemnation, and the enemy has no right to put condemnation on you (Romans 8:1; Colossians 1:13-14). The law has no right to put any demand on you (Romans 6:14; 7:4-6). There is no obligation on you to partake of the blessing in Christ.

The blessing in Christ, on the one hand, is your joy and satisfaction, but it is also the Christian life (Romans 5:1-2; 8:37-39; Galatians 2:20; Philippians 1:21; 3:8-11). It is Christ fulfilling the covenant and working in you that which is well pleasing in His sight by His own life (Colossians 1:10; Philippians 2:13). And God is dealing with you, not because of you individually apart from Christ, but because you are a member of Christ (Romans 8:1; Colossians 1:18; 2:10). He deals with us somewhat vicariously (Romans 5:12-21; 2 Corinthians 5:21). We are clothed with Christ, accepted in Christ, raised together with Christ, justified in Christ, and He is our life and our sanctification (Galatians 3:27; Romans 6:4; Colossians 2:12; 3:3-4; 1 Corinthians 1:30; Philippians 1:21; 3:9). He is everything (Colossians 3:11; Ephesians 1:3; 4:15).

To the degree that we understand this, our conscience gets settled (Romans 8:1; Colossians 1:22; 2:10; 1 John 3:19-20). And like Jewel always says, we are dead to 5 seconds ago (Colossians 3:3; Romans 6:6-7; 2 Corinthians 5:17). Our history does not disqualify or qualify us in the things of God (Romans 8:38-39; Philippians 3:8-9). It is not that we are growing some ability to stand before Him based on our merits, no (Ephesians 2:8-9; Titus 3:5). What we are learning is how completely the blood of Christ has reconciled us to God, made peace with us and God, and dealt with our past, including our 5 minutes ago, including our 1 second ago (Colossians 1:20; Romans 5:10; Hebrews 9:12-14; 10:10).

So that even if we just exploded in sin for some reason, we have just as much right to come straightforward boldly to the throne of grace and take our position as sons and heirs (Hebrews 4:14-16; Romans 8:15-17; Galatians 4:6-7). Because if we do not, how are we going to have any power to live righteously (Romans 6:11-14; 8:12-13; Philippians 2:12-13)? If we are hiding in our sins, we will not have the power to live righteously (1 John 1:5-10; James 4:7-10). But if we come forward and stand in the light, and do not care that it exposes us, we have an advocate with the Father, Jesus Christ the righteous (1 John 2:1-2; Hebrews 7:25; 9:14-15). He is our history, and He is our qualification (Hebrews 12:2; Philippians 3:8-9).

In one sense, it is a license to sin, because it says we can do whatever we want and still come to God (Romans 6:1; Galatians 5:13). And yet, if we do not come to God, we will stay in sin and condemnation (John 3:18; 5:24;

Romans 8:1; 1 John 1:5-10). But if we actually use our license, if we actually use the grace, and come to God on the basis of Christ's merit when we do, then we will not sin (Romans 6:1-2; 8:1-4; 1 John 1:7; 3:9). We will be washed, we will be cleansed, and we will be in His presence (1 John 1:7-9; Romans 5:1-2; 8:37-39).

To the degree that we know how to enjoy this as a rich spoiled brat who does not deserve to be in the Father's house and yet has everything freely provided for him and did not have to work for it, to that degree, we will also begin to model the behavior and characteristics of the house and the nature of the Father and the nature of the household, the divine nature (Romans 8:14-17; 2 Corinthians 3:17-18; Colossians 3:1-17; 2 Peter 1:3-4).

We do not get to partake of the divine nature unless we partake of the divine life, and that comes through the knowledge of Jesus Christ (2 Peter 1:3-4; John 17:3; Colossians 2:6-10; 3:1-4). And it is all of grace (Ephesians 2:8-9; Romans 5:1-2; 6:14; 8:37-39). We have to exercise our faith and come to Him and realize that God is not dealing with us and our history, but He is dealing with Christ (Hebrews 12:2; Romans 8:1; Colossians 3:1-4; Philippians 3:8-9). We are in the ark, and our salvation is in Christ, not in our own efforts (Genesis 7:1-5; 1 Peter 3:20-21; Ephesians 2:8-9).

In or Out of the Ark is the Only Thing that Matters

I went to a funeral of a friend of mine who committed suicide when I first became Christian, I was one of these zealous types that didn't think Christians could do that.

And, I was furious. Figured he was a fake Christian. You know, he wrote a big long suicide note about what a failure he felt like and how the apostles were blessed, but he couldn't be. Why? Because he was under legalistic teaching. But anyway, this was 25 years ago. He was under a performance mentality. He took his life. But a relative who gave the sermon used Noah's Ark said that there are basically 2 conditions. You're either on the ark or you're not. How do we know this guy was on the ark? Well, it was because of his profession. And that that was when I learned for the first time, really, that salvation is a matter of being in Christ, not what I do.

Growth in the Christian life is just becoming more and more confident. To walk around in the ark and act like it's your own. Maybe 1st couple weeks you just stay in this 1 room by the donkeys in the ark. You're sick because you're eating donkey food, and it stinks down there. You're still in the ark. But one day you realize that the gate is open from that little room, and you get out, and you walk all the way up to the bridge, where it's still just as dark because there's only one window on the other side of the ship. But, there's Noah, and he's having dinner with his family lit by candles. Maybe you think, "I slipped in. I'm not even suppsoed to be here. I'm a stowaway. You didn't even know I was here." Noah would say, well, pull up a chair. He's not going to throw you off the ark! He's going to feed you.

To enjoy that place at the table, you had to realize you could move around and not stay down there with the donkeys. Our growth is just a realization of how much God is dealing with us on the basis of Christ and our position in him and not on the basis of our condition. On the one hand every day we need to renew our understanding of our access that we have in Christ. On the other hand, there is a cumulative knowledge where we become more confident and more assured. And that's one of my favorite things to hear from people who listen to my videos. They say, "it used to take me weeks and weeks or months, after a sin, to come to God. Especially if it was a big one, before I could fellowship with God again. Now it's a couple minutes." And I'm like, yeah. That's that's the story. The story is how fast can you get back into the presence of god. That is the story of your victory. Can the enemy keep you thinking, oh, I don't even deserve to be saved, and God probably hates me and I'm probably not one of His children, and I probably wasn't really saved, and maybe I didn't believe, and maybe I'm going to drown after all! Or what are all the different doctrines the enemy uses to try to trip you up or make you feel like there's some debt you owe or demand on you.

The debts were canceled at the flood. None of those people can pay. They paid with their lives for all the wickedness and violence they did. The only thing left is to get on the ark. It's too bad nobody did. But the 8 that did were dealt with because they were on the ark. Once the water hit, it's because you're on the arc, not because you're this or that.

Genesis 9:1-7 KJV And God blessed Noah and his sons, and said unto them, Be fruitful, and multiply, and replenish the earth. (2) And the fear of you and the dread of you shall be upon every beast of the earth, and upon

every fowl of the air, upon all that moveth upon the earth, and upon all the fishes of the sea; into your hand are they delivered. (3) Every moving thing that liveth shall be meat for you; even as the green herb have I given you all things. (4) But flesh with the life thereof, which is the blood thereof, shall ye not eat. (5) And surely your blood of your lives will I require; at the hand of every beast will I require it, and at the hand of man; at the hand of every man's brother will I require the life of man. (6) Whoso sheddeth man's blood, by man shall his blood be shed: for in the image of God made he man. (7) And you, be ye fruitful, and multiply; bring forth abundantly in the earth, and multiply therein.

The Everlasting Covenant

So now let's focus on the covenant. Despite the above tangent, Noah is on dry land. God's covenant contains a new provision - the the death penalty. Here God is reasserting the dominance of man, the preciousness of man and his intention to bless man and reminding all creation that man was created in the image of god and is unique. None of the angels can say that. And believe me, the angels are watching this. 1500 years has passed since the creation of Adam, at least. And man has become so depraved and so wicked that God had repented that he made him and Destroyed him. And yet, here in this blessing, he's saying if you kill man, I'm going to require his blood, because he was created in the image of god. And then he's also blessing Noah. That's a big deal that there's a blessing again. I don't think there's a mention of blessing from Genesis 3 all the way till now. So this after the flood covenant is really profound. Just like our position in Christ, once we land on dry ground in Him, He's a really good place to be. But as we'll see, Noah and his descendants are by no means sinless. Yet from now on, God is dealing with people according to their relationship to his covenant that he's establishing with the seed, not based on their behavior. And that's why David and Abraham and Jacob and these people can do such ridiculous things but still be blessed. David had Uriah slain and had his wife and Bathsheba. There's just awful stuff. And yet because of the covenant, god remembers them. That's the other thing we saw in this chapter is last chapter that God remembered Noah. That's a covenant kind of word - God remembers us.

Genesis 9:10-18 KJV And with every living creature that is with you, of the fowl, of the cattle, and of every beast of the earth with you; from all that go out of the ark, to every beast of the earth. (11) And I will establish my covenant with you; neither shall all flesh be cut off any more by the waters of a flood; neither shall there any more be a flood to destroy the earth. (12) And God said, This is the token of the covenant which I make between me and you and every living creature that is with you, for perpetual generations: (13) I do set my bow in the cloud, and it shall be for a token of a covenant between me and the earth. (14) And it shall come to pass, when I bring a cloud over the earth, that the bow shall be seen in the cloud: (15) And I will remember my covenant, which is between me and you and every living creature of all flesh; and the waters shall no more become a flood to destroy all flesh. (16) And the bow shall be in the cloud; and I will look upon it, that I may remember the everlasting covenant between God and every living creature of all flesh that is upon the earth. (17) And God said unto Noah, This is the token of the covenant, which I have established between me and all flesh that is upon the earth. (18) And the sons of Noah, that went forth of the ark, were Shem, and Ham, and Japheth: and Ham is the father of Canaan.

Token of the Covenant

And then verse 11, I will establish my covenant with you, neither shall all flesh be cut off of any more by the waters of the flood, neither shall there be any more flood to destroy the earth. This is the token of the covenant which I made between me and you and every living creature that is with you For perpetual generations, I do set my bow in the cloud, and it shall be a token of a covenant between me and the earth. Now again, and it shall come to pass. When I bring a bow book cloud over the earth, the bow bow, I'm sorry, shall be seen in the Cloud. And I will remember my covenant. There's the word remember again. Which is between me and you, and every creature of all flesh. The water shall no longer become a flood to destroy All flesh and the bow shall be in the cloud, and I will look upon it.

Then I will recall the everlasting covenant between God and every living creature of all flesh that is on the earth (Genesis 9:16). And Noah said, "This is the sign of the covenant that I have established between me and all flesh that is on the earth" (Genesis 9:17). This sign is the bow, and we interpret the rainbow in the cloud. Any time the word for cloud is used (in Hebrew, "anan"), it is speaking of what is called a theophany, an appearance of God in glory (Exodus 16:10). He covers himself with a cloud (Exodus 13:21). Literally, there is no time that the word for cloud is used except in reference to God's appearance. It is a pillar of cloud (Exodus 13:21), when God appeared over the tabernacle (Exodus 40:34), over Sinai (Exodus 19:9), and when God filled the temple, so the priests were not able to minister (1 Kings 8:10-11). All the way through, it is the cloud of his glory that covers his presence, for no man shall see his face and live (Exodus 33:20).

It is not just the cloud up in the sky because of rain, although I believe there is something to that as well. But this cloud is a cloud that is a covering of the throne of God (Ezekiel 1:28). And it is associated with judgment and gloom, because it hides God's presence when he manifests, and it is often associated with judgments (Isaiah 4:5). The tribulation is called the dark and cloudy day (Joel 2:2), and it is because Christ is over the earth during that time. He is concealed in the clouds (Matthew 24:30). The whole earth is dark, but it is actually the appearance of his glory, for he is dealing with the earth in judgment (Revelation 6:12-17). And there is a rainbow around the throne (Revelation 4:3). In Revelation 5, the one who sits on the throne is like jasper, and there is a rainbow around the throne (Revelation 4:3). And in Revelation 10, when Christ stands up, I believe that is Christ. He has the book in his right hand. He has one foot on the land and one foot on the sea (Revelation 10:2). And it says that the kingdom of God had become his, Christ's actually. Let me read that:

Revelation 10:1-2: "Then I saw another mighty angel coming down from heaven, clothed with a cloud. A rainbow was on his head, his face was like the sun, and his legs were like pillars of fire. He had a little scroll open in his hand."

There is that rainbow again. That is the token of this covenant, the everlasting covenant (Genesis 9:16). And a rainbow was on his head, and his face was as it was the sun, and his feet pillars of fire, and he had on his right hand a little book open. And he set his right foot on the sea and his left foot on the earth and cried with a loud voice as with a lion roars (Revelation 10:1-3).

And when he had cried, the seven thunders uttered their voices (Revelation 10:3-4). The thunders go with the clouds, for they are a storm of judgment (Psalm 18:13). And He, the one who sits upon the throne, is clothed with the cloud, but he also has a rainbow around his head (Revelation 4:3). What is that? It is a token of a covenant (Genesis 9:12-17).

In Revelation 5, we see that the one who sits upon the throne is like jasper and sardius stone, and there is a rainbow around the throne (Revelation 4:3). This is the token of his covenant, and this covenant that he makes in Genesis 9 seems to be a covenant with all creation (Genesis 9:12-17). But it is not a covenant in the sense that there are no obligations on creation to keep their part of the covenant. Rather, it is part of the everlasting covenant that is referred to in Hebrews 13:20-21, which makes Christ the great shepherd of the sheep, and is the covenant with God, with the seed of the woman, the seed of Abraham, and the seed of David.

The first part of this covenant is that God will never again destroy the earth with a flood (Genesis 9:11). And this is good, because when God executes judgments, he remembers his covenant (Isaiah 54:9). During the tribulation, there will be many judgments on the earth, but God will be looking at the bow in the cloud (Genesis 9:16). The cloud comes and hides his presence, so when his presence comes, it is judgment for the wicked, but a blessing for the elect (Isaiah 26:20-21).

Jesus said that there will be great tribulations such as never been, has been, nor ever will be (Matthew 24:21). And if those days were not cut short, no flesh would be saved (Matthew 24:22). But for the elect's sake, those days will be cut short (Matthew 24:22). God does not wipe out the earth because of his covenant with Christ and the elect (Genesis 9:16). And it is because of this bow, this covenant, that God gave the earth to Christ, so he will not destroy it in a flood (Psalm 115:16).

At the end, there will be a purifying fire, but some people believe that the new heavens and the new earth are different heavens and earth (2 Peter 3:13). However, I tend to believe that it is this heavens and earth that will be purified and glorified, just like our bodies will be purified and glorified (Philippians 3:21). Our bodies are important, and God will transfigure them to be like the body of his glory (1 Corinthians 15:42-44). And when he does, he will catch us up into the cloud (1 Thessalonians 4:17).

For Noah, this would have been like a restoration of dominion and a blessing (Genesis 9:1-7). God was saying that people could not just come up and kill them, for they were created in the image of God (Genesis 9:6). And he was talking about this bow, a rainbow, that meant he would never do this again (Genesis 9:11-17). And Noah's days were blessed going forward (Genesis 9:28-29).

In conclusion, God deals with us in Christ for the sake of a covenant, and this covenant is the token of the bow that is literally around Christ's head and around God's throne (Revelation 4:3). When God appears in his throne of glory in the earth today, it is covered with a cloud, but if we could see through that cloud, we would see the bow (Exodus 13:21-22). This means that there is judgment for the wicked, but blessing for the elect, or blessing for those in Christ (Genesis 9:12-17). And we need to have that kind of view, for we are in a time right now where the world is coming under judgments, and we need to remember our position in Christ and God's covenant with us.

Chapter 25 - God Stands with Those Who Have His Testimony (Genesis 9)

Genesis 9:18-29 KJV And the sons of Noah, that went forth of the ark, were Shem, and Ham, and Japheth: and Ham is the father of Canaan. (19) These are the three sons of Noah: and of them was the whole earth overspread. (20) And Noah began to be an husbandman, and he planted a vineyard: (21) And he drank of the wine, and was drunken; and he was uncovered within his tent. (22) And Ham, the father of Canaan, saw the nakedness of his father, and told his two brethren without. (23) And Shem and Japheth took a garment, and laid it upon both their shoulders, and went backward, and covered the nakedness of their father; and their faces were backward, and they saw not their father's nakedness. (24) And Noah awoke from his wine, and knew what his younger son had done unto him. (25) And he said, Cursed be Canaan; a servant of servants shall he be unto his brethren. (26) And he said, Blessed be the LORD God of Shem; and Canaan shall be his servant. (27) God shall enlarge Japheth, and he shall dwell in the tents of Shem; and Canaan shall be his servant. (28) And Noah lived after the flood three hundred and fifty years. (29) And all the days of Noah were nine hundred and fifty years: and he died.

Genesis begins with the first blessed situation of rest in Eden, with man created in the image of God, given dominion, and everything subdued to him. All the animals are brought to him, and he names them all. Then, you have the uncovering of their nakedness. It's really interesting that they are naked and unashamed. They don't even know they're naked. But after eating from the tree of the knowledge of good and evil, the first thing they become conscious of is their nakedness. They become sin-conscious. The enemy's chief attack tactic is to bring you into sin-consciousness and self-consciousness. This causes us to hide from God.

Then Genesis records the fall and everything that happened up to the flood. This is about 1500 years of history. Now we have Noah, whose name means "rest." He brings all the animals to him and is brought through the flood as a picture of baptism, which is the termination of the old creation. He is set on dry ground on the day of resurrection with eight souls representing the new creation. The curse is at least some extent lifted or reversed, and God reaffirms the blessing that He spoke in the garden.

God blesses Noah and says that if anyone sheds man's blood, his blood shall be shed, for man was created in the image of God. This is the first time we see blessing since the fall, and it's the first time we see the statement that man is created in the image of God since the Genealogy that said that Adam was created in the image of God. God tells Noah that he has dominion over every creeping thing. It's a picture of the situation in Genesis 3 reinstated after a judgment. I believe that Genesis 3 records events after a previous fall of the angelic order prior to the creation of man.

It's interesting that in the story we're going to encounter today we will see another attempt to bring attention to man's nakedness. Noah is in the blessed situation of rest, and the curse has been reversed in a sense. There's a blessing there. He plants a vineyard, and a vineyard is plant life to tend, just like in the garden. They were given to tend everything, and they were also to eat of the fruit of all the trees. Noah plants a vineyard in his situation of rest, in his blessed situation with the restored mandate, and he becomes drunk from drinking from the vineyard. He's uncovered in his tent, he's naked. "Now, is that a sin? We assume that it's a sin, and we do know that in the New Testament it says, 'Be not drunk with wine, but be filled with the Spirit' (Ephesians 5:18). We've been given an alternative. But God created wine, according to the Bible, to cheer the heart (Psalm 104:15)."

So, is it a sin that he's drunk in his tent, enjoying the produce of his labor of cultivating a vineyard? Our Father is a husbandman, and there's going to be a wedding feast with wine produced from that vine, from all the fruit in our lives. That's going to be a satisfying enjoyment in the kingdom. Most people don't see this story this way, there's room for interpretation, but I believe we can see it as a picture, a type, a positive type. At the same time, you could say that being drunk in the tent and being uncovered was supposedly a sin. The law has not been given yet. There's been no commandment that says, "Don't drink to excess." He's in his tent, in the privacy of his own home.

But Ham came upon Noah's uncovered condition and drunkenness and clearly thought it was worth reporting to his brothers. This is playing out Satan's tactic. Satan, in the tree of the knowledge of good and evil, brought attention to Adam's nakedness and turned something that was neutral, if not positive, into something that's shameful. That's what the enemy loves to do. He wants to attack your conscience, boldness, and confidence before God by trying to make you ashamed, even of the good things that God has given you. Trust me, I know from experience.

God created Adam and Eve naked, and they were unashamed. God said it was good. But by the time the enemy was done with them, they were ashamed of it and it had to be covered. I'm not saying that we all need to go around naked, that's not the point. But it is not coincidental that the first thing that happens in this restored situation of rest is that the enemy, through Ham, tries to bring Noah into bondage and damage people's perception of Noah, stigmatize him, and call him a sinner, and fill the whole situation with shame after God blessed him and said he's created in the image of God. That's what's going on here.

"These are the three sons of Noah, and from them, the whole earth was overspread." There was Shem, Ham and Japheth. Ham is the father of Canaan. God will pronounce a curse on Canaan because of this incident. Remember that later, the good land is populated with the Canaanites. They're all enemies of God and they're to be killed, every man, woman, and child. It's pretty bad in the land when Israel is to take the land. They're intermarrying with the sons of Nephilim, so there's demonic stuff going on.

God said to replenish the earth, and this is a new start. It's really important, with this new start, how the family that's going to populate the whole earth perceives Noah and God's mandate. Who is this one that did all of this? He's the one who appointed Noah to be the ambassador and the representative of His work. Is God righteous? Anytime the enemy brings accusation to you and tries to bring shame and slander to you as a believer, what he's really trying to do is accuse God. You are secondary.

Remember the story in the Gospel when the Pharisees brought the adulterous woman to Jesus? She surely thought she was the center of the story; they were all ready to stone her. But it says that their eyes were on Jesus because they wanted to see what He would do. They were seeking ground to accuse Him. Is He going to uphold the law? Is He righteous? Yes, He's righteous. He is the righteousness of God (Romans 3:22). It is His absolute right to forgive whoever He wants. In the propitiation in Romans 3:25, He is the manifestation of God's righteousness, that God may be just and the justifier of those who believe in Jesus. The accusation in the court of heaven is against God first and foremost. He is being vindicated in His choice of the vessels that He uses and reconciles to Himself and represents Himself through.

He has chosen to identify Himself with the foolish things to confound the wisdom of the wise and the weak things to bring not the strength of the powerful (1 Corinthians 1:27). He's not ashamed to call us brethren (Hebrews 2:11). Jesus is familiar with our weakness, touched with the feeling of our weakness (Hebrews 4:15). It is important to recognize that we are foolish and have been given a high priest who can sympathize with our foolishness (Hebrews 4:15). We are lost sheep, weak, detestable, and obnoxious (Luke 15:4-7). Yet, God has chosen to express the message of his righteous kingdom through vessels like us. This is because it is all accomplished by Christ and not by man (1 Corinthians 1:29-31). It is the power of God, not of man, that saves through the foolishness of preaching (1 Corinthians 1:21). When man is brought into shame, the accusation is against God first. It is about God, not about us.

The Enemy's Tactic is to Bring Shame to God's Order

Noah was God's chosen ambassador at that time, the one who carries the promise of redemption. He is the one God chose to build the ark and bring everyone through. He is the head of God's government, and God's authority is behind who He justifies. Everything works together for our good by God's authority and power. The enemy's tactics are worked into God's story of how He brought us to an end of ourselves and revealed His unlimited grace and goodness towards us. When we are weak, His power is perfected in our weakness.

God is being vindicated through His identification with us or in spite of His identification with us. The situation with Ham accusing Noah is significant because it shows that God takes issues of government seriously. God's government is with His word, not human authority (Isaiah 55:11). In the wilderness, there were problems with people not understanding the authority behind Moses and Aaron (Exodus 16:6-7). They saw their human weakness and questioned why they spoke for God. However, God vindicated them by causing Aaron's staff to bud, representing resurrection and life (Numbers 17:1-11). The authority is with those who bear the testimony of Christ.

Noah became a husbandman and planted a vineyard. He drank wine and became drunk, which is a foolish state in the eyes of Ham. Ham saw his father's nakedness and told his brothers. Moses is the one who wrote all of this down. He writes to the children of Israel and wants to show them that this goes all the way back. God doesn't forget, and He takes issues of government seriously. Ham's actions are an attempt to defile everyone's consciousness about the situation that God has set up. It is reminiscent of Peter's vision in Acts 10, where God showed him that what He has called clean should not be called unclean. God's speaking produces cleansing and covering of sin. And restores your conscience to make you bold so that you can go forth in His authority, knowing that you represent Him. Peter went to Cornelius' house knowing he represented God and that God had sent him. Noah is positioned here with the knowledge that God had brought him through the flood and that he was the representative of God's move in life, right?

The enemy's tactic is to judge what God has called clean and to bring reproach against God? That's what's going on. You think, "Uh, it's just about Noah." No, no, this is a satanic attempt to bring shame into this situation. If Satan can bring shame to you, he shuts you down. That's why it's so important that people use the law and ordinances to bring people into condemnation and shame. That is our warfare. Those are our enemies, whether they are reconciled to God or not. Once they have that accursed gospel and they're calling what God has called clean unclean, they are working against the purpose of God and moving against His authority. And when they do it, and if you fall for it, you lose your effectiveness because when you're ashamed, you can't represent. That happened to Peter. Peter went to Cornelius' house, and then he came back, and the Jewish believers in Jerusalem persecuted him for eating with Gentiles. They were more mad that he was eating with Gentiles than profoundly moved by the fact that Gentiles could be saved. And at that point, if you remember, they didn't even believe Gentiles could be saved, and that was 10 years into the start of the church. They're confused. Why are they confused? Because their conscience is bound by ordinances and shame.

Later in Antioch according to Galatians 2, Peter was freely eating with the Gentiles as he should, giving them the message of reconciliation. But then when the Jews from James came, he shrank back from them and wouldn't eat with them anymore and even pretended like he had not been eating with them. What was that? That was shame through ordinances shutting him down. And it was a satanic attack. Paul had to set him free by rebuking him in front of everybody. You can read this account in Galatians 1 and 2. Satan, through the principalities and through ordinances, "Do not handle, do not taste, do not touch," brings people into bondage and shuts down the message of life. It's an attack on the gospel. It's an attack on God's authority. It's an attack on God's righteousness that He would associate Himself with sinners.

We are sinners, but God justifies us, and God is justified in choosing us and even giving us the ministry of reconciliation. We've received mercy; therefore, we have this ministry, you know, a genuine ministry, which is unto the administration of the fullness of times to head up all things in Christ. God's authority backs it, and it comes with resurrection life. It comes with the almond tree that buds and the rod that buds. People get renewed and set free and cleansed and washed through the ministry.

Satan attacks God's administration which is through man, by bringing shame and shutting man down. The issue in Genesis 10 is an attack on the character of God's move. Those who sided with God, Japheth and Shem, moved with God to cover. They didn't look. They walked backwards while covering Noah and averted their eyes. They would not look on Noah's nakedness. Remember, love covers the multitude of sins. They would not know him according to the flesh. They would not know him how Ham was trying to expose him. And that's important. It wasn't about Noah. It was about God.

The enemy tries to get your eyes on the messenger and his weaknesses and failures rather than on the message itself. Noah represented a message. We're nothing if we don't represent a message. But we have to understand that that message represents God's move. How does He move? By releasing life through the message. You know, Noah was a preacher of righteousness at that time. Is he a sinner?

Yes. Okay, and that produces a problem for people who have issues in their conscience. The principalities work through the fallen conscience of man to produce shame through ordinances.

Colossians talks about it, connecting the principalities with the ordinances when it says that Jesus blotted out the handwriting of ordinances which was contrary to us (Colossians 2:14). He blotted it out, took it out of the way on the cross, and He made an open show of the principalities, triumphing over them in it (Colossians 2:15). How? By blotting out the handwriting of ordinances, which is their ground to accuse us, which is their way of shutting down God's message. If Peter and his defiled conscience said, "I can't go eat with Cornelius because he's a Gentile," that would be Satan's victory over Peter's conscience to keep Peter, through his own wrong sense of righteousness, from delivering the message of life to the Gentiles, which would have been a thwarting of God's move (Acts 10:28). That's how significant it is when you are being attacked with condemnation from every side, and you're full of shame, and you're thinking you're defeated, and you're thinking you have no use before God. The enemy, he is not focused on you. You think it's all about you and God's mad at you. No, the enemy is trying to shut down God's move in life by causing you to call what God has called clean unclean (Acts 10:15). That's what shame is for. And the enemy loves to use shame to bring reproach against those that God has justified and made ambassadors of His message, to stigmatize the message and shut the message down. That's the focus.

So, it's really sad that Ham got caught up in this. But Shem and Japheth, their response to Noah's nakedness, was to cover it. Their response to Ham's uncovering of Noah's nakedness is to cover, and they walk backward, not letting themselves see Noah. And that's what Paul talks about, how we know not we don't know each other after the flesh. We have to know each other as a new creation in Christ. Same thing. They would not. They understood that this was significant. Sometimes people will do something that seems innocuous, but all of a sudden, the righteous feel like, "Whoa, this is significant," because there's a sensitivity to God's move in life. And so, they will circle the wagons, so to speak. You'll see them all move together all of a sudden. Shem and Japheth moved with God in life to cover Noah.

Noah Speaks for God

But again, I think it's all very interesting how it points right back to the same thing that happened with Adam. Satan tried to bring shame and reproach, and he did successfully. He tried to do it with Noah, but guess what? It didn't work. Noah awoke from his wine and knew what his younger son had done to him. And he said, **"Cursed be Canaan. A servant of servants shall he be to his brethren."** He said, **"Blessed be the Lord, God of Shem, and Canaan shall be his servant. God shall enlarge Japheth, and he shall dwell in the tents of Shem, and Canaan shall be his servant."**

This is a blessing, this is a prophecy, right? This is just like Israel later prophesying over the 12 tribes. Israel said that Dan is a cursed adder (Gen 49:16-17) and then their destiny unfolds exactly as Jacob prophesied, so that eventually Dan brought the tribes into idolatry and was a stumbling block to them. And Dan doesn't appear in the roster in Revelation 7 when the 10-12 tribes are sealed. Levi replaces him. He's gone. And that was prophesied all the way back in Jacob's time. These decrees mean something and stand throughout history. When you see the representative of God's move decreeing something like this, it's heavy.

The blessing in this prophecy points to Shem, the Lord God of Shem. Shem is going to be the continuance of the blessing and the birthright, the seed of the promise of the seed of the woman, and eventually the seed of Abraham, the seed of David. Christ is going to come out of Shem. Okay, so that's his blessing, and that's why he's the Lord God of Shem. And God shall enlarge Japheth, and he shall dwell in the tents of Shem. As we'll see in Genesis 10, the Gentile nations, the Western nations, really come from Japheth. It says they'll dwell in the tents of Shem, and the Western world has come to associate with Christ. I mean, you know, Christendom is associated with the Lord God of Shem. We are dwelling in Shem's tents.

Shem's descendants, Abraham, Isaac, and Jacob, dwell in tents. They didn't dwell in Babel; they dwelt in tents, and then there was the Tabernacle in the wilderness, right? And ultimately, all these things point to Christ. And Noah was naked in his tent, right? I think the tent is significant. And for Japheth to dwell in the tent of Shem means that they're dwelling in Christ. Ultimately, the Gentiles become blessed through Shem. So, that's the blessing. But notice that Noah doesn't curse Ham.

He curses Canaan, saying he'll be a servant of his brothers. A servant of servants shall he be to his brethren. Canaan shall be the servant of Shem, and Canaan shall be the servant of Japheth. I mean, he's getting subjected to everybody now. What is this? I used to think of this as Noah decreeing a curse on Canaan because of Ham's disobedience, and I've heard it that way. "Oh, you come against God's government like that, you're going to be cursed." Well, then why didn't he curse Ham? Ham was the one who did it. Why curse Canaan?

No, this is not about Noah exercising authority to show who's gonna do what because he said it. This is Noah demonstrating his clarity. Um, and God vindicating that he really stood with Noah, even though Noah was drunk, and you think he's foolish, even though he was uncovered. He is the representative of God's government, and he has the discernment and the vision to speak God's message and to accurately prophesy the destiny of these descendants because it's exactly how it all unfolds. World history unfolds from this chapter, the arrangement of nations and the blessings and the curse in a sense is all described in Noah's speaking which is full of clarity.

This didn't happen because Noah spoke it. Noah is just showing that he's clear. God is vindicating him. Who do you listen to? Who should you listen to? You should listen to those who clearly articulate the truth because that's the one that God is standing with. Um, he goes with his message, you know, in spite of the vessels he chooses, and he chooses vessels that are often offensive and obnoxious in order to hide the message from those who won't get it because they're self-righteous and deceived. Now, Ham did take a turn here because nothing good comes out of his descendants. Cush, his other son, is the grandfather of Nimrod that produced Babel. Babel is the source of all the abominations in the earth, the mother of all abominations in the earth. Everything that's filthy and vile in this order after the flood comes from Babel which proceeds from Ham's line. They rebelled against God and obviously had a view of God that he was evil. We'll see more of that in Genesis 11.

Ham Takes the Way of Cain

Ham's sin is similar to Cain's. Cain refused to recognize that God had justified Abel. Maybe Abel was drunk, maybe Abel sinned, you know. See, when self-righteous people bring reproaches against God and who he vindicates and who he justifies, they go down a predictable line when they double down in hatred of those who God justifies. What we're going to see in the next chapter is just like a recount of Genesis 4, which is Cain's line of actions, negative activities, and they go out from God.

You see the same thing with Ham's line in the Table of Nations. You'll see, we'll see. It's all negative. And yet, Ham himself isn't cursed. And but that event somehow galvanized in his mind that "Jehovah is not the God I want to serve, and I don't want to be associated with his people either."

That's the close of that story. Then Noah lived after the flood 300 years, and all the days of Noah were 950 years, and he died. So, this is the big significant event after the flood. The enemy tried to bring reproach to God's government, and it worked to an extent because Babel and Nineveh comes out of it from Ham's line, and all the negative things, the Canaanites, so many negative things are brought into the earth through Ham's descendants because of his view of God and what he passed on.

But Noah is not pronouncing a curse on him here as a punishment. I believe he's God vindicating Noah as his representative by his prophecy, showing that, no, he's the clear one. You thought he was drunk and naked in his tent? Well, he was in his tent, and is it really a shame to be naked before me? You know, being in the tent means before God, that's in your secret place. You know, was Noah sinning? I don't know, but Ham got indignant. That's why I say it's just like the sin of Cain to bring accusation against God and those who He justifies.

When religious people are offended, it's often because they think that what God has called clean is actually unclean. And it's the work of the devil, it's the work of a spirit, it's a work of the principalities to try to bring ordinances against God's children, to find ground to condemn their behavior and say, "See, God's not righteous and associating with people like this."

Remember that this is Moses putting this story together in the midst of dealing with the Israelites who are constantly questioning his authority. And he's the most humble man on earth, it says (Numbers 12:3). He didn't think he had any right to do anything. He threw himself at the face of God, at God's feet, and worshiped every time to intercede for the people (Exodus 32:11-14). And one time God said, "I'm gonna destroy him and I'll just create a nation out of you." He said, "Heaven forbid, don't do that" (Exodus 32:10-14). He did not have a high estimation of himself, and the people didn't have a high estimation of Moses either.

But God wasn't interested in Moses being something. God was interested in God being represented (Exodus 3:10-12). And that's what he puts his seal on, is those who have the testimony (Revelation 12:17). Remember Aaron's rod that butted as a sign that God's authority was with him ended up in the Ark (Numbers 17:1-11). If the testimony of God testifies of those who testify of Him, we have the testimony as the sons of God (Romans 8:16). We have set our seal that God's record is true (John 3:33). We have the testimony of the Son, God's testified concerning His Son, and that is in us (1 John 5:9-12). That is our authority to speak, and you are qualified if you've received mercy to be an ambassador of God's message of reconciliation (2 Corinthians 5:18-20).

Somebody said on my wall, he gave a really good comment in the last message, saying that we've been given a message of reconciliation, and our message is about

Christ, not about ourselves. Our message is Christ. Noah's message was not his own righteousness; it was Christ's (Genesis 6:8-9). And Christ is the one who justifies sinners (Romans 3:24-26). And Paul said, if while we seek to be justified by Christ, we are found to be sinners, does that mean Christ is a minister of sin? God forbid (Galatians 2:17). In other words, your fallen humanity does not stop God from being able to represent His message through you. In fact, we can do nothing against the truth. We can only confirm it (2 Corinthians 13:8). Let God be true and every man a liar, right (Romans 3:4)? And that, my lie, it bounds to His glory, according to Romans. But that doesn't mean we do evil that good could come (Romans 3:8). But we are the ones God's chosen, and we believe the message. We have the evidence of His testimony in ourselves, and that is our "aaron's rod" (1 Corinthians 1:26-31). And we should be bold enough to speak (Ephesians 6:19).

Paul said to the Philippians, "I want you to walk in a manner worthy of the gospel, so that whether I'm with you or not with you, I can behold your order and the steadfastness of your faith. That in one mind, you're striving for the gospel, in nothing being terrified of your adversaries, which to them is a token of perdition, but to you of salvation, and that from God" (Philippians 1:27-28).

The enemy tries to work to bring reproach against the conscience of the saints, to shut them down in an attempt to shut down God's move. Don't fall for it. That's why we want to let no one steal our crown (Revelation 3:11). It topples your confidence so that you won't speak for the Lord. If you're in shame and condemnation, there's no way you're going to share the gospel with anybody. You might share laws and regulations, but you won't share the gospel, which points to Jesus Christ, not me (Romans 1:16).

We're enjoying Genesis as a grace book, and we're discovering the line of grace in it all.

Chapter 26 – God Divides when Babel is around (Genesis 11)

Genesis 10:1-32 KJV Now these are the generations of the sons of Noah, Shem, Ham, and Japheth: and unto them were sons born after the flood. (2) The sons of Japheth; Gomer, and Magog, and Madai, and Javan, and Tubal, and Meshech, and Tiras. (3) And the sons of Gomer; Ashkenaz, and Riphath, and Togarmah. (4) And the sons of Javan; Elishah, and Tarshish, Kittim, and Dodanim. (5) By these were the isles of the Gentiles divided in their lands; every one after his tongue, after their families, in their nations. (6) And the sons of Ham; Cush, and Mizraim, and Phut, and Canaan. (7) And the sons of Cush; Seba, and Havilah, and Sabtah, and Raamah, and Sabtecha: and the sons of Raamah; Sheba, and Dedan. (8) And Cush begat Nimrod: he began to be a mighty one in the earth. (9) He was a mighty hunter before the LORD: wherefore it is said, Even as Nimrod the mighty hunter before the LORD. (10) And the beginning of his kingdom was Babel, and Erech, and Accad, and Calneh, in the land of Shinar. (11) Out of that land went forth Asshur, and builded Nineveh, and the city Rehoboth, and Calah, (12) And Resen between Nineveh and Calah: the same is a great city. (13) And Mizraim begat Ludim, and Anamim, and Lehabim, and Naphtuhim, (14) And Pathrusim, and Casluhim, (out of whom came Philistim,) and Caphtorim. (15) And Canaan begat Sidon his firstborn, and Heth, (16) And the Jebusite, and the Amorite, and the Girgasite,

(17) And the Hivite, and the Arkite, and the Sinite, (18) And the Arvadite, and the Zemarite, and the Hamathite: and afterward were the families of the Canaanites spread abroad. (19) And the border of the Canaanites was from Sidon, as thou comest to Gerar, unto Gaza; as thou goest, unto Sodom, and Gomorrah, and Admah, and Zeboim, even unto Lasha. (20) These are the sons of Ham, after their families, after their tongues, in their countries, and in their nations. (21) Unto Shem also, the father of all the children of Eber, the brother of Japheth the elder, even to him were children born. (22) The children of Shem; Elam, and Asshur, and Arphaxad, and Lud, and Aram. (23) And the children of Aram; Uz, and Hul, and Gether, and Mash. (24) And Arphaxad begat Salah; and Salah begat Eber. (25) And unto Eber were born two sons: the name of one was Peleg; for in his days was the earth divided; and his brother's name was Joktan. (26) And Joktan begat Almodad, and Sheleph, and Hazarmaveth, and Jerah, (27) And Hadoram, and Uzal, and Diklah, (28) And Obal, and Abimael, and Sheba, (29) And Ophir, and Havilah, and Jobab: all these were the sons of Joktan. (30) And their dwelling was from Mesha, as thou goest unto Sephar a mount of the east. (31) These are the sons of Shem, after their families, after their tongues, in their lands, after their nations. (32) These are the families of the sons of Noah, after their generations, in their nations: and by these were the nations divided in the earth after the flood.

How God Remembers History

This is called the table of nations (Genesis 10:1-32). When God talks about nations, he means it from this table.

I live in America. Here, we are a hodgepodge of nations. We all come from this table. When God thinks of us, he doesn't think of America, he thinks of the table - the families we come from (Genesis 10:5). I don't believe that God is so concerned with national boundaries as he is with people and languages and genealogies (Acts 17:26).

Ephesians says that every family in heaven and earth is named by the Father (Ephesians 3:15). He knows us a lot more intimately than we know ourselves, and he knows us according to a history that we've lost all our connection to.

I'm adopted, and I didn't know who I was most of my life. Now I have had the benefit of learning who my biological parents were and reconnecting to some of that family. Still, though, my culture, I've been uprooted from that culture. But I wonder how much God knows me in respect to that culture. When God deals with the nations at the end, he will deal with them largely based on these roots. For example, if you look at Ezekiel 38, for example, which is where we get one of the most specific outlines of that endtime events, these nations come up by their names in this table. Today we call them "Turkey" or Iraq, Iran, and Pakistan. But in the table, and in Ezekiel, they're named by their origins - Persia, Togarmah, Sheba and Dedan, etc. They can be traced based on histories, and we can determine what nations these are today. But God remembers them according to older things.

Matthew 25 talks about the sheep and goats nations (Matthew 25:31-46). We tend to think since America and Britain have supported Israel, God will consider them "sheep nations." We think, Russia and China are gonna be the goats. But those are arbitrary man-made distinctions. That's not what God's looking at. God's looking at where you really came from. That's why this table is very important. If you want to find out who the people are that God refers to throughout the Bible, he's looking at this view. And remember, it's playing out according to destinies pronounced by Noah over Ham, Shem, and Japheth. Ham's son Canaan is going to serve both Japheth and Shem. Shem gets the blessing. This blessing is related to the seed. It's the same blessing that came upon Abraham, and was passed to Isaac, and Jacob, but ultimately rests on Christ, the blessed One (Genesis 9:25-27). And Japheth will be enlarged too and even dwell in the tents of Shem. The "tents of Shem" is an interesting phrase. Abraham Isaac and Jacob dwelled in tents in contrast to Babel. These prefigured the tabernacle, in which God dwelled among the people in Israel in a tent. Of course, Christ is the tabernacle of God, the meeting place between God and man, the great tent. And many of the Gentile nations have come to dwell in Christ, who is the real "tent of Shem."

God cursed Canaan, and the Canaanites are the Hittites, the Jebusites, the Dergashites, all those "ites" that had to get dispossessed from the land. And they were to be wiped out utterly. God is not playing around when it comes to these things. He remembers everything. He remembers things that we don't remember. Jesus said anyone who gives a disciple in His name shall not lose his reward (Matthew 10:42). God remembers everything. And if you are blessed, God remembers everything positive, everything that's in

Christ, everything that you've done in Christ, everything that you felt because of Christ. It's all remembered by God. And so, he's good in that respect. What is the significance of Genesis 10? To us, maybe it is just a bunch of names.. Well, this is what God remembers and this is how God deals with the earth and how things are distributed (Genesis 10:1-32).

I hate to say it, but there's a reason why the Western nations are prosperous. The Gentile nations were very prosperous. Well, because God said he would enlarge them (Genesis 9:27). There's a reason why the Semitic people, not just the sons of Abraham, but definitely the sons of Abraham, have a religious bent. It's the Lord God of Shem (Genesis 9:26). It seems unfair why some have and some don't. I believe that there are decrees and blessings on the nations according to Genesis 9. God means what he says. However, the good news is that if you come to dwell in the tent of Shem, you're blessed. The best place to be is in Shem's tent. And in there, there's no Jew or Gentile, but Christ is all in all (Galatians 3:28). So the real blessing is to be cut out of Adam, grafted into Christ, and made partaker of His blessing. But there are still the nations, and God deals with them and remembers them and has a destiny for them. There are Gentile nations in the millennium. There are Gentile nations apparently in the new heavens and the new earth. The glory of the nations will be brought into the New Jerusalem. God has a plan for everything.

The body of Christ is the place to be because you get reckoned according to Christ and not according to these statuses. However, these statuses do affect where you live when you live and what God works with to bring you to Christ. This is like the background material of your carnal or genetic genealogy, lineage, background, environment, etc. One thing I notice is that in the mentions both of the sons of Japheth and the sons of Shem, there is a mention of division, the dividing of the earth and the dividing into nations and families, which is a positive thing (Gen 10:5, Gen 10:25). It's a move of God in contrast to Ham's line, out of which came Babel, which tried to unite everything.

Worldly unity is of the devil, and God always works by dividing his people out to keep them free from contamination and error, and for our sake, we are told to divide (2 Corinthians 6:17). Jezebel and Baal always want everybody to be united. Actually, Babel is Semiramis and Nimrod's religion, which is the origin of Baal worship, which is a false Christ. And Jezebel was the priestess of that religion. They're all about unity through guilt, through manipulation, and through fear of being shut out. People are led into this false unity where they're directed to worship a false Christ, and sometimes thinking they're worshiping the real Christ. But God brings clarity by dividing us out. That's what it says in 2 Corinthians, "Come out of her, my people, and touch not the unclean thing." It's talking about false teachers. You have to separate from elements. Today, the church, the institutional church, is a part of the Babylonian mystery system or the Mystery Babylon. She thinks she's the church, but she's not. She's directing people to the stern taskmaster, to Baal, and not to Christ. And she does it through flattery and manipulation.

She says, "let's all stay together and let's make a name for ourselves so that we won't be scattered!" She rests God's move to divide and spread out. All that is associated with the curse. We are told of the unity of the body of Christ, but this is not a worldly unity where everyone is in lock step and staying together. It is the unity of the vine that spreads out and bears fruit in clusters, always increasing. It doesn't need to be centralized and outwardly controlled because the life of the vine is in all the branches.

Japheth line - God's work to Divide

The sons of Japheth were Gomer, Magog, Madai, Javan, Tubal, Meshech, and Tiras. And the sons of Gomer: Ashkenaz, Riphath, and Togarmah. A lot of these nations show up in Ezekiel 38's description of a (yet future) attempt by the nations to invade Israel, called the "Magog invasion". And the sons of Javan: Elishah, Tarshish, Kittim, and Dodanim. These were the isles of the Gentiles divided in their lands, everyone after his tongue, after their families, in their nations.

Now, what's interesting is that in the line of Japheth, the bible mentions Gomer, Magog, Madai, Javan, Tubal, Meshech, and Tiras. But we're only told about Gomer and Javan and their sons. Why are they significant? The dividing work of God is evident in the isles of the Gentiles, as they were divided into different lands, each with its own language, families, and nations. Although we don't have much information about the activities of these groups, it is interesting to note that only the sons of Japheth who participated with God in the dividing work are listed by name. This division is further emphasized in Genesis 11, where God confounds the languages of the people at the Tower of Babel, causing them to scatter. This scattering was a protective measure to prevent the unification of mankind under the influence of the Antichrist, as Satan is always attempting to establish his seed in positions of power.

During the time of Babel, the sons of Japheth's great-grandsons, who were alive at that time, played a role in God's plan to divide people and protect them from the tyranny of Babel. Babel was a place of tyranny, and it is important to note that the sons of Ham, specifically Cush, Mizraim, Put, and Canaan, were also associated with Babel. Canaan, in particular, was cursed by Noah. The sons of Cush, such as Seba, Havilah, Sabta, and others, are associated with present-day Saudi Arabia. The sons of Mizraim are associated with Egypt. The significance of the other sons of Ham, such as Put and Canaan, is not explicitly mentioned.

Ham's Line – The opposition to God's Purpose

One notable figure among the descendants of Ham is Nimrod, who is described as a "mighty one" in the earth. The word used to describe him, "gibberim," is the same word used in Genesis 6 to refer to the Nephilim, who were giants and tyrants. Nimrod is believed to have gained access to the knowledge of the pre-flood civilization through occult sorcery and underwent "apotheosis," transforming himself into a god. He married a prostitute named Samuramas, who is considered the mother of all filthiness and abominations on earth, associated with sorcery, temple prostitution, child sacrifice, and cannibalism. These practices were attempts to deify man and gain access to the tree of the knowledge of good and evil. According to occult lore, the pre-flood civilization was led by "ascended masters" who walked openly with the fallen angels (although the occult calls them watchers and the gods of old) deriving their powers from them. Nimrod is a pattern for subsequent god-kings in the world empires such as Babylon, Persia, and Egypt and Rome.

The influence of Nimrod and the occult practices associated with him can still be seen today. Helena Blavatsky and Alice Bailey, who "channeled" books supposedly authored by these ascended masters (which means they went into a trance and let these beings write through them) provide insights into these practices. Alice Bailey even formed the Lucifer Publishing Agency, later renamed Lucis Trust, which is the official publishing arm of the United Nations. The architectural symbolism associated with the United Nations building, such as the unfinished Tower of Babel, the capstone, and the pyramid on the dollar bill, all point to the anticipation of a future leader who will bring about the return of those days. This leader will continue the idea of apotheosis, where man becomes like a god, tracing back to the tree of the knowledge of good and evil.

Nimrod, the firstborn of Cush, firstborn of Ham, established his kingdom in Babel, Erech, Akkad, and Shinar. The land of Shinar is significant, as it is associated with wickedness (Zech 5:8-11). From this land, Asher went forth and built Nineveh, Rehoboth, Calah, and Resen. It is worth noting that Asher is not listed among the sons of Ham but is from the lineage of Shem! This mixing of lineages between the sons of Japheth, Shem, and Ham resulted in tangled destinies, was another reason that required God's division.

Nineveh, known for its wickedness, was shown mercy by God because of their ignorance. God sent Jonah to Nineveh to call them to repentance, as they did not know their "right hand from the left." This act of mercy towards Nineveh can be understood in the context of God's faithfulness to the fact that He is the Lord God of Shem, and Asher, who built Nineveh, descended from the line of Shem! It is likely that Nineveh and even Jonah were unaware of this historical connection. But God Remembers!

The dividing work of God is evident in the division of the isles of the Gentiles and the scattering of people at the Tower of Babel. The descendants of Ham, particularly Nimrod, played a significant role in the wickedness associated with Babel. The occult practices and desire for apotheosis can be traced back to the pre-flood civilization and continue to influence society today. The mixing of lineages among the sons of Japheth, Shem, and Ham resulted in tangled destinies, necessitating God's intervention. God's mercy towards Nineveh can be understood in the context of His faithfulness to the lineage of Shem, from which Asher, the builder of Nineveh, descended.

Mitzraim, from whom came Ludim, Anamim, Lehabim, Naphtuhim, Pathrusim, Casluhim, and Caphtorim, the ancestors of the Philistines (Genesis 10:13-14). Then there's Canaan. We have Sidon, his firstborn, and Heth, and the Jebusite, the Amorite, and the Girgashite, the Hivite, and the Arkite, and the Sinite, the Arvadite, and the Zemarite, and the Hamathite (Genesis 10:15-18). These are, and afterward, were the families of the Canaanites spread abroad. The border of the Canaanites was from Sidon as you come from Gerar to Gaza, as you go on to Sodom and Gomorrah, Admah and Zeboiim and Lasha. All these cities are significant.

Remember who he's talking to. This is Moses talking to the children of Israel about the lands they're about to possess. Okay, there's a reason why he's telling them this story. Yes, it's to record faithfully God's record, but also to introduce the Israelites, to remind them of who they are, to give them their background, and to show them what covenant God is dealing with when He's dealing with them and what promises and what He's doing, and to fill them in on the background of Ham and Canaanites, the ice in the land that they're about to possess.

The Blessed Line of Shem, Establishing the Covenant

Shem is mentioned last, but he's the blessed one, the father of all the children of Eber, the brother of Japheth, the elder. These are honorable. The way he says this is very honorable and decorative. The father, the children of Eber, and the brother of Japheth, and the elder. Even to him were children born. The children of Shem, Elam, Asshur, Arphaxad, now Arphaxad ends up being, I think, the like the great-great-grandfather of Abraham. The children of Aram, Uz, and Hul, and Gether, and Mash. And Arphaxad begat Salah, and Salah begat Eber, and unto Eber were born two sons. The name of one was Peleg, for in his days the earth was divided, and his brother's name was Joktan. There's the division of the earth again, and a lot of people believe that that's the physical earth, the tectonic plates, the continents being separated. So, through Japheth, uh, the families were separated out from Babel, but in Peleg's time, which was probably not Japheth, did I say Japheth? Uh, Japheth, his grandson, during their time, uh, the nations were divided, which was the work of God. And during Peleg's time, who was probably a contemporary, uh, the earth was divided. Both of those are works of God. They're positive moves to divide out God's people who are going to be blessed from this whole situation in Babel because there's mixture. Asshur shouldn't have gone and created Nineveh. That shows how much he was impacted by the culture at Babel, creating another great city that turns out to be exceedingly wicked.

Anyway, Joktan begat Ahmodad and Shiseila from other names, uh, and their dwelling was from Misha as you go to.. We'll leave off there. These are the sons of Shem, after their families, after their tongues, in their lands, after their nations.

These are the families of the sons of Noah, after their generations, in their nations. By these were the nations divided in the flood, after the earth, after the flood. Okay, so that's Genesis 10, and obviously, I didn't do it justice. There are more thorough histories that can be investigated if you want to learn about these lines.. But I do see the positive division with God's move through the Japheth's line. I see Ham being isolated and singled out, set up as a backdrop against which God's light will shine through Shem's line. With Shem, I see God calling his people out of the world system to rest an inheritance, moving toward the city whose builder and maker is God.

Chapter 27 The Background and the World we are Called Out Of (genesis 11)

Genesis 11:1-9 KJV   And the whole earth was of one language, and of one speech. (2) And it came to pass, as they journeyed from the east, that they found a plain in the land of Shinar; and they dwelt there. (3) And they said one to another, Go to, let us make brick, and burn them throughly. And they had brick for stone, and slime had they for morter. (4) And they said, Go to, let us build us a city and a tower, whose top may reach unto heaven; and let us make us a name, lest we be scattered abroad upon the face of the whole earth. (5) And the LORD came down to see the city and the tower, which the children of men builded. (6) And the LORD said, Behold, the people is one, and they have all one language; and this they begin to do: and now nothing will be restrained from them, which they have imagined to do. (7) Go to, let us go down, and there confound their language, that they may not understand one another's speech. (8) So the LORD scattered them abroad from thence upon the face of all the earth: and they left off to build the city. (9) Therefore is the name of it called Babel; because the LORD did there confound the language of all the earth: and from thence did the LORD scatter them abroad upon the face of all the earth.

In Genesis 10, the Table of Nations, what stood out to me this past week was God's act of dividing. It is God who separated the nations into tongues—a positive move. Ham's line, as we'll see, is associated with Babel, while Japheth and Shem's line are distinguished through God's act of division. This is described in Genesis 10, which serves as an overview of the nations that were divided as a result of the events in Genesis 11, focusing on Babel—the first world empire (Genesis 10:5, 20, 31).

As we delve into Genesis, all of this sets the background for what Abraham was called out of. What constitutes the world? What is the world system? In this chapter, we confront Babel, which signifies confusion. Some have said that the Bible tells a tale of two cities: Jerusalem and Babel. From Babel emerges the world empires, ultimately led by the Antichrist—the final world leader opposing Christ. He is a false Christ, an Antichrist. The term "Antichrist" denotes a replacement (in the latin it is called vicar, which shows the irony of the pope calling himself the "vicar of Christ"). To those not firmly grounded in the scriptures and lacking the Spirit—the testimony of Jesus Christ—to guard them against the strong delusion, he will appear as the messianic hope (Genesis 11:1-9; Revelation 13:1-18).

Evil manifests itself largely unchecked in today's world. Hitler could not have perpetrated his atrocities if the church, serving as the restrainer, had merely focused on suppressing evil. Throughout history, including the inquisitions and persecutions under the Catholic Church's system, diabolical evil has prevailed in various forms over the past 2,000 years: from the gladiatorial arenas to the Holocaust and everything in between.

Restraining Strong Delusion

The Holy Spirit, as the Spirit of truth and the bearer of God's testimony regarding His Son Jesus Christ within us, convicts the world of sin and righteousness. It convicts the world of sin because it does not see but believes, and concerning judgment. All of this is encapsulated in the person of Jesus Christ. The Spirit bears witness to the reality of Jesus Christ, thwarting Satan's attempts to introduce his Antichrist, although he has tried. Hitler, operating under a demonic influence, sought to establish a thousand-year kingdom, with himself as a god-king, desiring the nations to worship him—a lineage tracing back to lore associated with Nimrod (John 16:8-11).

Despite Satan's desire to bring forth his seed, he has not yet succeeded in manifesting the man of lawlessness, whose "coming is after the working of Satan with all power signs and lying wonders" (2 Thessalonians 2:9). This is because the restrainer is specifically holding back strong delusion—not just general evil, but strong delusion. God has declared that He will allow those who did not receive the love of the truth to fall into strong delusions so they will believe the lie. This will coincide with the final revelation of the man of sin, whom people will worship as a false Christ. He will come after the working of Satan with all power, signs, and lying wonders to deceive those who are not sealed with the Spirit and do not have the testimony of Jesus Christ. The testimony of Jesus Christ preserves one from delusion. This is why it is not possible for the elect to be deceived—not merely preserving from evil, but from delusion. A delusion is forthcoming upon the whole earth, yet for now, the church is present with the testimony of Jesus Christ.

A unique aspect of the tribulation is that the 144,000 from the 12 tribes, the seed of Abraham, will be sealed and will have the testimony of Jesus. They will be unable to be deceived. Furthermore, everyone who believes through their witness will also be sealed and unable to be deceived, thus they will not accept the mark of the beast. You may wonder, what relevance does this have? This topic came to mind suddenly because its roots lie in Babel. Babylon represents the narrative of an opposing system, one that opposes God and will eventually bring forth the man of sin. Many, myself included, believe that he will have some connection to Nimrod, who is identified with Gilgamesh. Nimrod is the central figure behind various legends the world reveres—a personality deeply rooted in history (Revelation 13:16-18; Revelation 14:1).

The Bible speaks of the beast that will ascend out of the abyss as one who "was not, was, and is not, and yet is" (Revelation 17:8). John indicates that he is of the seven, yet he is also the eighth, implying that he is one of the former heads of a world empire who will re-emerge as the eighth. He is both one of the seven and the eighth—a fascinating concept. He emerges from the abyss, a place where the angels who sinned, described in Genesis 6 as those who went after strange flesh, are kept until the day of judgment—the day of the Lord. They are set to be released. Nimrod, as we observed in the previous chapter, became a gibborim, using the same term Genesis 6 employs for the mighty men of renown. Nimrod is the figure all occultists regard as the prototype of their envisioned world brotherhood of man, world empire, age of enlightenment, and final Luciferian age, believing it will manifest in a person.

This individual founded Babel and was contemporary with Abraham. Even before Abraham's divine calling, out of nowhere, when God appeared to him, Abraham, a descendant of Shem, was in the line of Shem. Noah proclaimed that the Lord God of Shem would be blessed. There is a continuous lineage from Shem and his descendants through Arpachshad, down to Eber. During Eber's days, possibly during his son Peleg's time, the earth was divided—a divine act. It was during this period that God responded to Nimrod's actions at Babel by calling out His people to continue His narrative of His city, Jerusalem. Abraham looked to a city whose builder and maker is God, opposing Babylon or Babel.

At the conclusion of the Bible's narrative, two cities emerge: Mystery Babylon, embodying all the evil characteristics of Babylon and destined for judgment, and the new city, Jerusalem, descending from heaven. While many attribute Mystery Babylon solely to America, its origins trace back to the early world empires post-flood, specifically Babel, associated with Semiramis and Nimrod. Semiramis, believed to be Nimrod's wife and a prostitute, allegedly established the first world religion. Exploiting the promise of the seed of the woman, she proclaimed her son, Tammuz, as Nimrod's incarnation on earth, demanding worship unto death.

According to mythology, Nimrod's death led Semiramis to deify him to solidify her religion. Nimrod had already adopted symbols such as the dragon, the sun, associating himself with the light bearer and the serpent. Semiramis deified him, declaring Tammuz as Nimrod's earthly embodiment, while she assumed the role of queen. Within the Babylonian religion, the queen of heaven, associated with the sun, proclaimed herself as the mother of God. Though historical details are murky, the mother-child worship originated from Babel, under Semiramis's influence, or whoever she may have been. At the core of these "mystery religions," making pacts with the devil, Semiramis's spirit of witchcraft persists beyond death, often identified with Satan, sometimes portrayed as androgynous, possessing both male and female traits, symbolized by the Baphomet.

At the division of Babel, the priesthood of this religion infiltrated every tribe and tongue, adapting to evolving languages and customs. Nimrod, also known as Baal or Tammuz, within this unholy trinity, represents a false Christ. His character fragmented, with idols symbolizing different aspects of his persona. Across various religions, the diverse gods are mere fragments, alluding to this unholy trinity. This idea aligns with what is called the "perennial philosophy," asserting a universal theme underlying all religions, with Lucifer, the Lightbearer, at its core. This belief system, veiled in symbols and rituals, hides its true essence, known only to initiates who progress through layers of understanding until they grasp the ultimate secret: Lucifer is the architect of this world and its destiny.

Although the Bible declares that the kingdoms of the earth belong to Satan, followers of Jehovah, through Jesus Christ, anticipate the destruction of this order, replaced by one founded on love, righteousness, and mercy and on the finished work of Christ. The imagery in different mystery religions leads back to the tree of the knowledge of good and evil, the deification of man, and Nimrod. Today's superhero lore revisits different aspects of Nimrod's personality that have been fragmented.

In the future, there will come a time of strong delusion when someone will deceive the world with lying signs and wonders. However, the elect will not be deceived because they have the testimony of Jesus Christ. This testimony has been passed down through the prophets, starting with Abel and continuing through Abraham. God was already separating the line of Japheth and Shem before Abraham was separated out. Abraham had a background and understanding of what was happening.

Separation

Abraham's calling is similar to our sanctification, which involves being transformed by the renewing of the mind through the knowledge of Jesus Christ. The spirit testifies of Jesus Christ, and we have the seal of the spirit, which prevents us from being deluded. Abraham's witness caused him to believe in the promised seed who would crush the serpent's head. Before Abraham, God was already at work in the line of Japheth and Shem, separating them from the world system of Babel.

Abraham's faith moved him away from Babel, just as we are not compatible with the world. We are strangers and pilgrims, just like Abraham, to Mystery Babylon or Babel. Nimrod, depicted as a false Christ, garnered worship from many, including Jezebel, who introduced Baal worship into Israel (1 Kings 16:30-33; Revelation 2:20). She subverted the worship of Jehovah with that of Baal, even replacing the priesthood with Baal eunuchs (1 Kings 18:19). The people, misled, failed to discern the distinction, as seen in the stoning of Naboth when they thought they were serving Jehovah but were really doing the bidding of Jezebel, dedicated to Baal and based on lies of "children of Belial" (another name for Baal) (1 Kings 21:1-16). Elijah intervened to clarify the true worship of Jehovah. Without the knowledge of Christ, people cannot understand the distinctions. The word is a two edged sword to bring a distinction and a separation based on these very issues. This is why Jesus promised Pergamum, where Baal worship was being introduced to the church in the form of the "doctrine of Balaam," that he would come and fight them (the Baalamites) with the "sword of his mouth."

We cannot be part of the world and part of Christ. We must be separated through the knowledge of God's testimony. This is why we look to the knowledge of the testimony as evidence of God's work in someone's life. God reveals His Son to us, just as He did to Abraham, and believing in Him justifies us and makes us heirs. We are currently immersed in Mystery Babylon, the present world system that influences our morals and our view of God through non-stop media.

The world today in a way is deeper, more developed and complex and all-pervasive than what Abraham was being separated from. We are swimming in a "toxic stew." For Abraham to get away from the world's influence, he could dwell in a tent apart from it all. If he wanted to shut it all out, he could go into his tent. We, on the other hand, go into our "tent," turn on the TV, and keep an eye on our phones. Babylon is like the Matrix. It's everywhere, it permeates our atmosphere and environment. It is the present world system. According to the book of Revelation, there is a commercial, religious, and political aspect to Babylon. All of this bears weight on our understanding of what work is, how value is measured, as well as our values about family, how life is lived, how nations exist, etc. All of the natural concepts are rooted in Babylon. This is a "mystery" city that manipulates our values and what we think is important. Christians getting involved with any cause other than Christ is usually just a path for them to be manipulated and taken advantage of because it all comes from the same world system.

Religious Babylon

But then there's religious Babylon, where Christ is replaced with the false Christ. This can be seen even from the Bible. When the Jews went down into Babylon, they came up with the Talmud and the Kabbalah, which are Babylonian mysteries injected into their interpretation of the scripture. The same thing happened again when Origen started allegorizing the scripture and the Catholic Church emerged. Now, we've spent the last 500 since the reformation, with God recovering us out from all of that by revealing the plain truth from the scriptures, especially in Paul's writing. We have seen a recovery since justification by faith, a recovery of focus on Christ, a recovery of the truth of our death with Him, the significance of our baptism into Him, the fact that He's our life, our satisfaction, our enjoyment and that He's building up the body of Christ to be the new Jerusalem. These thigns were in the scripture but the scripture was not available to everyone and was handled by wolves that deliberately mishandled the truth from the pulpits for a thousand years, which the world calls "the dark ages." If only they knew how dark it was!

This body of truth, the knowledge of Christ, the testimony of God regarding His Son, is a calling that transforms us out of our present world, mirroring Abraham's separation. What Abraham knew of the promised seed, the promised land, and the heavenly city whose builder and maker is God catalyzed his transformation and withdrawal from the world. While the principle remains the same, we are blessed with deeper revelations and a greater understanding of our status in Christ. We are seated with Him and raised with Him, co-heirs of His inheritance. Now that He has risen, so have we.

Given that we are more deeply entrenched in Mystery Babylon than Abraham was in Babel, God amplifies the flow of the water of the Word, providing us with a stronger stream of the knowledge of Christ. We should anticipate the unveiling of greater truths concerning our identity in Christ, our access to His riches, and His comforting presence through His Word. Christ, ultimately, will present

His Bride as glorious, without blemish, having sanctified her "through the washing of the water of the word." Peter affirms that through the knowledge of Christ, an abundant entrance is granted for us to enter the Kingdom confidently. When the enemy raises a standard, our Lord responds with a flood, as God raises a standard against him.

Indeed, the abundance of revelation concerning the person and work of Christ is our divine calling. It is God's summons to extricate us from the grip of this world system, particularly from the false religious notions that advocate the worship of Baal. In ancient times, this idolatrous worship centered around Tammuz, the son of Nimrod, the original god-king, whom they demanded be worshipped as the promised seed (Genesis 10:8-10; Jeremiah 10:2-5).

Sanctification is Separation from the Hard Taskmaster

Within Christianity, there exists a false Christ—a hard taskmaster—who often usurps the true focus of Jesus and places emphasis on human effort for righteousness, sanctification, or reward (Galatians 1:6-9; Colossians 2:8; Romans 9:32-33). This false Christ mirrors Nimrod and the spirit of Babel, epitomizing the attitude of "Let us build this city to make a name for ourselves, that we would not be scattered," as depicted in Genesis 11:1-9. This narrative sets the stage for God's call to His people, following His mention of a separating work in Genesis 10:32.

Nimrod serves as the archetype of subsequent god-kings in empires. Pharaoh, for example, symbolized by Satan himself, demanded the Israelites toil relentlessly, mirroring the false Christ's call to labor endlessly (Exodus 5:6-9; 2

Corinthians 11:13-15). Conversely, God's directive for His people to celebrate a feast to Him represents liberation from toil and a transition to abundant provision—a concept exemplified by the promised land flowing with milk and honey (Exodus 3:8; Deuteronomy 26:15; Psalm 34:8).

The narrative of Genesis 10 and 11 marks the commencement of God's sanctifying work among His people. Sanctification, far from separation to toil, entails separation from toil unto Christ, who is our true feast and inheritance (1 Thessalonians 5:23; Ephesians 1:11-14). The edifices of God are not constructed by human hands (Acts 7:48; Hebrews 9:11). We are separated unto a heavenly city, whose builder and maker is God Himself (Hebrews 11:10; Revelation 21:2).

Chapter 28 God Separates His Called By Giving Them A Language to Speak of His Covenant (Genesis 11-12)

Genesis 11:10-26 KJV These are the generations of Shem: Shem was an hundred years old, and begat Arphaxad two years after the flood: (11) And Shem lived after he begat Arphaxad five hundred years, and begat sons and daughters. (12) And Arphaxad lived five and thirty years, and begat Salah: (13) And Arphaxad lived after he begat Salah four hundred and three years, and begat sons and daughters. (14) And Salah lived thirty years, and begat Eber: (15) And Salah lived after he begat Eber four hundred and three years, and begat sons and daughters. (16) And Eber lived four and thirty years, and begat Peleg: (17) And Eber lived after he begat Peleg four hundred and thirty years, and begat sons and daughters. (18) And Peleg lived thirty years, and begat Reu: (19) And Peleg lived after he begat Reu two hundred and nine years, and begat sons and daughters. (20) And Reu lived two and thirty years, and begat Serug: (21) And Reu lived after he begat Serug two hundred and seven years, and begat sons and daughters. (22) And Serug lived thirty years, and begat Nahor: (23) And Serug lived after he begat Nahor two hundred years, and begat sons and daughters. (24) And Nahor lived nine and twenty years, and begat Terah: (25) And Nahor lived after he begat Terah an hundred and nineteen years, and begat sons and

daughters. (26) And Terah lived seventy years, and begat Abram, Nahor, and Haran.

What we're doing is looking at God's move in grace in Genesis, with a focus on the revelation of Jesus Christ and God's move to bring Him forth. We've seen so much about how God has dealt with his people from the beginning. According to Christ, he dealt with Abel and rejected Cain because Cain rejected Christ (Hebrews 11:4).

Cain rejected the way that man could be brought into fellowship with God by presenting the first thing of the flock as an offering for sin with the fat portion. Abel understood that because he was a prophet and had the testimony of Jesus Christ. To be a prophet means that you see God behind everything (Genesis 4:4, Revelation 19:10). I think about Elijah when he was with Elisha and the armies of Syria were around them. Elijah asked God to open Elisha's eyes, and God did. Elisha could see tens of thousands of angelic chariots surrounding them. There's a spiritual reality based on God's faithfulness to his word (2 Kings 6:17).

Being a prophet doesn't mean having an ability to see something supernaturally in a vision. It means understanding unseen things because of confidence in the testimony of God's word and the ways of God in relation to his covenants. All of his covenants center on the person and work of Christ. Having a prophetic vision, seeing Christ, understanding the testimony of God concerning the Son, puts you in a position to see things others can't see by faith.

How do I know that the calamities in my life and the consequences for my bad decisions will work together for good? How do I know that God is not angry at me and that he's lovingly dealing with me through them all to teach me to depend on him and manifest his life in me? I know that from the word. It's a prophetic vision that allows me to see the true nature of things behind things, so I don't misinterpret all my circumstances.

That's what it means to have a prophetic vision. It means discerning what God is doing. Unfortunately, we are at a time when so-called prophetic people have no clue what God is doing. They know nothing of his heart and reject the testimony of Christ and the scriptures. They're not in the word and not operating in faith. They peddle false doctrine based on fleshly experiences, visions, dreams, and encounters with sensual spirits and doctrines of demons. We have this wrong idea of prophets. A prophet is someone who is so constituted with the word of God's testimony that they move with God, agree with God's judgment, and see the nature of God based on what God has established in his covenants. When God establishes his covenant, we see his grace, his nature, and his mercy.

God established his covenant with Noah and the seed, which is ultimately Christ. Even though God repented that he made man because man's thoughts were only evil continually, he preserved Noah for Christ's sake. Noah understood that and was justified because he believed it. He was preserved for Christ's sake so that God could have a new start in a new day, in a new world, with a new human race. The old human race was judged, and now God is dealing with a group of people he calls out from among the human race to be separated unto his testimony and purpose, which is related to Christ. Just like Noah and Abraham, we don't have a purpose apart from Christ. Everything apart from Christ is vanity.

Abraham was said to be a prophet because he believed in Christ. We know this from Romans 4, Galatians 3, and Hebrews 11. He understood the promise of the seed and redemption and had everything that the line of prophets had. In the first six chapters of Genesis, we saw a line of life that understood the need for an altar, an offering, and the promise of the seed of the woman. Based on their faith in the seed of the woman and their understanding of sin, God's grace, and his covenant, they offered up the first thing of the flock, called on the name of the Lord, and walked with God. They understood that judgment was coming and that God did not destroy the righteous with the wicked. Eventually, they participated with God in the building work of preservation, Noah's ark.

This is the prophetic vision, and we see it outlined in Hebrews 11, the "hall of faith." It's not about the great men of faith and their valor. Faith is not a work; it's a vision. The focus of Hebrews 11 is what they saw by faith. They did things because of what they saw. Why did Abraham dwell in tents rather than live in Babel? Because he sought a city whose builder and maker is God. Why did Moses choose to suffer the afflictions of Christ with the people of Christ rather than indulge in the pleasures of Egypt? Because he had a vision that, according to God's covenant, he was going to separate a people and put them in the land as an inheritance for them and bring them into rest. It was the vision of what God was going to do that caused people to move forward.

Sharing God's Vision As A Friend

Now, we're in Genesis 12, and we want to see this with a prophetic view. Don't think of the prophets as special; think of yourself as prophetic. Paul desired that everyone could prophesy. When you see the testimony of Christ, your eyes are opened. When you look at the Bible in the light of the testimony of Christ, you see things that others don't see. Cain, carnal people, and works-oriented people who don't understand the testimony of Christ or the move of God don't understand his grace, his kindness, or his purpose to cause us to inherit all things with Christ. Christ and that it's all related to Christ. Without Christ, there is no purpose. All they see is commandments and flesh and the works they think they should generate. Why? Because they have no vision. When they read the Bible, their eyes are closed. They don't read it for anything but moral lessons so that they can work on themselves. Well, that's not how we're looking at the Scripture. We're looking for Christ. We're looking at God's testimony. And the more we see of His testimony, which is how He moves in mankind to bring forth Christ before the church and now in the church, the more our eyes are opened to see the goodness of God, the grace of God, the kindness of God. And we become His friends. He says, "Now you're my friends."

Jesus said, "A slave doesn't know what his master is doing; but I have called you friends, for all things that I have heard from My Father I have made known to you" (John 15:15). Abraham was the first to be called a friend of God (James 2:23). That's why God shared with him His plans regarding the judgment of Sodom and Gomorrah. He knew that Abraham, being a man of vision, understood God's heart and character (Genesis 18:17-19). Abraham knew that God would not destroy the righteous with the wicked (Genesis 18:23-32). Based on his knowledge of God's nature, Abraham interceded for Sodom and Gomorrah (Genesis 18:22-33). That's the kind of best friend you can have, you know. And that's what we are (John 15:14-15).

And that's what it means to walk with God. Once you see God's heart, then you can walk with God because you understand His nature and you start interpreting things in the light of it. And so, you're in a position to cooperate with God and not get dismayed when conflict comes or when the devil attacks because you know what the stakes are and God's move is. But when you're blind and the devil attacks, you don't know what the stakes are, you don't know what God's move is (Proverbs 3:5-6).And so, you think, "Oh, I must have done something bad and now God's mad at me. And that's why I'm being judged or getting sick or having these things happen to me. I did something wrong." Really? You think that's who God is? No, God's intention in Christ is to comfort you at every stage. But that requires a prophetic vision.

The comfort works while we look not to those things which are seen but to the things which are unseen. And Christ is wrought into us. We don't judge things by the flesh and by our circumstances. We judge by, we learn to judge by the testimony of Christ. That's how we interpret what God's doing in our life, in the world. What is He trying to accomplish? What does He say He's going to do? And because we believe it and we know His nature, our prayers are affected. The way we pray, what we pray about. Blind people don't pray for the building up of the body of Christ. Blind spiritually blind people pray, "Bless me, forgive me of my sins, keep me from doing this, keep me from doing that. Use me, God, use me, God. Make me useful, clean me up so I can be useful." They want to be a tool and an employee and a slave.

But when you see God's heart, you say, "Oh Lord, I pray that people would have a spirit of wisdom and revelation in the full knowledge of You. I pray You'd enlighten the eyes of their heart. I pray You give us a glimpse of the riches of Your glory so that Christ can be put on display before us. And as we behold Him, we know that He's worked into us and that Your purpose is accomplished. That You're building up the church. Lord, let the church be built up. Let the word be glorified. Let the word go forth and produce life. Wash people, renew people, bring them into the freedom they have in Christ, out of bondage and into this liberty of the sons of God, the spirit of sonship. Lord, allow us to speak of these things clearly as we ought. Help us to speak the mystery of Christ. That's prophetic prayer. That's praying according to God's heart.

And you know when you pray like that and talk like that, the legalists will accuse you and say you're behaving badly, you're sinning, God's going to get you, He's going to judge you. And if they can't think of why, they'll make up accusations. So don't be surprised when religious people suddenly start accusing you of all manner of evil because you speak of Christ. It shows where their heart is. We want to be prophetic when we look at Genesis. We don't want just to see it as an old collection of old stories. We want to see God moving and what He's doing.

The Background and the Call

So Genesis 11 is the background of Abraham's call. And in Genesis 10, we talked about Nimrod boming from Ham's line. Ham generated Canaan that populated the good land to be in opposition to God putting His people in that land as an inheritance. And Ham generated Cush who begat Nimrod who developed the world system to seduce God's people and keep them from wanting God's inheritance, their inheritance. That's really what the world system is. It is a circus to attract you and draw you away from Christ and what He is. And it presents a false Christ and misrepresents God, makes Him the hard taskmaster. In the world, everyone's job is to build Nimrod's kingdom, Baal's kingdom, the false Christ kingdom, the hard taskmaster's kingdom. If you are in the prophetic line and you're called, you're called out of that.

There can be no fellowship between the two lines. Just like in Genesis 4 and 5, there were two lines. There was a line of Cain and then the line of life in Genesis 5 with Seth, Enosh, Enoch, Methuselah, and Noah, Lamech. They were on the line of life. They had the testimony of Jesus Christ, and they were separated to that testimony. And they had an altar, offered up the first thing of the flock, called on the name of the Lord, walked with God, and were preachers of righteousness. And then there was the world, Cain's line, which went out from the presence of God and built cities and named them after themselves and developed the world system at that time.

The same principle is operating here in Genesis 10. Ham's line generates things that are in opposition to God and to seduce God's people. Cain's cities and musical instruments, agriculture, all the things that were developed from his line would have been an attraction. And eventually, the idea is to pollute the line of life. And it must have gotten pretty bad because God decided to destroy them all. We know there was angelic stuff going on too, fallen angels and all that. But with Nimrod in Genesis 10, we saw that Asshur went forth out of Shinar and created Nineveh, the same way Nimrod created Babel. And Nineveh was another wicked city. But I was surprised to discover that Asshur the line of Shem. What's he doing dwelling like Nimrod and the sons of Ham and building cities like that?

The world system is seductive. And the world system made up of orphans. Living in the world is like living as an orphan being rejected from God, knowing you are alienated from Him, and not being willing to make peace with Him through the blood, but instead going your own way. And here we see in Genesis 11 that Babel was created. And I don't; there's not that much detail about it, so I'm not going to emphasize that much detail about it. But one thing Josephus said was that Babel was made of a certain brick that was waterproof. They were wanting to protect themselves from another flood. this is unbelief and a denial of God's covenant. Remember, these are Noah's sons. They knew the rainbow promise that God would never do that again. Also, accoridng to the Bible, they started migrating east, back towards Eden. Second of all, they built the city on the plain of Shinar to reach the "gates of heaven." And it was in rebellion and opposition to God by Nimrod. The book of Jasher called him "the hunter of the souls of men." They hated Jehovah. They hated the God of the Bible. Their view was sometihng like, "look what He did to the world. He destroyed it! We're going to build a city that's waterproof so He can't get us this time." All of this is a denial of God's word.

So there are two groups of people: Noah and his line, Japheth and Shem, or at least Shem. The God of Lord God Hashem (of Shem), those people believed God's covenant. How do we know that? Well, they had an altar and a tent. You know, Abraham was a friend of God. He had an altar. You'll see him in this story making altars occasionally and offering up something to the Lord. And he believed in the promise of the seed, and he knew God's purpose was to preserve life, create life. But in Babel, the idea is God's purpose is to destroy and judge unless you build something that can protect yourself from it.

And that's what Masons believe too. That's why they wear their apron in their coffins. They believe somehow that's going to protect them from the judgment of God. Babel is essentially a religious place with a false Christ, Nimrod, married to Semiramis who fashioned herself the "queen of hevaen," and Tammuz, who is the so-called son of God (a counterfeit). Jeremiah mentions this when he said "I beheld another abomination, women weeping for Tammuz and making cakes to the queen of heaven." That points all the way back to this religion with its false Christ. They capitalized on the promise of the seed of the woman and said, "We have to build a city." Nimrod said, "We have to build a city to protect ourselves from the judgment."

This is what religion does. Religion has the false Christ, the false taskmaster Christ who wants to judge and obliterate everybody and gives you virtue and religion in the things you build as a kind of protection against the judgment of God, which is just like the aprons that Adam and Eve sewed out of the fig leaves. Remember, we saw that the word for apron was the same word that people girded themselves for battle. They were putting on armor. People have a view of the judgment seat of Christ. We've talked about this with rewards, that you need to protect yourself from God's judgment. They don't understand. They've come to Zion. They don't understand that it's a whole new atmosphere of rejoicing and celebration, pleasure and gladness that's in the city of the living God. They don't know what the Bema seat is. They think you're going to be beaten for your faults and your sins, even though Jesus already bore it.

No, He bore that so that all that remains is what will be celebrated. Wood, hay, and stubble, can be burned off in the twinkling of an eye when we are changed. So corruptible works will be lost. But you yourself are standing in that day rejoicing. I believe that firmly now. How you see the judgment seat of Christ is very much related to how you see God, how you see His covenant, how you see whether you walk with Him, whether your eyes are opened. And people who see the judgment seat of Christ, the Bema seat of reward, as a fearful place for a believer don't understand it. And they're looking at it in the light of how the false Christ has been presented, the hard taskmaster.

He's there to beat you, and you better protect yourself. So they do "good" (dead) works, not springing forth from the rejoicing in the life in them, but to build up some protection against that day. And that's what Babel was. The root of Babel is, number one, we will exalt ourselves to heaven. We're going to find a way in. Okay, it was a gateway to heaven, a gate to the heavens. Some people think it was some interdimensional portal. That may be a bit far, but they were definitely doing some occultic stuff. Josephus said the stones were all names of blasphemy. They hated God but did all this in the name of being godly, in a sense. But it's a false god. Baal is a false god. Tammuz is a false god. They had a false god who pretended to be Christ. He's the prototype of Antichrist. Antichrist being a replacement for Christ, pretending to be the seed of the woman, but not carrying you on the basis of His work, but rather as a taskmaster demanding your work, which you must do to protect yourself from wrath.

Babel was made out of waterproof stones in a complete denial that God had said in a covenant that He would never flood the earth again, even though man's heart is wicked. God said I know His heart is evil since His youth, but I'll never do that again. I'll set My bow in the cloud. So based on His promise, Noah and his descendants through Shem, leading up to Abraham, walk with God, just as they did in the line of life prior to the flood. They know that they have nothing to do with Babel. And as we saw, it was Japheth's line and Shem's line through which God divided the nations. These are the "good guys," and the division is God's work.

Separated Out

And remember, He divided the nations because of what was being attempted at Babel. So His move is to separate His people out from that. The whole earth was one language and of one speech. You might be tempted to say "oh good, unity!" No, that's Babylonian unity! And it came to pass as they journeyed from the east, they found a plain in the land of Shinar, and there they dwelt. They said to one another, "Go, let us make brick, burn them thoroughly." And they had brick for stone and slime they had for mortar. And they said, "Go, let us build a city and a tower whose top may reach unto heaven, and let us make us a name, lest we be scattered upon the face of the earth."

This is about identity. It's about being reaching heaven. I think that the idea was they were going to climb into heaven, assault the God of heaven, and put their god in its place, according to Josephus and other sources. They looked at Him, Jehovah, as a usurper. That's the secret of the Luciferian religion. They believe that Satan's seed is the legitimate god, and Jehovah is the usurper, apostate, or whatever. It's really bad, but that's the root of Luciferianism in this age and it has its roots at Babel.

And the Lord came down to see the city and the tower, and the children of men that which the children of men built. And the Lord said, "Behold, the people are one, and they have one language, and this they began to do. And now nothing will be restrained from them, which they have imagined to do." And remember, every imagination of their heart is only evil continually. That has not changed after the flood. The only people that's not true of is those who have had their imagination purified by beholding the vision of God's testimony and His covenant and His purpose and His will, which is us. Why the knowledge of His will separates and sanctifies you. We're separated and sanctified by the washing of the water, the word. We need to have a vision. Otherwise, we will think the way Babel thinks about God, and we'll build ourselves something to protect ourselves from God instead of opening ourselves up to Him as children, knowing that He intends our good and everything is working for our good, even though we all like sheep are counted as for the slaughter every day.

You know, we go through trials, but we know God's purpose behind all that and what He's really doing in this universe related to Christ. And so we don't despair in our trials, knowing our momentary light affliction works in us an exceeding weight of glory that's not worthy to be compared to these momentary light afflictions, right? You have got to have a vision to be able to rejoice in God in your trials. Otherwise, you say, "Well, I need to build up something to protect myself because..." God's trying to judge me again.

God said, "And let us confound their language, that they may not understand their speech." So God scattered them abroad from thence the face of the whole earth, and they left off to build the city.

Now, I used to think that all happened in one moment miraculously. Suddenly, everybody in one second couldn't understand each other. But when I read Genesis 10, I see that it was in the days of Eber, the son of Arphaxad, that his son Peleg is during his days that the earth was divided. The earth was divided physically, maybe that's the platonic movement the plates, I don't know. So God was doing, I believe it's more of a gradual. The tower would have been a multigenerational work, like the cathedrals, the Catholic Church. In the medieval times, it was modern Babylon in a very literal sense. And they had these building projects that were really temples to Baal, pretending to be temples to God. They took generations to build, right? Your grandfather was working on it, and your grandfather's grandfather. It's the great work. Masons love multi-generational building projects that get whole cultures wrapped up in their religion. Nimrod is the father of the Illuminati and the masons. It's important to realize because God's separating work is a process.

Divided when God's People Learn His Vocabulary

It's really important that we see through Abraham's story that his separating work is a process of God visiting his people again and again and over time making more and more clear the purpose for which he's called them. This is the assurance that they have, that he's going to bring it to pass, securing their trust through his faithfulness. He doesn't demand that you obey him when you don't believe him, and he doesn't demand that you believe him without leaving a record and assuring you and teaching you through your life how faithful he is. He demonstrates himself on behalf of the righteous. If you're justified and fit by faith, your life is a proving ground where God's going to prove to you that number one, your flesh doesn't work, number two, God does work in spite of your flesh. And he brings you into the blessing one way or another, but he has to prove it to you so that you'll walk with him, and that takes time.

Religionists don't like time. They think that they get saved and then instantly now they're going to obey God. Well, obey what? What have you seen? They may say, "I'll look in the Bible. Here it says I'm supposed to love my wife." Neverv mind that this verse is sitting in a context of description of Christ and the church. Did you see in Colossians when it refers to the same thing, he's talking about the new man? What's the new man? What's the new creation of God? I don't know. I'm just gonna get a bunch of marriage books and learn how to love my wife. That's not it. God wants to visit you and see the people of God learn a new vocabulary. And that's one of the reasons why the language divides. Seed, promise, altar, sin, justification, blessing, rest, good land, Christ, the triune God, the body of Christ. All the language we learn from the Bible concerning God's purpose separates us.

You know, there's a lot of people who don't understand what we're talking about, and so they say, "Oh, it's a cult." Why? Because they don't understand the language. The language itself is a work of division, and one of the problems in Christianity is that everybody speaks a different language. It's total confusion. Very few are speaking the language of God's testimony, but that in itself produces a division because God's testimony and the language surrounding it produces a culture, circumcision.

Abraham eventually was defined by a culture that was a linguistic culture based in language surrounding God's covenant. If you know God's covenant, you have a language that other people don't have. You talk about things that they don't. That separates you. But ultimately, God confounded their languages. However, I believe that happened over time. (Genesis 11:7)

So the Lord scattered them abroad from thence the face of the earth. They "left off to build". Shem and Japheth would have separated out and left off from building the city. Shem, Ham, and Japheth, all were brothers, but their descendants, because of the blessings and the curses because of Genesis 9, they had very different trajectories. (Genesis 11:8)

Shem's line was separated out to dwell in tents, which are a type of the tabernacle, because out of them is coming Christ, who is the tabernacle of God and the church, the habitation of God. Shem's line is about God's city, whose builder and maker is God, which is in contrast to Babel. They were all building Babel, but as God confounded their languages, one of the ways he did this was to provide the called people with a language that was unique because they believed in the covenant. (Genesis 11:9)

When God gives His people a clear language, all the other speaking of people who don't understand God's language becomes nonsense and vain jangling. At Babel they talked about God's judgment and the flood. They said "he's going to kill us all and you better build up a name for yourself." But the people of God said, "No, there's a covenant. Don't you remember the everlasting covenant? Where's your altar?" (Genesis 11:6)

As soon as God made that covenant, Noah made an altar. Those are two words, covenant and altar that were not understood by the Babylonians. All right, where's your walk with God? Why aren't you calling on the name of the Lord? Abraham did all those things just like they did in the days before the flood. It's a continual line of God's vocabulary, his language, his covenant, his purpose, and separating people out by it.

So therefore the name of it is called Babel because there the Lord did confound the language of all the earth. And from thence did he scatter them abroad upon the face of all the earth. (Genesis 11:9)

The scattering abroad is not a bad thing. The church grows by scattering, not by gathering together. When there was a revival, there was a revival in Jerusalem in the book of Acts, right? But then there was a persecution. God allowed that. Why? Because through the persecution, the Jewish believers were scattered. They wouldn't leave Jerusalem. Jerusalem had become Babylon at that time, in a way. An Earthly-rooted gate to heaven, but the gate was closed and the hard taskmaster had replaced Jehovah through the corruption brought in by the baylonian mysteries in the Talmud.

They didn't have the right gospel anymore. And it was a mix of Babylonian and Jewish practices. They had the Talmud, they had the Kabbalah, they had all kinds of stuff. But God separated his people out through the gospel, restoring to them a language of grace, regenerating them, showing them something about the body of Christ. And then through persecution, scattered them from Jerusalem. Otherwise, they would have stayed in Jerusalem. But he scattered them. It was during the scattering that you saw Gentile churches start to crop up everywhere, and the gospel was going out from Jerusalem to the uttermost parts of the world.

The scattering work is a good thing from God to get his people out of that environment. If you've been a Christian and you've tried the institutional churches and you've been in and out and you keep finding no rest there because nothing there matches your conscience which is anchored in the testimony of God, you've been scatterd. You've been scattered and you may be alone, you may feel alone. You're outside the gate suffering with Christ. Let us go out to him outside the camp bearing his reproach. There's a scattering that's from God, there's a division from God to divide you out from the false Christ taskmaster and set you up for rest and grace. And we'll see Abraham's life was typified by not building, but dwelling in tents, resting in God's provision, to varying degrees of perfection as his faith grew by God's visitation. Remember, this whole thing is the background of Abraham's call.

Back to the Line of Life

> **Genesis 11:9-11 KJV   Therefore is the name of it called Babel; because the LORD did there confound the language of all the earth: and from thence did the LORD scatter them abroad upon the face of all the earth. (10) These are the generations of Shem: Shem was an hundred years old, and begat Arphaxad two years after the flood: (11) And Shem lived after he begat Arphaxad five hundred years, and begat sons and daughters.**

Okay, so then after he scatters them, what does he say? These are the generations of Shem. So now he's focused again on the line of Shem. This is the line of life. This is, just like Genesis 5, after he told of Cain and his deeds and the tragedy where Lamech said, "I killed a man and God's going to avenge me sevenfold." That's that last work in the line of Cain, to speak of vengaence. Lamech's little speech about boasting that he killed someone and he was going to be avenged. Right after that, God moved and described the line of life. Look at the verses:

Genesis 4:24-26 KJV   If Cain shall be avenged sevenfold, truly Lamech seventy and sevenfold. (25) And Adam knew his wife again; and she bare a son, and called his name Seth: For God, said she, hath appointed me another seed instead of Abel, whom Cain slew. (26) And to Seth, to him also there was born a son; and he called his name Enos: then began men to call upon the name of the LORD.

Then God gives us Chapter 5, the "book of the generations of Adam." When God has a book, it means this is what He remembers. Adam's generations in that book don't have anyone on Cain's line in it. By the way, this tells me Adam was saved. In this line, instead of boasts, we see God remembers they called on the name of the Lord, spoke of the judgment of God, were preachers of righteousness, and said, "God's gonna comfort us concerning our toil." The Lamech in that line named Noah, comfort, rest, because God's going to comfort us concerning our toil. He is the opposite of the Lamech in Cain's line!

It all comes down to language. Your speech eventually reveals what line you're on. The Lamech on the line of Cain spoke of vengeance and boasting in his own evil deeds. But the Lamech in the line of life named his child Noah because he knew God was going to comfort us from the toil because of the curse. This means that Cain didn't believe that God was going to comfort anybody. He never reconciled to God; neither did his descendants. But the line of life, they did. That's why they had an altar, that's why they walked with God, that's why they called on his name because they knew he's the God of all comfort, the Father of mercies. Again, who do you see? If you are a prophet with the testimony of Christ, you will see a very different kind of God than those who do not have that language. And it's going to come out in your speech eventually.

We see the same thing here. Nimrod's got the false, he hates Jehovah, he takes the symbol of the dragon and the sun, exalts himself like Satan, becomes a giborrim, marries Semiramis, and starts this mother-child cult. She does with a false imposter Christ, Tammuz, and herself as the mother of God, hijacking the promise of the seed of the woman and then building up this weapons system and defense mechanism against the judgment of God, totally in denial of God's covenant, totally in denial of God being a God of grace and mercy.

But God separated his people, the line of Shem, from all that by His promise. Their belief in covenant promise gave them a new language and a new direction. How did God divide the nations? He confounded their language. What is the primary thing? What is the difference between the language of Babel and the language of God's people? Well, there's the language of a false Christ taskmaster with all of his works and a misperception of God's nature and a misperception of the judgment. And then there is the true seed of the woman, the promise of Christ, the blessing, the rest, the comfort, the inheritance.

Abraham's going to be told that he's got an inheritance. These are, and there's an altar for sins, there's forgiveness, there's mercy, there's comfort. I don't have to build anything, I'm just going to dwell in a tent as a stranger and a pilgrim. That's my testimony. It's language that produces this. God's language, his word, versus the world's language, which comes out of the world system made out of Satan's lies about God.

Okay, so then he starts recounting. This shows God's focus. There's a little blurb about Babel, and the main point is that God confounded their language to separate out his people, and they eventually left off building the city. Praise God. And again, this is a process. Sanctification is a process. When you become saved, you're still building Babel. You still try to build it up. You don't know how involved Babylon you are until you really start to see grace and see the difference between man's religion of Baal and the true Christ. And that comes from growing in the knowledge of Jesus Christ through the milk of the word, his language. They left off from building the city. By this, they were separated from it. As their language changed, that's the point. That's what it is. He confounded their language. Praise God.

Genesis 11:10-26 KJV These are the generations of Shem: Shem was an hundred years old, and begat Arphaxad two years after the flood: (11) And Shem lived after he begat Arphaxad five hundred years, and begat sons and daughters. (12) And Arphaxad lived five and thirty years, and begat Salah: (13) And Arphaxad lived after he begat Salah four hundred and three years, and begat sons and daughters. (14) And Salah lived thirty years, and begat Eber: (15) And Salah lived after he begat Eber four hundred and three years, and begat sons and daughters. (16) And Eber lived four and thirty years, and begat Peleg: (17) And Eber lived after he begat Peleg four hundred and thirty years, and begat sons and daughters. (18) And Peleg lived thirty years, and begat Reu: (19)

And Peleg lived after he begat Reu two hundred and nine years, and begat sons and daughters. (20) And Reu lived two and thirty years, and begat Serug: (21) And Reu lived after he begat Serug two hundred and seven years, and begat sons and daughters. (22) And Serug lived thirty years, and begat Nahor: (23) And Serug lived after he begat Nahor two hundred years, and begat sons and daughters. (24) And Nahor lived nine and twenty years, and begat Terah: (25) And Nahor lived after he begat Terah an hundred and nineteen years, and begat sons and daughters. (26) And Terah lived seventy years, and begat Abram, Nahor, and Haran.

Restating the genealogy in Genesis 10, it mentions that in the days of Peleg, the earth was divided (Genesis 10:25). So it was generations into building up Babel that God was working to separate his people. Sarah lived after he begat Nahor 200 years. Nahor begat Terah, who is Abraham's father. And Terah lived, and we've got Abraham, Nahor, and Haran. Now these are the generations of Terah: Abraham, Nahor, Haran. And Haran begat Lot. And he is married to Milcah. Abraham and Nahor took them wives. The wife of Abraham was Sarah, or Abraham with Sarah. The wife of Nahor was Milcah, the daughter of Haran. And Lot, Abraham's nephew, went with him. And his brother Nahor took Milcah, his brother's niece, and married her. That's just a glimpse into the culture, but also it explains why it was so hard for Abraham to leave.

God instructed Abraham to leave his family and everything behind, yet he didn't fully comply initially (Genesis 12:1). This highlights the strong bond and duty within the family unit. Taking Lot with him was a matter of righteousness, showing that serving God doesn't mean abandoning family (Genesis 12:4). Jesus cautioned against nullifying God's commandments through tradition, emphasizing the importance of honoring parents (Matthew 15:3-6). Family is a gift to God, and dishonoring parents goes against this principle (Exodus 20:12). Abraham's actions, though initially hesitant, ultimately honored his family, as evidenced by God's patience and eventual separation (Genesis 11:32, Genesis 13:5-9). God knows how to separate individuals according to His plan (2 Corinthians 6:17). Obedience to God may involve difficult choices, but separating oneself from family in disobedience contradicts God's sovereignty (Luke 14:26). Abraham's obedience, despite initial hesitation, demonstrates his understanding of God's call (Hebrews 11:8).

Sarah was barren, and she had no child. That is mentioned there because that's important. Obviously, we're talking about the seed. It has to come supernaturally. Terah took Abram and his son, and Lot, the son of Haran, his son's son, and Sarah. So, Terah is the one who moved out, and they went forth from Ur of the Chaldeans to go to the land of Canaan. Terah is the one who moved to the land of Canaan? I thought Abraham was called!

And this is where I believe that God had already been working for generations in the people of the line of Shem. He doesn't always tell you to go. You get to a point where you can't take it anymore because your conscience is constantly satisfied with God's language, and it doesn't match Babel. You have to go because you're just not compatible. That's God's work too, every bit as much as Him commanding you to go.

And they came into Haran and dwelt there, and the days of Tara were 205 years, and Terah died in Haran. The Lord had said to Abram, "Get thee out of thy country, from the kindred, and from thy father's house, unto a land I will show you." We discover here that God had already called Abram, and so this shows that God is moving in sovereignty. Terah to Haran, his house. Haran apparently had land in Canaan, and in the cleaning up of all the family business after Haran died, they ended up living in Haran.

Abraham was slow. God had already told him to come out, but Abraham had to honor his family and stay with them. Was he disobeying God? No, he was waiting on God to sovereignly arrange his circumstances to fulfill what only God could fulfill. That's what grace is. Grace rests and waits on God. Grace does not try to do it yourself.

Terah moved, but was it Terah's decision? Abram was caught between, "Do I honor my family or do I follow God?" He had been told to separate from his family, and yet he can't because then he'd be dishonoring his family. That can't be right either. They're believers, apparently, right? You don't get to leave your marriage. There's a lot of things that people do thinking they're obeying God that violate very basic principles. No, you have to wait on God for Him to arrange the circumstances. Eventually, Terah moved them all, and then Terah died. Then Abram was free.

And then it says, "Now Abram, God had told Abraham to leave," past tense. So that's why I say it's a process. In this sense, sanctification can be viewed as a process. Separating you out is a process. Don't go before God has moved. He'll tell you what He wants. He'll give you a vision of it. He'll give you the language for it, and it'll make you incompatible with everything around you. But then you may be forced to have to wait on God because you've got obligations, and we don't think like that.

But this shows that God honors. It's not that He honored the obligations. It's just that He's not going to let anything stop His purpose with Abraham. Abraham has a little freedom.   God is compassionate. He knows how to work all things together for your good. He knows how to get you where you need to be, and He's not worried about time. He's not in a hurry, obviously, because Abraham is 75 here. I think Abraham doesn't have Isaac until he's 100.

This is the end of Volume 1 of the Genesis Commentary

For More Books and Information, visit:
https://www.christiansneedthegospel.com

Made in the USA
Columbia, SC
17 October 2024

44598962R00265